ALSO BY

CLIFFORD H. POPE

THE GIANT SNAKES   1961

REPTILES ROUND THE WORLD   1957

THE REPTILE WORLD   1955

THESE ARE BORZOI BOOKS

PUBLISHED BY *Alfred A. Knopf* IN NEW YORK

TURTLES

of the United States & Canada

TURTLES

OF THE

United States & Canada

CLIFFORD H. POPE

ILLUSTRATED WITH 99 PHOTOGRAPHS

NEW YORK: ALFRED · A · KNOPF

1 9 7 1

THIS IS A BORZOI BOOK,
PUBLISHED BY ALFRED A. KNOPF, INC.

Manufactured in the United States of America

Published August 14, 1939; second printing, February 1946; third printing, September 1949; fourth printing, December 1961; fifth printing, January 1967; Sixth printing, November 1971

Published in Canada by Random House of Canada Limited

TO
MY WIFE

PREFACE

Although this is a book primarily about the habits of turtles, I have included keys and diagnostic descriptions so that any chelonian of the United States can be identified at least as to its species. In contrast to the brief descriptions the life histories have been fully presented, the facts being based on all the available technical publications and many authoritative popular articles as well. More than eight hundred papers on American forms of this group are in existence, and these, with few exceptions, have been perused in search of interesting facts. The major task has been the collation of such extensive material. In spite of this, many a reader will be surprised to see how little is known about the habits of our common turtles; I am, for example, disappointed in being unable to describe the courtship of more than a very few species.

Yet if all our turtle life histories were well known, a book no longer than this one would be a mere catalogue without running text, or, for that matter, popular interest. A librarian once told me that if all her borrowed books were turned in at once, she would be forced to close the library, as there would be no room even on the floor for anything but books. So it is with the turtles: if they marched up in a brigade to report,

species by species, on life histories, I should be in more of a
predicament than that librarian with all her volumes returned!

I firmly believe that the average individual is just as interested in fundamentals of science as are the scientists themselves, but it is patent that these basic facts must be presented
in familiar terms as free as possible from technical language.
On the other hand it is not complimentary through unwar-
ranted simplification to give the reader credit for no mental
application whatsoever. Hence I have included a limited number of technical characters that can be determined without
dissection.

ACKNOWLEDGMENTS

My wife, Sarah H. Pope, assisted in the preparation of this book from beginning to end by cataloguing and organizing information, checking almost every fact, reading, typing the entire manuscript, correcting proof, and attending to endless minor details. To her I am most deeply indebted for all this as well as for constant encouragement.

The generosity and courtesy of the Directors of the Zoological Society of Philadelphia, represented by Freeman M. Shelly and Roger Conant, General Manager and Curator, respectively, of the Zoological Garden Staff, and the skill of its photographer, Mark Mooney, Jr., enable me to present a unique series of original portraits of American turtles from life. I cannot easily express my appreciation of this invaluable help and co-operation, which entailed great labour and expense.

Mr. John T. Nichols put at my disposal the results of years of work on the habits of the Common Box Turtle; Mr. James W. Atz brought many interesting references to my notice and lent me books and articles from his private library; Dr. Archie F. Carr, Jr., sent me the latest results of his researches on the species of *Pseudemys*, enabling me to give the only satisfactory arrangement of this puzzling group; Dr. Norman Hartweg supplied information and sent me an unpublished manuscript on the Kinosternidæ. For all this assistance I am indeed grateful.

Through its Curator of Reptiles and Amphibians, Karl P. Schmidt, the Field Museum of Natural History aided by permitting me to study their collection of American turtles, as did the New York Aquarium through its Director, Charles M. Breder.

Interesting photographs adding greatly to the value of this book have been contributed by Drs. Francis Harper, William T. Davis, Robert T. Hatt, and Mr. E. Ross Allen. Mr. Douglas Cullen took several pictures especially for use herein and Dr. Robert P. Van Dusen, Director of the Philadelphia Aquarium, willingly permitted Mr. Mooney to photograph the seaturtles of his collection. Mr. Edmond Malnate lettered the first two illustrations.

Miss Hazel Gay and her staff cheerfully found for me scores of books and articles in the stacks of the library of the American Museum of Natural History, thus greatly facilitating my search of the literature.

For the help and encouragement of the following friends I am grateful: Messrs. Charles M. Bogert, James Kezer, Robert Devine, George Johnson, M. Graham Netting, Samuel F. Hildebrand, and Robert S. Mathews.

The General Biological Supply House, Chicago, generously supplied a triply injected turtle for dissection.

CONTENTS

CHAPTER VI

CHAPTER VII

CHAPTER VIII

CHAPTER IX

ILLUSTRATIONS

☼

TURTLES
of the United States & Canada

TABLE OF MEASUREMENTS

The measurements of eggs and hatchlings are recorded in millimetres and for the sake of uniformity all fractions are given in
decimals. The following table shows inch fractions in both six-
teenths and decimals with their equivalents in millimetres.

Inches (Decimals)	Inches (Sixteenths)	Millimetres
.06	$\frac{1}{16}$	1.6
.1		2.5
.12	$\frac{1}{8}$	3.2
.19	$\frac{3}{16}$	4.8
.2		5.1
.25	$\frac{1}{4}$	6.4
.3		7.6
.31	$\frac{5}{16}$	7.9
.37	$\frac{3}{8}$	9.5
.4		10.2
.44	$\frac{7}{16}$	11.1
.5	$\frac{1}{2}$	12.7
.56	$\frac{9}{16}$	14.3
.6		15.2
.62	$\frac{5}{8}$	15.9
.69	$\frac{11}{16}$	17.5
.7		17.8
.75	$\frac{3}{4}$	19.1
.8		20.3
.81	$\frac{13}{16}$	20.6
.87	$\frac{7}{8}$	22.2
.9		22.9
.94	$\frac{15}{16}$	23.8
1.00	1	25.4
1.25	$1\frac{1}{4}$	31.8
1.50	$1\frac{1}{2}$	38.1
1.75	$1\frac{3}{4}$	44.5
2.00	2	50.8
2.50	$2\frac{1}{2}$	63.5
3.00	3	76.2

CHAPTER I

TURTLE BEGINNINGS
and WAYS

ORIGIN AND RELATIONSHIP

The turtle is most familiar to us in its liquid form, but to enjoy this book (as well as our soup) we must go deeper than the soup pot and learn that turtles are reptiles along with snakes, lizards, crocodilians, and lonesome *Sphenodon* of the New Zealand region. Now, reptiles are vertebrates, or back-boned animals, lower than birds and mammals, higher than fish and amphibians. In fact they are the " highest " of the cold-blooded vertebrates, or groups which do not have heat-control mechanisms, but rather must be satisfied with a temperature approximating that of the air, earth, or water surrounding them.

Having so easily put turtles in their place, most of us will want to go farther to learn why a turtle is only a turtle and not something better or even worse. Sounding the bottom of this matter would get us too deep into animal architecture, but we can at least learn a few attributes that you or I should have to possess in order to qualify for admission to that soup pot. As already hinted, we should have to boast a vertebral column in our backs and be as cold as we shall actually be one sad day.

Having narrowed our pursuit down to back-boned cold-bloodedness, our next step is to single the turtle out from this formidable category. By far the best characteristic to use here

3

is the possession of locomotor appendages with complex bony skeletons, usually in the form of hands or feet rather than thin (or even fleshy) fins. Thus we throw the fish right out of the running, leaving in only the reptiles and amphibians (frogs and salamanders). Our next point is the most effective eliminator, for it pushes the fishes still further out of the way, gets rid of the frogs and salamanders, and even reaches upward to differentiate further the bird-mammal group. This important point is the dry horny outside covering of the vast majority of reptiles, contrasting with the "slimy" and scaly one of the fish, the scaleless, usually moist skin of frogs and salamanders, the feathery covering of birds, and the hairy coat of mammals, including almost naked man.

At last only reptiles are left to worry us: snakes, lizards, crocodilians (crocodiles and alligators), chelonians (turtles), and that lizard-like critter of the New Zealand region known as *Sphenodon*. Among these a turtle is readily recognized by its complete lack of teeth and its shell, with parts of which the backbone and ribs are more or less fused.

This shell is indeed the most remarkable and one of the most effective armours ever assumed by fish or four-footed animal. It has proved so excellent that turtles have relied upon it in essentially the same form for some 175,000,000 years while other whole groups of weird creatures both large and small have flourished and vanished, leaving only their remains in the rocks for the edification of inquisitive fossil-hunters. The turtles too have left their trail, but they still carry on and probably are as flourishing today as ever they were in the past. We should really respect these stolid reptiles, who might well shake their toothless heads at us and boast: " We watched the dinosaurs rise, reign, and vanish; and even as they disappeared, your earliest insignificant ancestors were still running over the ground on all fours, not as yet even remotely resembling an ape."

STRUCTURE

No matter how much at ease a turtle may appear to be in its bony box, let it be understood that "getting that way" was not easy, and remaining that way has minor drawbacks as well as major advantages. The chief benefit of being boxed up is too obvious to require elaboration; a visit to any collection of mediæval armour will readily convince one that man has long been envious of the turtle's protected position in life. The shell of a tortoise may even weigh a third as much as the total animal, so wearing a suit of mail proportionately as heavy would be no light task.

This shell consists of two distinct parts: the carapace covering the back of the animal, and the plastron protecting its belly. These are joined together on each side by a narrow bridge. Plates 1 and 2 show these structures more clearly than could any description.

But how did these lowly creatures attain this position and get so much of their skeleton outside of the rest of it and of them? Although fossils have helped little in solving this major problem in turtle evolution, embryology and Dr. Ruckes have given us a fair idea of how the carapace, a close combination of ribs and bony plates, manages to arrive on the sunny side of the limb supports or girdles. The forerunner, or "anlage," of the carapace largely accomplishes this as follows:

First appearing as a raised area in the centre of the embryo's back, the anlage grows outward in all directions, expanding in a manner suggesting the flow of very thick molasses. Just beneath the anlage the ribs form independently, but soon come so much under its influence that their subsequent positions and relations are largely determined by its growth. As a consequence the ribs remain comparatively straight, never curving downward and around to meet on the lower side of the body as do ours, for example. The growth of this external anlage is so rapid and its influence on the ribs so pronounced that the limb girdles are soon enclosed without being given a fair chance to assume their usual exterior position. Thus we see that the girdles do not migrate inward, as some students have maintained, nor the ribs assume the initiative and get themselves on the outside, but the anlage or forerunner of the carapace directs development to its own advantage and, incidentally, to that of the turtle. The embryo as a whole grows in a side-to-side direction much more rapidly than in an up-and-down one, producing the characteristic flattened shape of the turtle.

The carapace, with its great rigidity and strength, robs the trunk vertebræ of their chief function, putting them in the position of the horse in a motorized civilization or labourers after the slump of 1929. Some vertebræ and many of their muscles, thus thrown out of work, completely disappeared. In contrast to these the bones of neck and tail retain their mobility and importance. In fact, retraction of the head and neck require special muscular development. The turtle's neck has eight vertebræ; that of nearly all mammals only seven.

Finally, one can readily see that the immobility of the ribs and the rigidity of the shell called for new ways of aerating the lungs. This difficult problem has given inquisitive mankind almost as much trouble as it must have once given the turtle. The latter solved it largely by substituting movement of the limb girdles for that of the ribs: to fill the lungs the bones of the shoulder girdle are rotated inward and forward while those of the pelvis are moved backward and downward. It is often stated that leg and neck movements pump air in and out, but at best these are of minor importance in breathing. Chiefly because a turtle has such thorough ventilation of its large lungs and a low rate of oxygen-consumption even for a cold-blooded vertebrate, it can hold the breath for a long time. This has been one source of annoyance in studying its respiration;

a victim vexed beyond a point by an experimenter simply refuses to respire for two or three hours at a stretch!

SIZE

When it comes to size, a turtle need feel apologetic only before the very largest animals, fossil or living. In fact, it would have taken a *Brontosaurus* to make the Cretaceous marine *Archelon* blush with shame at its mere twelve feet of length and (probable) ton of avoirdupois. (An *Archelon* alive today in its native South Dakota would bring more than blushes to the faces of her inhabitants.) Coming to comparatively modern times, only a million or so years back, the gigantic *Colossochelys atlas*, perhaps the largest turtle that ever cast a shadow on this earth, plodded over the hills of northern India, no doubt alarming our not too distant ancestors by its four to five feet of stature and seven-foot shell.

Even today the giant tortoises weighing a few hundred pounds, the hard-shelled sea-turtles of equal bulk, and the pelagic Leatherback sometimes boasting three-fourths of a ton, are not to be sneezed at even by *Archelon, Colossochelys,* or any other reptile for that matter.

Thus we see that during tens of millions of years turtles have been weighed in Nature's balance and not found wanting.

THE SEXES

External sexual differences in turtles are fairly numerous, but inconspicuous and usually of an entirely practical nature. For example, the most universal difference is in the greater distance between the anus (through which the penis is extruded) and the base of the tail in the male (see Plate 32), a character obviously correlated with efficiency in copulation. Male Kinosternidæ have, in fact, carried the matter far beyond the joking-

point and developed grasping devices on the hind limbs as well
as a positively prehensile tail. Another common but by no
means universal character belonging in this same carnal category is the concavity of the male plastron contrasting with the
flat or even slightly bulging one of the female. All this indicates that, in matters of sex, the turtle keeps his feet firmly on
the ground and probably could not be taught the meaning of
the term " sex repression." This is the more surprising when
we consider the inconvenient shape of the turtle.

The female is usually larger than the male; among the soft-
shelled turtles the female attains even two to three times the
bulk of the male. In a few species the male slightly exceeds the
female in size. The larger size of the weaker sex may be tentatively linked with its need of extra space for developing eggs.
Some might say that this, too, facilitates copulation, since a
relatively small male undoubtedly more easily maintains a
balance during such union.

The most striking external sexual differences among vertebrates, such as brilliant plumage and gaudy fur coats, are
generally held to be correlated with the selection of mates.
Turtles do not boast anything really striking of this kind, although in some species fairly obvious colour differences are
evident: The male's colours may be obscured through a general darkening, or minor differences in head or neck patterns
and eye colour may exist. Just how much these help in sex
recognition I do not know.

It would not be fair to let the long fingernails (see Plate 60)
of the Painted Turtle and relatives go unmentioned, even
though they are more appropriately treated under courtship.
When the male Painted Turtle grows fingernails two or even
three times as long as those of his mistress, he does not do so to
prove his indolence, as Chinese gentlemen used to do, but to
give his loves a sensual thrill by tickling their lores.

REPRODUCTION

While I was walking along a country road with an elderly lady we came to a bridge; below the bridge was a stream and by the stream a rock; on the rock sat a turtle. My companion, glancing at the lonesome reptile, casually dropped the remark: " I don't see how they do it." If this had been south of the Mason and Dixon's Line my confusion might have been great, because explaining the facts of life to a lady in the south is not always easy. Being in the north, I managed to explain without undue embarrassment that a male turtle, unconscious of its awkward shape, finds no difficulty in mating, his love-life, in fact, lasting just as long as courtship and copulation, and only by the purest accident does he bestow his favours on the same lady twice. Moreover, she pays no attention to the white objects resulting from their union after these are once safely buried where heat of the sun or of decaying vegetation can promote development; *he* would not recognize one of his eggs even if he saw it.

All turtles are alike in having this rather casual way of reproducing their kind, so in their world a children's nurse and a dentist would starve to death at about the same rapid rate. Nevertheless, as a group, turtles have advanced beyond the fish stage of external fertilization of the egg, and the amphibian one of dependence on water as a medium of egg and larval development.

Just as in other higher animals, courtship to a turtle is a necessary preliminary to copulation. A giant tortoise's idea of love-play is to approach a prospective mate uttering all the while deep resounding roars and, once arrived at her side, violently to pound her with his massive bulk for minutes on end. These caresses are accompanied by continuous roaring and vicious nipping of her legs. The object of his tenderness does not try to escape nor does she even draw in her legs. Finally

he mounts her broad matronly back to begin their final stage
of their married life. Strongly contrasting with this terrestrial
courtship is the really touching way the American species with
long fingernails arouse their mates. The male Painted Turtle,
for example, swims toward a female until, with forelimbs out-
stretched, he can just reach her face, which he proceeds to
stroke by moving his slender nails rapidly up and down. A
sufficient amount of such caressing apparently opens her mind
to more intimate advances.

Copulation itself has been carefully described for only a
few of our species. As already stated, the male assumes the
usual superior position.

Mating regularly takes place in this country during the
spring; autumn union is also not uncommon and even in summer the sexes sometimes come together. It is highly probable
that in many species a single mating suffices to fertilize not
only all the eggs of that season but diminishing percentages of
those for two, three, or even more seasons to come. This fact
was well established for diamond-back terrapins by scientific
study of their artificial propagation.

In the United States turtles usually nest during June and
early July, thus allowing the eggs several weeks for incubation
and hatching before the onset of severe weather. Hatching,
or at least actual emergence from the nest, is sometimes delayed until spring, the advanced embryos or hatchlings actually
hibernating *in situ*. This of course occurs most commonly in
the northern states and Canada.

As a rule the nest is a flask-shaped hole in which the eggs are
buried under a few inches of dirt, sand, or decaying vegetable
matter. The sea-turtles, however, make a secondary pit in the
bottom of a broad shallow excavation. The nesting female is
nearly always oblivious of her surroundings; the approach of
a person or even a sharp blow may go unnoticed. Natives frequently hold a receptacle under the tail of one actually ovi-

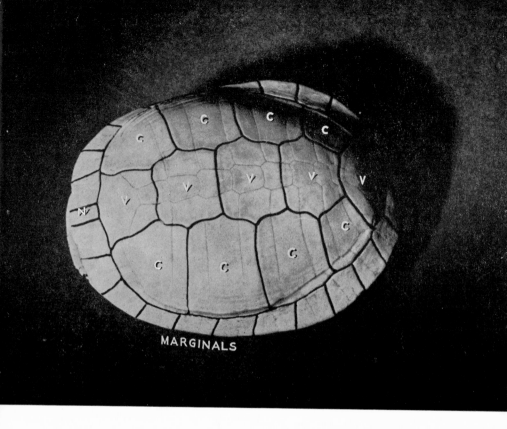

MARGINALS

THE SHELL OF A TURTLE FROM ABOVE

1. This is a photograph of the upper shell or " carapace " of a Central Painted Turtle from Michigan viewed from above to show the names of the superficial horny shields, all of which are of utmost importance in identification. Although the actual shields have been removed, the positions that they occupied are outlined in black and the name of each shield is indicated by a letter, except in the case of the numerous surrounding marginals.

N stands for nuchal, which is single and lies just above the neck
V " " vertebral
C " " costal

The faint lines are the sutures between the bony plates of the shell. Obviously little correlation exists between bones and shields.

The Central Painted Turtle is used here only to illustrate a typical but by no means universal arrangement and number of shields. (*Photograph by Mark Mooney, Jr., lettering by Edmond Malnate.*)

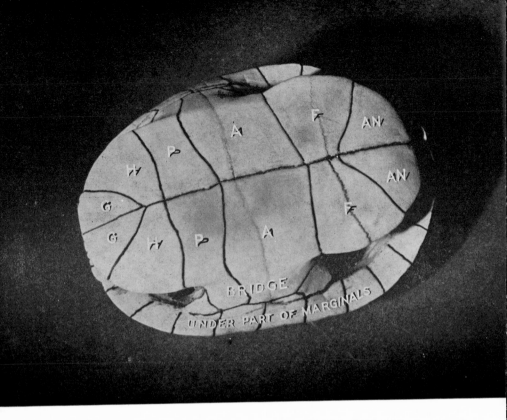

THE SHELL OF A TURTLE FROM BELOW

2. The same Michigan shell is here viewed from below to show the shields of its lower part or " plastron," the " bridge " connecting carapace and plastron, and the under parts of the marginals, which are " folded " over the edge of the shell.

> G stands for gular, which lies just under the neck
> H " " humeral
> P " " pectoral
> A " " abdominal
> F " " femoral
> AN " " anal

The small triangular " axillary " shield lies at the front extremity of the bridge, the slightly larger " inguinal " at its opposite extremity (neither is lettered).

In some groups of turtles a row of shields on either side along the marginals separates them from the pectorals and abdominals and are known as " inframarginals."

The sutures of the underlying bones are rather obscure with the exception of the conspicuous one under the lower " F." (*Photograph by Mark Mooney, Jr., lettering by Edmond Malnate.*)

positing and thus receive the eggs " hot off the griddle."

The most interesting thing about the nests is not their structure but rather the technique and implement of construction. Although bound forever to land by the necessity of burying its eggs in the earth, the turtle has become adapted to life in almost every warm environment, and in becoming adapted the hind limbs have changed in form: flipper for the seas, stump-shaped limb for deserts, and webbed toes for the fresh waters. In spite of these changes the same annual digging must be and is accomplished by hind legs alone, no matter what their shape. The three-hundred-pound sea-turtle crawls out to make a nest with deft movements of a huge paddle-shaped limb; the Desert Tortoise selects a spot in a sandy waste and skilfully reaches the same end with its elephant foot; the river species ascends a bank and digs with its webbed toes, using them something like a hand. Each species knows how to get the same result with its particular tool. Mother Nature has readily changed the form of a leg from stump- to flipper- to paw-shape, but never produced a turtle egg able to develop anywhere except in the earth, or an embryo able to grow, well protected from danger, within the body of the female. In many species, especially the sea-turtles, this necessity of laying on land forces the adult to expose itself to the one great danger of existence, and makes bird and mammal fodder out of myriads of tender hatchlings.

At hatching time the shell of any egg suddenly becomes a tomb instead of an incubator and the helpless embryo must promptly turn into a Houdini or perish. Because advanced turtle embryos develop on the tip of the snout a hard structure known as the " egg-tooth," zoologists have quite naturally assumed it to be responsible for the fissures that appear in the shell at the time of emergence. Recent studies have surprisingly shown that other factors are involved in this jail-breaking process. The egg-tooth, in fact, has even been proved quite useless in certain species, rapid absorption of water by the egg content being responsible for the distention and ultimate rupture of the shell, often at a spot remote from the hatchling's snout.

The gauntlet of danger run by some embryonic and young turtles makes one wonder how survival is accomplished. The sea-turtles, perhaps the worst sufferers, combat their enemies by sheer fecundity. The female lays, at intervals of two weeks during the rather brief breeding season, four to seven clutches, each composed of about a hundred eggs. The land and fresh-water species of this country produce relatively few eggs at a time and seem to lay but once a year. Many of the smaller kinds deposit but two to six, some of the larger as many as fifteen to twenty-five eggs to a nest; others lay clutches of intermediate size. The Common Snapping Turtle has been known to deposit as many as forty eggs at a time.

THE EGG

Most turtle eggs are elliptical in shape, but some — those of sea-turtles, for example — are spherical or nearly so. The Common Snapping Turtle lays objects astonishingly similar to Ping-pong balls in size, shape, and, when fresh, ability to bounce. (As a matter of fact, Ping-pong balls are slightly larger.) The Snapper's egg is relatively big for a chelonian although the giant Loggerhead sometimes produces one 2.12 inches (54 mm.) in diameter. (See Plates 22, 26, 55, 88, and 97.)

The shell, either flexible or brittle, is always devoid of pattern and it is never pigmented like that of so many bird eggs. This is presumably because all turtles bury their eggs, which consequently do not have to be camouflaged.

But these are relatively minor points. The really important facts about vertebrate eggs involve " inside information " and a little knowledge of evolution. We must know that the reptiles, in contrast to the outright aquatic fishes and the amphibious amphibians (salamanders, frogs, and cæcilians), were the first vertebrates to free themselves as a group from the necessity of either living or breeding in water. This was accomplished by evolving a cleidoic or " closed-box " type of egg. In escaping from this bondage of water they paved the way for the development of birds and mammals, including man; obviously they deserve our undying gratitude and esteem. A cleidoic egg is by no means a simple structure, because, in addition to having a shell to hold its parts together and prevent desiccation, it must either provide nourishment, water, and gas for embryonic growth or allow for the procuration of these through the shell. To use a barnyard illustration, the yolk of a hen's egg is its supply of nourishment, the white is its water reserve, and a space just inside the shell holds some of the necessary gas.

The turtle compromised by providing a good supply of yolk, a limited amount of white, and a permeable shell readily permitting the passage of water and gas. Responsibility for placing the egg where it can get additional gas and water was left with the female. A sea-turtle egg by weight is about six, forty, and fifty-five per cent shell, white, and yolk, respectively, whereas the corresponding figures for a hen's are roughly eleven, fifty-six, and thirty-three. The bird egg has a better shell and a larger water reservoir, but relatively less yolk.

All this sounds simple enough, but there were complications. For example, what about the waste products given off by the growing embryo? Would they not poison the whole egg by being constantly resorbed? This little difficulty was taken care of by breaking down these products into insoluble uric acid instead of into the soluble urea as the fish and amphibians had previously done, and still do, for that matter. This insolu-

ble uric acid is readily segregated in the closed egg; the urea
of the submerged fish and amphibian egg is dissolved away as
fast as it is formed; the blood stream of the parent removes it
in the mammals.

It is a standing joke among professional reptile-men that few
of them can identify the young of even our common chelonians. Apparently the Creator did not keep these " pros " in
mind when He made infant turtles so different from their parents! Among many other points, the shell of the hatchling is
round, or at least much more nearly so than that of the adult,
and the tail is proportionately much longer. Generalization on
the numerous colour differences cannot be made except in
regard to the more sharply contrasted patterns of the young.

The Creator did not keep the young turtles too well in mind
either, since He left them soft, defenceless, and, perhaps, too
brightly ornamented. Consequently their first year of life,
like that of suckling *Homo sapiens* unblessed by modern medi-
cine but cursed by too much " civilization," is the critical
period of existence. Compensation in the form of an astonishing ability to hide and a sweet independence of food has
been granted the infant turtle. Possibly we should put it this
way: Only the little ones that have been given these attributes
are still with us. Everyone who has searched for turtlets away
from their nests knows how hard they are to find; even the
ubiquitous box turtles are rarely caught in swaddling-clothes.
In strong contrast to the ever hungry new-born mammal
the late-summer- or fall-hatched turtle readily winters on a
stomach still innocent of food and is even able to live weeks if
not months on the same virginal digestive tract after emergence
in the spring.

LONGEVITY AND GROWTH

Every turtle is commonly thought to be a potential Methuselah that grows about as fast as a stone. There is considerable truth in the first part of this belief, but very little in the second.

Large giant tortoises are always cited as examples of creatures that must have watched the centuries roll by, whereas actually one of these Goliaths weighing 350 pounds *may* be no more than twelve years old. At least an individual confined in California increased its weight from 29 to 350 pounds in seven years. Three others, kept in Houston, Texas, weighed from 7 to 13 pounds in 1928 and balanced the scales at 179 to 183 in 1937, an annual increase of 21 to 22 pounds per turtle. The straight lengths of their shells in 1937 were about double what they had been in 1928. Probably in the tropical climate of their native Galapagos Islands these reptiles require not more than ten to twelve years to reach sexual maturity; I hazard a guess that the average turtle of the United States matures and attains some three-fourths of its ultimate size in five to seven years, but continues to grow at least as many years more.

As for age, there is no doubt that turtles outlive not only all other reptiles but every other vertebrate as well, including man himself, the champion among mammals. The individual tortoise positively known to have lived the longest survived at least 152, perhaps 200 years of life on Mauritius, where accidental death overtook it in 1918. This centenarian-plus was the last surviving individual of its kind and deserves at least a commemorative monument. Even the humble Common Box Turtle sometimes lives a century. Thirteen species of this group have remained alive during 41 or more years of captivity, so the chances are good that many of the 250 known kinds not infrequently pass the half-century mark.

Accurate age-determination depends on three factors:

rapidity and method of growth, and existence in a climate that causes regular interruptions in growth.

We must understand that (in certain species) each horny shield of the shell increases in size peripherally, and when growth is periodically retarded or suspended, as during hibernation, the rings of horn added during seasons of rapid growth stand out so conspicuously that age can be easily determined from their number. This retention of all the successive layers of horn produces a low pyramid of sorts on each shield. In other species, however, the old shields are regularly cast off and growth-ring counts cannot be made with any degree of success.

Just after maturity, rate of growth abruptly slows down and the new horny rings cannot be made out clearly; attrition soon wears off the tops of the pyramids, leaving a relatively smooth and indecipherable shell.

WHERE TURTLES LIVE

Compared to snakes, lizards, frogs, and toads, the two hundred and fifty species of turtles inhabiting this globe seem like a meagre assortment, what with both snakes and lizards exceeding this number some tenfold, frogs and toads about seven. Going on down the scale, however, we find that there are scarcely two-thirds as many kinds of salamanders as of turtles, and just over a score of crocodilians (crocodiles and alligators). After all, our turtles make a fair showing, especially when we recall that this show of theirs has been going on without intermission for a cool 175,000,000 years.

But where do these quarter of a thousand species live? Their home is the warm belt of this sphere because, like all other reptiles, they cannot survive in permanently frozen regions. Even among reptiles their penetration to the north is relatively restricted. In North America, for instance, they reach extreme southern Canada only in limited numbers, and in milder eastern Europe they go but eight degrees farther poleward.

Within the temperate parts of the earth the turtles have made themselves at home in every major type of environment from the dry land through the fresh waters to the seas. In the last their conquest is quite complete; on the first they have become adapted to life in mountains, on plains, and even in deserts. Some of their greatest triumphs have been made on isolated oceanic islands such as those of the tiny Galapagos Archipelago, lying six hundred miles off the coast of Ecuador. One of the saddest tales of turtle history and human avarice was enacted here when whaling and other vessels of the last century removed literally tens if not hundreds of thousands of giant tortoises. Islands where they once swarmed in vast hordes are now almost if not entirely devoid of them. Thus man, the arch enemy of wild life, destroys in a few score of years what Nature laboriously evolves through scores of millenniums.

Leaving our six marine forms out of consideration (because half of them are cosmopolitan in distribution), this country boasts a rich assortment of turtles: twenty-five thoroughly aquatic and four strictly terrestrial species; four aquatic ones with strong terrestrial tendencies; a single terrestrial one with aquatic inclinations. The fresh waters of North America can justly claim a lion's share of indigenous chelonians, whereas the continent itself harbours about a quarter of the living species.

HIBERNATION

The cold-blooded turtle, like all other reptiles, has little or no ability to keep its body either warmer or cooler than its surroundings and therefore must be careful to stay in earth, air, or water with temperature above freezing and below, let us say, 100° F. It is interesting to note that the Common Snapping Turtle, for instance, becomes uncomfortable at a body temperature of 80° F. and rarely survives one of 102° to 105° for half an hour. The higher figure is astonishingly near the point fatal to man himself.

Obviously winter presents its problems to the turtle world; not only difficulties of heat maintenance arise, but food troubles crop up. What could animals living largely on insects, other invertebrates, and plants so conspicuously absent in winter do for food even if there were no heating crisis? Wings might bear them safely southward and, indeed, a flying turtle would be a sight for sore eyes. Nature, however, has given them a much simpler solution; is it not easier to go a foot or so toward China than a thousand miles or more to the tropics?

Once safely ensconced in the relatively warm mud of pond, lake, or river bed or snugly buried below the frost line under a foot more or less of earth or leaf mould, the turtle has little to fear and plenty of time for dreamy meditation. There is no danger of starvation for an animal able to survive months without food even when normally active; lack of movement and the greatly slowed-up bodily processes during hibernation ensure survival on the available supply of fat. Nor does fear of suffocation disturb the sleeper's dreams, because the small amount of oxygen required to keep the low fires burning is readily secured even in submerged mud or under water itself. It must be remembered that cold water holds more oxygen in solution than warm.

Æstivation, a state of suspended animation somewhat similar to hibernation, tides turtles and other animals over periods of dry heat. Little is known about æstivation of North American chelonians; it is possible that more species resort to it than is now realized.

SUNNING

Most aquatic turtles are so fond of basking in the sun that doing so must satisfy some need. Perhaps general health is promoted and growth stimulated. Doubtless also the warmth of the solar rays is pleasant, since almost any confined turtle will edge up against a hot pipe or radiator. Leeches and other external parasites are at least temporarily banished by prolonged exposure to the sun, and growth of algæ on the shell is retarded.

The recent discovery that even sea-turtles bask on remote beaches is interesting because it was previously thought that the water was deserted only by females about to nest.

This habit of leaving the water to sprawl in great numbers on logs or bank surely has its disadvantages. Certain enemies are quick to see basking individuals and thus get a clue to their whereabouts. Man himself is a good example. The surprising alertness of sunning groups is good evidence that such caution is a necessity; carelessness in this regard might be synonymous with rapid extinction.

FOOD AND FEEDING

The average human being fortunate enough to attain ripe old age uses three sets of teeth; turtles, on the other hand, have managed to pull through several tens of millions of years with no teeth at all. It is true that old fossil *Triassochelys* did have teeth in the roof of the mouth, but we need not be too concerned about them, since the last set has not been in use outside of a museum for more than 150,000,000 years. Like many other true statements, the foregoing one about the lack of teeth in living turtles is a little misleading because not a few species do have structures with some right to be called " teeth." These are serrations and projections of the sharp horny edges of the jaws (see Plate 75) and, less often, of the ridges inside the mouth.

This lack of true teeth is not surprising when we realize that a turtle's jaws are only seizers and choppers, not real masticators of food; nor do they have to engulf relatively huge objects as do the extensible jaws of snakes. The claws of the forelimbs help a great deal in tearing up large pieces, and the thick tongue subsequently manipulates them on the inside. After passing the jaws, the food enters a digestive tract fundamentally like that of man except that it terminates in a cloaca instead of a rectum. Now, the cloaca not only is the receptacle for all the outgoing waste products of digestion but serves as a vagina in the female and the place where the penis is lodged in the male. The contents of the urinary bladder must also pass through this all-important vestibule which opens to the exterior through the anus.

The relative length of the combined large and small intestines varies considerably from species to species, being in some as many as seven times as long as the shell, in others only three. The large intestine is enormously developed in the herbivorous Gopher Tortoise.

Although sharing with other reptiles the ability to fast for months on end, turtles will feed as regularly and almost as often as mammals, consuming a surprisingly large amount of food (see Plate 59). The aquatic species prefer to swallow with the head submerged, the prey sometimes being thus drowned. Digestion is slow at best, and its rate varies considerably with the temperature of the animal, which is always about the same as that of its immediate surroundings. Experiment with one species showed that raising the temperature of its stomach from 64° to 84° F. a little more than doubled the rate of digestion. It is patent that the cold-blooded reptile can live on less food than the warm-blooded mammal or bird, and, combining with this low fuel requirement a great capacity for fat storage, we have a partial explanation of the average turtle's ability to live a year or more without eating. Cold-bloodedness has its advantages, for a turtle at least.

As an example of chelonian food requirement the following illustration given by Dr. Benedict is interesting: The standard energy needs of a nine-and-a-half-pound South American Tortoise with a shell eleven and a half inches long at a temperature around 63° F. would be supplied for approximately four weeks by six and a half ounces of banana.

High specialization in choice of food is rare among chelonians. Most species do not confine themselves to either plants or animals, and a moderate number occasionally devour carrion. Only the more tender parts of plants are consumed, presumably because of the mechanical difficulty of reducing tough fibrous structures to bits small enough to be swallowed. Succulent leaves and stems and delicate blossoms are habitually sought out. As far as I know, no turtle has developed a habit of digging for roots.

Small invertebrates such as earthworms, snails and slugs, thin-shelled bivalves, crustaceans, and insects, larval or otherwise, form the great bulk of the animal food, whereas young adult or larval cold-blooded vertebrates also frequently fall victim to the more robust kinds. Small mammals and birds rarely, comparatively large ones still more rarely satisfy turtle appetite. This does not, of course, include the eating of individuals found dead.

Their carnivorous feeding habits put these reptiles either astride or on the beneficial side of the fence from man's point of view although, under certain conditions, more harm than good may be done by a very few of the largest species. The plants consumed are of little or no economic significance.

Turtles drink regularly when water is available and some

species have considerable capacity to store water in recepta-
cles, paired or single, known as cloacal bladders and connected
with the exterior through the cloaca.

ENEMIES AND DEFENCE

A turtle's shell is obviously its best protection from besetting
dangers of all kinds, and, indeed, the scores of millions of years
throughout which shell and turtle have stuck close together
is excellent proof of this pudding. I cannot resist men-
tioning a unique exception, a land tortoise that starts life with
a bony shell of sorts which it rapidly proceeds to lose by re-
sorption so that the adult is the most remarkable of chelonians:
a soft-shelled land tortoise. The horny outside shields of
course remain, but form only a soft, flexible covering due to
the lack of support, a condition that the flat " softy " makes
use of by its habit of hiding in crevices between the many rocks
of its arid stony habitat; once well ensconced, the reptile in-
flates its lungs, thus rendering extrication extremely difficult.
This wily creature has virtually given up the hardness of its
shell to make still harder rocks its chief haven of refuge!

In spite of æon-long dependence on a shell, the turtle does
not depend on it altogether for defence. Hatchlings are masters at the art of concealment; adults, not so bad at this same
game, rely also on wariness and flight, and some even add more
positive methods such as biting and clawing or voiding excre-
tory matter and water from the cloaca and bladders. By taking certain species, the ferocious snappers and the docile box
turtles among them, we can even correlate aggressiveness with
degree of shell development; but this analogy must not be
pushed too far. Unsavouriness caused by musky excretions or
by ill-flavoured flesh is also a common means of defence. The
delicious diamond-backs, for example, are sadly in need of this
weapon to save them from turtle soup. In strong contrast to

snakes, turtles have never made much use of the gentler art of bluffing.

If the shell is the turtle's best protection, we may reasonably conclude conversely that the most perilous periods are when the shell is either lacking or incompletely developed. The really critical stage is spent in the egg, as then it is that most individuals meet their end, almost in advance of their beginning! The pages to come are full of references to destruction of nesting sites by hungry mammals (see Plate 4), including an almost naked, two-legged species well known to every reader of this book. The next most hazardous part of chelonian existence is early infancy, when the shell is soft and the quite defenceless turtlet of mouthful size for most enemies, a dainty tidbit for the larger ones.

Finally, the adult female faces considerable danger while nesting (see Plate 38), not only because of her usual conspicuousness due to the selection of a sunny spot, but because she is ordinarily too preoccupied to heed the approach of an enemy; both male and female often suffer from exposure during copulation for the same reason.

Let us suppose that turtles, suddenly become supreme on earth, are bringing to formal judgment their major enemies. Man himself heads the list of offenders. After disposal of Public Enemy No. 1 an array of four-legged egg- and baby-eaters such as bears, raccoons, and skunks are charged with turning nesting sites into free-lunch counters. Birds open to much the same indictment include a shameless fat reprobate, the flightless insular landrail of the Indian Ocean, known to subsist on terrestrial tortoise eggs. Sea-turtles riot at the sight of frigatebirds, so fond of gathering on beaches to gulp down thousands of hatchlings on their first trip to the sea.

Several large reptiles do not escape this court of justice, because monitors and other big lizards frequently exhume and devour turtle eggs, and the stomach contents of alligators constantly include at least a small and sometimes a large percentage of chelonian remains. All the crocodiles are found just as guilty. Numerous predaceous fish of good size are rightly accused of swallowing tender aquatic hatchlings as they arrive in the water, and of taking occasional bites out of the flippers of giant marine kinds; sharks of swallowing adolescent sea-turtles whole.

The non-parasitic invertebrates are relatively innocent, but of the parasitic forms a multitude of tiny pale pests lodge in the turtle's innards, not to mention others decorating his " out-ards." The guilt of these insidious enemies is of staggering proportions, rivalling that of man himself.

SENSES AND INTELLIGENCE

The head is an important part of all land vertebrates not only because it houses the brain and starts food down the " red lane " but also because the important senses of sight, smell, taste, and hearing are located there. The organs of these senses are the gateways through which the outside world is largely recognized, so some but not necessarily all of these gateways must be open in every group of animals.

Turtles themselves nicely illustrate this point. Although possessing well-developed middle and inner ears, they cannot hear in the ordinary sense of the term. At least, no one has indubitably proved them capable of responding to sound-waves transmitted through the air, and some very careful experiments have been carried on. This question is especially interesting because courting and mating turtles are well known to grunt and even make other sounds. Presumably turtles once heard or else they would not have such complete ears; now they simply use other senses to replace this lost one. Astonishingly slight vibrations transmitted to the skin or shell through solids are quickly noticed and the slightest tap on the shell is felt.

Even when vision is cut off a shy turtle cannot be easily approached.

Their sight is keen. Distinguishing between red, yellow, green, blue, and violet, as well as between black and white, their total range of colour perception approximates that of man himself. Especially interesting is the fact that colours at the red end of the spectrum are more readily recognized and it is just these that so frequently adorn the turtles themselves.

Exactly how good the senses of smell and taste are has not been accurately determined, but they are generally considered to be at least weakly developed.

Most surprising of all is the turtle's ability to learn. Certain species have been taught to discriminate between patterns of vertical and horizontal black and white lines, and to run mazes. Their behaviour was indeed found to be about on a par with that of various mammals. The memory is also fair.

RELATION TO MAN

It is little wonder that turtles have always attracted special attention. Certainly if these reptiles were known only from rare fossils, they would be counted among the great show pieces of every natural-history museum, and biologists would endlessly conjecture just how such boxed-up creatures ever managed to breathe and otherwise live normal lives.

Mythology, folk-stories, and current popular beliefs the world over are rich in turtle lore, but perhaps in no country has this lowly animal been granted such an exalted position as in China. The *Book of Rites* named the tortoise as one of the four benevolent spiritual animals, and through the centuries it has been honoured as emblem of longevity and symbol of righteousness. One wise tortoise even prophesied the downfall of an ancient dynasty, whereas in recent times the renowned Li Hung-chang was ordered by imperial edict to offer sacrifices to the tortoise for protecting the dikes of " China's Sorrow," the treacherous Yellow River. Strongly contrasting with this, the epithet " turtle," in vulgar language, connotes a low degree of sexual depravity and becomes an expression of vile abuse. The insult is often modified by substituting the term " turtle egg," or the really elegant admonition to " roll away."

Also in ancient China the will of the Supreme Ruler was ascertained by reading cracks that appeared when turtle-shell bones were scorched. I have tentatively identified burnt fragments used in such divination as belonging to the extinct Chinese species *Pseudocadia anyangensis*. The heavy responsibility thus placed on this turtle was apparently too much for it.

Probably even older than Chinese divination are the more practical uses of turtles as articles of diet and adornment. Turtle soup and " tortoise shell " are familiar in every country and I doubt that one could find a more widely known dish or raw material of the arts. Thanks to their world-wide distribution, the edible Green Turtle and the beautiful Hawksbill have for centuries obligingly supplied all but the frozen races of mankind with these two foods, one for their bottomless stomachs, the other for their still more abysmal vanities.

In the United States the delicately flavoured diamond-backs are the only chelonians that a democratic government has deigned to rescue from threatened oblivion. The culture of diamond-backs is now on a permanent basis, whereas other similarly handicapped species face extinction. Although the soft-shelled turtles are among the most delicious of all our kinds, they are not well known in markets, being consumed for the most part locally. Some of the big forms of the genus *Pseudemys* and their larger relatives rank well in popularity and market consumption. The fortunately stinking musk and mud turtles often meet an untimely end, not because of their suitability for food, but because of an appetite too much like

3. Unfortunate " Orphan Annie's " tail even was not spared a coat of paint! She now enjoys life in the Philadelphia Zoological Garden little the worse for wear, thanks to the promptness with which the paint was removed. Such victims of an extraordinary sense of humour soon succumb unless rescued as Orphan Annie was. (*Courtesy Zoological Society of Philadelphia, photograph by Mark Mooney, Jr.*)

4. An unidentified mammal robbed this nest in northern Michigan. If turtles were human, a glance at this picture would be to them like the mention of the Black Death to a European of the Middle Ages. The needle's eye through which every turtle must pass is its period of incubation and infancy, during which it is still soft and therefore vulnerable to the attack of nest-robber and baby-eater.

(*Photograph by Robert T. Hatt.*)

5. Common Musk Turtle (*Sternotherus odoratus*) from the region of Philadelphia with a carapace 4.50 inches long. (*Courtesy Zoological Society of Philadelphia, photograph by Mark Mooney, Jr.*)

6 [LEFT]. Common Musk Turtles (*Sternotherus odoratus*) from New Jersey. Some of the sexual differences described in the text are illustrated. The female, with head and tail almost hidden, has a carapace 3.78 inches long, whereas that of the male measures 3.84 inches. (*Photograph by Douglas Cullen.*)

7 [RIGHT]. Young Common Musk Turtle (*Sternotherus odoratus*) from Talbot County, Maryland, with a carapace 28 millimetres long. (*Courtesy Zoological Society of Philadelphia, photograph by Mark Mooney, Jr.*)

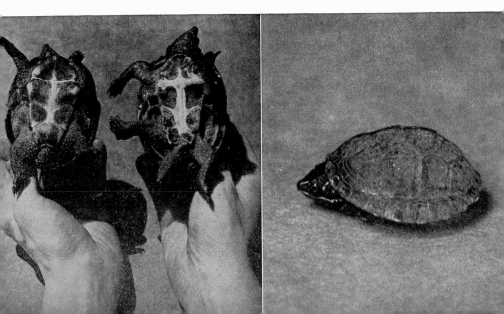

that of a fish, a similarity which frequently makes them the victim of thwarted irate anglers. The Common and Alligator Snappers are the only other kinds that habitually arouse the ire of man. Their sin is the occasional slaughter of game fishes and aquatic birds, both domestic and wild. These formidable reptiles also do some good as scavengers and destroyers of harmful animals. They are often eaten, especially in Philadelphia (see Plate 23). Species not mentioned in this paragraph on the whole go unmolested and, in this respect, are much more fortunate than their unjustly persecuted relatives, the snakes.

There is no doubt that some chelonians are valuable destroyers of noxious insects and other invertebrates, but this aspect of their economy is little understood and calls for careful separate analysis of the habits of each and every species. (See the remarks in the section on food and feeding above.)

CARE OF BABY TURTLES

Although few people keep adult turtles in confinement, literally tens of thousands have pet turtlets. These infants are products of a large traffic originating chiefly in the Gulf states. For the benefit of this host of owners I give here blanket directions for the care of the species (Map and Troost's Turtles) which usually get into circulation. The very young of most of the aquatic kinds will respond fairly well to this same type of treatment.

CONTAINER. An aquarium arranged so that it is about equally divided between water and dry land makes the best home for these baby turtles. The water should be deep enough to allow the occupants to eat and swim under the surface. It is best to use a readily moved water-container and keep it free of everything solid except objects such as flat stones and pieces of cork or wood under and on which the turtles can hide and bask at will. The stones should be arranged to form a miniature cave. Cleanliness is advisable on general principles, although a little contamination is not necessarily fatal.

TEMPERATURE. Since most trade specimens are of southern origin, they require a high temperature, ranging from 75° to 85° F., preferably about 80°. A sharp nightly fall in temperature is very harmful, so during cold weather the vivarium should be heated with an aquarium heater or an electric bulb, or, in default of these, covered with a blanket. All clean water put in the container must be at about room temperature to avoid sudden chilling of the turtles.

SUNLIGHT. Sunlight is extremely important in maintaining health. In winter a sun-lamp is the best substitute. The sun's rays should enter the vivarium direct, but those that pass through ordinary glass are better than none and are useful in keeping the temperature up and making the pets feel at home. It must be remembered, though, that any reptile is readily killed by a direct summer sun from which it cannot escape.

FOOD. For city pets, raw chopped lean beef or fish is suitable food; in the country, living worms and other soft-bodied invertebrate animals are ideal, their movement helping considerably to arouse appetite. Lettuce or other tender vegetable leaves may also be given occasionally. A pinch of bone-meal (or the raw crushed backbone of a fish) and a drop or so of cod-liver oil should be mixed with the food as often as possible. The dried " ant eggs " commonly sold in pet-stores are not recommended, nor is a straight diet of house flies advisable.

A little experience will indicate how finely to chop the food. It must of course be in pieces small enough to go down readily, and the smaller the pieces, the more easily the ingredients can be mixed in, but when too finely divided, the inevitable remnants will rapidly spoil in the tepid water. (Most aquatic turtles prefer to eat with the head submerged.) Semi-weekly feedings will suffice and care must be taken to determine whether any food is consumed; its apparent disappearance does not always mean that it has been eaten. Indifference to food in winter is not necessarily a sign of illness, as it is often the result of a tendency to hibernate in spite of living in a warm environment.

BLINDNESS. Improper food, lack of sunlight, and low temperature are prone to cause the eyes to remain closed. Washing the lids twice a day with cotton soaked in warm boric-acid solution and improvement of food and surroundings are all that can be done as a cure.

PAINTED TURTLES. Victims of an extraordinary sense of humour are the thousands of tiny waifs with gaily painted shell. A typical example is " Orphan Annie," shown on Plate 3. The paint must be flaked off as promptly as possible with a razor blade or sharp knife because it seriously interferes with the growth of the shell.

SOME EXPLANATIONS

NAMES. The use of the words " turtle," " tortoise," and " terrapin " is in a state of exasperating confusion. British reptile-men prefer to reserve each of these names for a particular group of the reptiles in question, thus giving them true scientific significance, but in the United States the tendency is to call all chelonians " turtles " and to think of fresh-water species with a market value as " terrapins," strictly land forms with stump-shaped hind limbs as " tortoises." I have followed the American usage, not only because I am writing about American turtles, but also because this is by far the simplest solution of the problem.

The question of common names for each kind of turtle is also vexed, but here I have truly chosen a single one for each species and subspecies in hopes that, if appropriate, it will be generally accepted.

TERMS. After learning from a study of Plates 1 and 2 that

the upper part of the shell is the carapace, the lower part the plastron, and becoming familiar with the names of the shields or horny plates covering the shell, one should have little difficulty placing a turtle in its proper species or even subspecies. Subspecies are subdivisions of a species that merge one into another in an intermediate area (or areas) between their ranges. Individuals from this area (or areas) resemble both (or all) of the subspecies and are called " intergrades "; the existence of these intergrades necessitates the use of the special term " subspecies." Representatives of different subspecies (of one species) found in places remote from a region of intergradation often differ noticeably from one another and therefore cannot be left out of this book. Not infrequently common names are regularly applied to strikingly different subspecies. The Painted Turtles (Eastern, Central, Southern, and Western) best illustrate this point. Because subspecies are strictly geographical, they can be identified on the basis of distribution alone.

MEASUREMENTS. Measurements of the shell, unless otherwise stated, are straight, not taken along the curve. As explained in the beginning of Chapter VIII, the sea-turtles form the only general exception. In the carapace and plastron widths the greatest width is usually meant.

IDENTIFICATION OF AMERICAN TURTLES

For the benefit of those not accustomed to identifying animals or plants it is necessary to state that a " key " is a scheme by which one is quickly led to the name of a species. To use the key one must understand the various terms contained in it and then proceed, specimen in hand, to make the indicated choices. For example, in the following key, " A1 " at the very beginning calls for determination of the nature of the shell and of the snout. If the former is hard and the latter not projected into a proboscis, go to " B1 " immediately below, in which the form of the limbs is brought in focus. If the limbs are like flippers, look for " B2 " and learn that you have a sea-turtle, treated in Chapter VIII. Should the limbs of your specimen not resemble flippers drop to " C1," count the shields on the plastron, and continue to " run " the key in this same manner.

The key below should cause no difficulty except perhaps in the characters distinguishing Chapter IV from Chapter VI. Fortunately the brevity of the former makes it a simple matter to turn to it and quickly determine whether the specimen being identified is by chance either the Wood, the Pacific Pond, or Muhlenberg's Turtle. (The Spotted Turtle is recognized at once by the yellow spots on the carapace.)

The key fails completely in the identification of very young Blanding's and box turtles because plastral hinges are not evident until some time after hatching. The carapace is never hard during the first few months of life and the tail is often proportionately longer than it will later be, but these facts should not mislead, because no choice is based entirely on them. Many other astonishing changes in growth are dealt with in the chapter introductions or under the various species.

When patterns are called for, any obscure component colours can be brought out by wetting the shell or skin.

KEY TO THE TURTLES OF THE UNITED STATES
AND CANADA BY CHAPTERS OF THIS BOOK

A1: Carapace hard and covered with horny shields; snout not projected into a soft proboscis.

    B1: Limbs not in the form of flippers; salt-marsh, freshwater, or land habitats.

        C1: Plastron (exclusive of bridge) with four or five

pairs of shields usually preceded by an unpaired one.

D1: Tail much less than half as long as carapace and without a dorsal crest of tubercles; plastron (exclusive of bridge) with five pairs of shields usually preceded by an unpaired one.

> MUSK AND MUD TURTLES
> *Chapter II*

D2: Tail much more than half as long as carapace and with a conspicuous dorsal crest of tubercles; plastron (exclusive of bridge) with four pairs of shields preceded by an unpaired one.

> SNAPPING TURTLES
> *Chapter III*

C2: Plastron (exclusive of bridge) with six pairs of shields.

D1: A hinge across plastron just in front of middle, dividing it into two movable lobes.

> BLANDING'S and BOX TURTLES
> *Chapter V*

D2: Plastron without hinge.

E1: Hind limbs not stump-shaped, toes more or less webbed; aquatic habitats; widely distributed.

F1: Head and neck without longitudinal yellow stripes or, if any are evident, carapace with numerous small yellow spots.

> SPOTTED, WOOD, PACIFIC POND, and MUHLENBERG'S TURTLES
> *Chapter IV*

F2: Head and neck usually with longitudinal yellow stripes (the diamond-back terra-

pins of salt marshes excepted).
DIAMOND-BACK TERRAPINS,
MAP, PAINTED, PSEUDEMYD,
and CHICKEN TURTLES
Chapter VI

E2: Hind limbs stump-shaped; toes without sign
of web; dry-land or desert habitats; found
only south of 36° N. Lat. in east, 38° N. in
west.   GOPHER TORTOISES
Chapter VII

B2: Limbs in form of flippers; marine habitat.   SEA-TURTLES
Chapter VIII

A2: Carapace soft and flexible, covered with undivided
skin; snout projected into a soft proboscis.
SOFT-SHELLED TURTLES
Chapter IX

CHAPTER II

THE MUSK *and* MUD TURTLES

Family KINOSTERNIDÆ
Genera *STERNOTHERUS* and *KINOSTERNON*

The musk and mud turtles comprise a New World family of only four genera and about twenty species, the genera *Sternotherus* and *Kinosternon* having, respectively, three and fourteen of the twenty. The family is distributed from central South America northward to extreme southeastern Canada. Unfortunately almost no fossil remains have been found, so the early family history is a matter of conjecture. Anatomical relationship to the snapping turtles is evident.

In this family the males are unique among turtles in having two opposing patches of horny scales on the inner side of each hind limb. The tail is also unusual in being prehensile and ending in a blunt nail. During courtship and copulation the male uses tail and hind limbs in securing a firm grasp on the female's shell, the opposing patches of scales and the prehensile tail enabling him to do so. The old belief that the former were rubbed together to produce a sound (stridulation) is apparently erroneous. (See the account of mating under the section on reproduction of the Yellow Mud Turtle.)

IDENTIFICATION

The recognition of a member of the family Kinosternidæ is a simple matter after one has become familiar with any of its species, but the uninitiated need some definite characters to go by.

The plastron (see Plates 8 and 15) is by far the best point of attack since the number of shields in it as well as the relation of its two more or less movable lobes combine to distinguish a musk or mud turtle of the United States from any other chelonian of this country. There are five pairs of large plastral shields plus an unpaired one at the forward extremity which is small or even lacking in the Keeled Musk Turtle. Each of these paired shields makes contact with its mate on the midline or is separated from it only by skin. The two movable lobes of the plastron are hinged to a fixed transverse section spanning the space between the edges of the carapace. In Blanding's Turtle and the box turtles the lobes of the plastron have a common hinge without an intervening immovable section.

Additional characters that will help are: the pair of small fleshy barbels on the chin and the usual lack of outward flare to the lower border of the carapace; and the presence on the bridge of small shields separating the marginals of the carapace from the large shields of the plastron.

In using the key given below, two points must be kept in mind: first, the distinction between the "quadrangular" and "triangular" shape of the pectoral shields (which lie just in front of the anterior hinge) is not absolute, the "triangular" ones sometimes having a very short fourth side along the midline suture of the plastron; second, the fact that all very young members of this family are more or less keeled makes the alternatives relying on presence or absence of keels somewhat unreliable. A good precaution is to read the section on the young under each species, thus avoiding confusion on this and various other points, such as the juvenile rigidity of the plastral lobes.

The Musk and Mud Turtles

KEY TO THE SPECIES OF *Sternotherus* AND
Kinosternon FOUND IN THE UNITED
STATES AND CANADA

A1: Pectoral shields quadrangular in shape (*Sternotherus*).
  B1: Gular shield well developed; side of head with or
    without two yellow stripes.
    C1: Side of head with two yellow stripes.
                                   COMMON MUSK TURTLE
    C2: Side of head without two yellow stripes.
                                   SOUTHERN MUSK TURTLE
  B2: Gular shield small or absent; side of head without
    two yellow stripes.   KEELED MUSK TURTLE
A2: Pectoral shields triangular (*Kinosternon*).
  B1: Carapace with three longitudinal yellow stripes.
                                   STRIPED MUD TURTLE
  B2: Carapace without three yellow stripes.
    C1: Ninth marginal shield roughly triangular in shape
      and distinctly higher than eighth.
                                   YELLOW MUD TURTLE
    C2: Ninth marginal neither triangular nor distinctly
      higher than eighth.
      D1: Carapace with three longitudinal keels or at
        least traces of them.   SONORAN MUD TURTLE
      D2: Carapace with a median keel or none.
                                   COMMON MUD TURTLE
                                   MISSISSIPPI MUD TURTLE
                              or STEINDACHNER'S MUD TURTLE

For assistance in making this key I am indebted to Dr. Norman E. Hartweg, who is studying the Kinosternidæ.

COMMON MUSK TURTLE

Sternotherus odoratus (Latreille)

[PLATES 5, 6, AND 7]

IDENTIFICATION. The carapace of the adult is without a keel or with a mere trace of one extending along the middle line. A well-developed gular shield is always present and the shields of the carapace are not overlapping. Two yellow stripes run along either side of the head. The carapace is dull olive or brown, with or without dark spots or streaks.

SIZE. The size of this species is clearly shown by the following analysis of Evermann and Clark's carapace lengths (measured along the curve) of one hundred and seventy-one Indiana specimens:

Longest carapace	5.37 inches
Weight of this specimen	7.75 ounces
Number of additional carapaces	
5 or more inches long	10
Number 4 to 4.99 inches long	104
Number 3 to 3.99 inches long	52
Number less than 3 inches long	4

Dimensions of a female from Union County, New Jersey, follow:

	Inches	Millimetres
Length of carapace (straight)	3.75	95
Length of carapace (along curve)	4.31	110
Width of carapace (straight)	2.75	70
Width of carapace (along curve)	4.25	108
Length of plastron	2.94	75
Width of front lobe of plastron at hinge	1.37	35
Height of shell	1.56	40

YOUNG. The highly arched carapace of very young individuals (see Plate 7) is nearly as wide as long (22.5 × 19 mm. in one case) and has three keels. It is rough and almost black. The lateral keels are lost early, but traces of the vertebral one may even persist throughout life. Both lobes of the plastron are rigid, whereas in the adult the front lobe is freely, the rear slightly movable.

THE SEXES. Sexual differences (see Plate 6) have been made the object of special study by Risley, who finds that:

The tail of the male is longer and ends in a blunt nail; that of the female may have an acutely pointed terminal nail. The tail of the female, but not of the male, has a row of tubercles down the middle of its upper side and is generally the more tuberculate.

The concave plastron of the male is narrower across the posterior edge of the humeral shields. The bridge connecting it with the carapace is also narrower in males than in females. The length of the male plastron is less than seventy per cent, that of the female more than seventy-two per cent of the carapace length. The amount of skin between the plastral shields is greater in the male, the female therefore having larger shields on the lower shell.

The male has two patches of horny scales on the inner side of each hind limb and a wider head, but its carapace is slightly narrower.

These differences do not make their appearance until the third or fourth year of life.

EGG. The elliptical eggs vary considerably in size and shape, but their average dimensions are 27.1 × 15.5 millimetres. The hard white shell is thick and brittle.

LONGEVITY. One individual of this species lived twenty-three, another thirteen, and four more nine years in captivity.

GROWTH. Risley believes that a carapace length of more than 3.15 inches indicates an age of at least ten years; that ages of two to seven years can be determined with accuracy by growth-ring counts; that males become sexually mature in their third or fourth year, females not until they are nine to eleven years old.

MOULT. The shields of the carapace and plastron are shed periodically according to Risley, but, if such is the case, I fail to see how he determined age by growth-ring counts.

DISTRIBUTION. Widely distributed over extreme southeastern Canada and the eastern United States.

In the north it occurs from southern Maine westward through the region of Lake Ontario across the southern half of the lower peninsula of Michigan, and the southern third of Wisconsin. To the west it is found throughout Illinois, over the southern half of Missouri, the southeastern corner of Kansas, the eastern third of Oklahoma, and the eastern half of Texas.

HABITAT. A little more than half of about fourscore habitat records of this common reptile divide their most popular haunts between streams of various sizes and ponds. Next come lakes, rivers, and ditches, but even with these the numerous types of aquatic situations frequented are not exhausted since there are scattered records for pools, lagoons, bayous, marshes, swamps, bogs, sloughs, and canals.

A muddy bottom is almost indispensable, and abundant aquatic growth attracts large populations. Watercourses with considerable current are inhabited, the turtles living in the deeper quieter stretches where the current is not swift enough to keep mud from settling. In fact, a preference for deep water has been noticed by several observers.

HABITS. This is an aquatic bottom-loving reptile typically seen crawling on mud under quiet water. It is a weak swimmer and progresses clumsily on land. Nevertheless, I have seen a small individual make astonishing, mouse-like dashes. Thoroughly aquatic adaptations are proved by the ability to live for months without visible ill effects in a straight-sided aquarium affording no footing out of water.

Most observers agree that the water is seldom left except by females ready to lay, but Newman found northern Indiana individuals of all sizes wandering freely and even feeding on land. He mentions picking up four males during heavy rain, and I suspect that these terrestrial excursions are correlated with rain or at least with localities and periods of great humidity. Perhaps members of unusually large populations finding food scarce in the water desert it to forage on terra firma.

Conant and Bailey secured some evidence that the Common Musk Turtle deserts a region in which the water has been made brackish by man's interference with natural conditions, whereas the Common Mud Turtle remains. This explains the reputation the former species has of being less coastwise in range than the latter.

The temperament can scarcely be called good, since wild individuals hiss, hold the mouth open threateningly, and frequently resort to biting when handled.

HIBERNATION. That this species sometimes hibernates gregariously is shown by an old report of the discovery of two hundred and thirty-nine specimens in one site, and the following part of a recent account by Thomas and Trautman:

"On March 28, 1927, we found a large colony of hibernating *Sternotherus odoratus* in the drained bed of a canal north of Buckeye Lake, Licking County, Ohio. The canal had been partially drained during the winter, and to complete the drainage, a steam shovel had cut a narrow ditch along each inner bank of the canal. During the ditching operations the shovel uncovered from the bed of the canal a colony of turtles that had been segregated in an area of approximately 45 feet in length by 6 feet in width. We estimated a total of 450 turtles in this small area. Only the one species was found in the aggregation.

" Almost all the turtles were dead, except perhaps 6 living individuals which were in the shallow water of the newly-created ditches. Apparently the removal of the water from the hibernating turtles, and exposure to a minimum temperature of approximately 15° F., had been sufficient to kill these animals. In the remaining half-mile of canal which we investigated, no turtles of this species were found. Because of disturbed conditions it was impossible to determine the exact depth in which the aggregation had been hibernating, though it appeared that they had been from a few inches to a foot beneath the surface of the soft, mucky bottom."

The other references to hibernation amount to little save one which suggests that winter is sometimes spent in shallow burrows away from water.

The published dates for first appearance fall from March 3 to 25 in Ohio, Indiana, and Michigan. In the early spring specimens may be found resting among aquatic plants and in débris under shallow water.

SUNNING. All accounts agree that the sunning habit is but poorly developed. In spite of this, specimens, especially in the spring, float or rest just below the surface when the sun is bright, and an occasional one even crawls out to bask on a log or other projecting object. The young are said to sun out of water more frequently than the adults.

MATING. The extensive researches on this turtle by Risley have brought out one extremely interesting fact: namely, that active spermatozoa are present in the male from September to May. In other words, the hibernation period merely interrupts the reproductive activity of this sex; presumably mating does not take place during the winter sleep. Field observers have reported autumn copulation, but the most active mating undoubtedly occurs in the early spring. The fact that motile spermatozoa have been found in summer in spent females shows what provision is made for the propagation of this species – spring and autumn mating and the ability of male cells to live in females for weeks if not months! This long survival of the spermatozoa is not so surprising when we recall that they apparently thrive for several years in the female Diamond-back.

The spring usually finds the sexes together in shallow water near shore, which of course is quickly warmed and therefore conducive to early activity. After the middle of May (in southern Michigan) the males disperse, leaving the females in the shallows to await laying time. Ovulation takes place in that locality between the 15th and 20th of May, the eggs remaining in the oviducts some twenty to thirty-five days while the albumen and shell are being secreted.

During courtship the male takes the aggressive, following the female about, and the former mounts the latter to affect union. In one copulating pair the female was "lying prone, as if dead."

NESTING. In southern Michigan the great majority of eggs are deposited "during the last twenty days of June and the first five of July." New nests have been located as late as July 17 in western Tennessee. Indication of occasional late nesting exists in reports of gravid females taken in Indiana in the autumn and a Wisconsin nest discovered near the end of September. Whether the eggs deposited late ever tide over the winter is not known.

Laying may take place at any time from early morning until twilight, and possibly at night, although no one has witnessed such nocturnal activity.

The nesting habits of this turtle are chiefly remarkable for their lack of uniformity, brought out by the following summaries:

The site may be well above ground on top of a rotten stump, under a fallen log, in a bundle of rushes drifted together, or almost anywhere near water, such as in a cow-track, in a mass

8. Southern Musk Turtles (*Sternotherus minor*) from Marion County, Florida, with carapaces 4.75 and 3.44 inches long. (*Courtesy Zoological Society of Philadelphia, photograph by Mark Mooney, Jr.*)

9. Southern Musk Turtle (*Sternotherus minor*) from Ware County, Georgia. (*Photograph by Francis Harper.*)

10. Striped Mud Turtle (*Kinosternon baurii*) with a carapace 3.75 inches long. (*Courtesy Zoological Society of Philadelphia, photograph by Mark Mooney, Jr.*)

11. Striped Mud Turtle (*Kinosternon baurii*) that has lived in captivity since 1913, as described in the sections on longevity and captivity. The characteristic head and carapace stripes of the species are not evident. (*Courtesy William T. Davis, photograph by Carlton Beil.*)

of muck, or on the bare surface of the ground. A strong tendency toward gregariousness is often exhibited, dozens of nests being found intermingled under one log or similar object. Muskrat houses are favourite sites for such congregations. Contrasting with this are the not infrequent discoveries of single eggs lying about unburied. A point of considerable interest in this connection is the astonishing resistance of the thick- and brittle-shelled eggs to desiccation, a fact presumably correlated with their occasional exposure to the effects of the sun and air, which are usually fatal for turtle eggs. Cagle reports that many uncovered eggs contain healthy embryos.

The female may either lay her eggs in the open, as already remarked, cover them with a thin layer of débris, conceal them in soft material under or in a log or stump, or barely bury them in a shallow hole dug by her hind feet. Her tendency to lay either in or under some large object is most unusual, since an open sunny place is nearly always selected by other chelonians. At times, however, she gives her offspring " decent burial " in a creditable way little inferior to that of species with more stable habits. The following observation made in southeastern Wisconsin by Cahn serves as an illustration:

" In one instance the nest was in the sand about 150 feet from the pond in which the turtle lived. At 6:20 on the evening of June 22, the female came slowly out of the water and paused for about ten minutes at the water's edge while she looked about with her head raised to the fullest extent. Satisfied that all was well she headed off through the tall reeds straight for the patch of sand; there was no uncertainty in movements. Arriving here she paused again for a few minutes, her head again erect. Then she walked deliberately out to nearly the middle of the open area and began to dig. The process was slow and leisurely, the dirt being scraped away with alternating strokes of the hind feet, and piled up into two small heaps on each side of the hole. When the depth of the hole was about equal to the length of the carapace, she deposited her eggs therein, after which she filled in the hole again with her hind feet and headed straight back to the water. The time required for the digging, laying, and covering was forty-seven minutes, during which time she paid no attention to anything around her. When I dug the nest out I found it to be semicircular in shape, the roof arched to conform to the curvature of the carapace. The hole descended at an angle of 50° to a depth of four and a half inches, and contained three eggs."

Newman saw a female dig with all four feet and even her snout. Since all other observers, however, have seen only the hind limbs used, it is better to conclude tentatively that these alone are normally made to serve as shovels.

The number of eggs laid at one time varies from two to seven, but the usual range is from three to five. A clutch of nine has been taken from the oviducts of a large female. Risley found that eggs kept in a laboratory where the temperature occasionally went up to 98° F. hatched in sixty to seventy-five days after deposition, whereas others placed in the basement and rarely exposed to a temperature higher than 77° F. required about ninety days to incubate. This well illustrates the effect of temperature on rate of development.

BEHAVIOUR OF HATCHLING. Laboratory experiments by Noble and Breslau lead them to conclude that hatchlings " find their way from the nests to the water primarily because they are attracted toward large areas of intense illumination "; also that the attraction of areas of great humidity is weaker than that of light. The further conclusion that the strong tendency of the hatchlings to climb uphill in the dark facilitates escape from the nest is especially interesting in view of the erratic nesting habits of the species. Exposed and lightly buried hatchlings emerging at night presumably hurry uphill until the bright horizon of the dawn brings them down again!

FOOD AND FEEDING. Although chiefly carnivorous, the Common Musk Turtle sometimes eats water plants and other vegetable matter. The animals devoured make up a long list of small aquatic and even terrestrial creatures: earthworms, larval insects and winged adults, small mollusks, crayfish, minnows, tadpoles, and so forth. Scavenger tendencies have been proved by observations of individuals feeding on various kinds of dead animals as well as on cow dung and kitchen refuse.

Subaqueous feeding is the rule, proved, nevertheless, by exceptions. Food is usually hunted on the bottom. An article too large to be swallowed whole is held by the jaws while the claws push against it, tearing the main mass away from the part in the mouth.

ENEMIES. Oddly enough no one has actually determined what creatures are responsible for the empty shells of Common Musk Turtles sometimes found lying about. In one case circumstantial evidence pointed to American and fish crows, in another, involving a series of observations, to muskrats.

The tiny young must make dainty morsels for land as well as aquatic enemies. The eggs are dug up and eaten by skunks, raccoons, and probably other kinds of mammals. Risley thinks that it may be crows and herons that dig great numbers of eggs out of muskrat houses.

Leeches frequently parasitize the Common Musk Turtle, whose aquatic habits play into the hands of such parasites.

DEFENCE. Biting is one of the chief defensive tactics of the Common Musk Turtle. The head is extended slowly toward an offending object, the speed of the movement being suddenly increased just before the goal is reached. The head is then quickly retracted, the jaws retaining their grip. The great length of the neck enables the turtle to seize a hand holding the forward or middle part of the shell. The bite is not severe enough to pierce the tough skin of one's hand. A hatchling has been seen to bite upon escape from its shell.

A specimen surprised on land may readily be seen to exude a yellowish fluid from two glands opening along the border of the carapace on either side: one near the point where the hind edge of the bridge meets the carapace, and the other about midway between the forward edge of the bridge and the head end of the carapace. The secretion has a strong musky odour, the purpose of which is undoubtedly defensive.

A frequent rank growth of algæ on the shell also protects the animal through rendering it relatively invisible. But, as explained in the following account by Evermann and Clark, animals as well as plants make use of the shell:

" During the late summer and early autumn of 1906, many small Musk Turtles were seen surrounded by a white halo which was conspicuous at a distance, very much resembling the general appearance of Saprolegnia on fishes. It was found upon examination that the white growth consisted of a dense growth of a stalked branched protozoan, *Opercularia.* Later it was found that larger Musk Turtles harbored considerable masses of the protozoan on the plastron, this being frequently entirely covered, so that the turtles were practically botanical gardens above and zoological gardens below. Neither the alga nor the protozoan appears to do the turtles any injury. The algæ above may assist the turtle in concealment; the protozoan below is self-supporting, feeding on minute organisms."

CAPTIVITY. The rather bad temperament, strong odour, secretiveness, and ungainly appearance of the Common Musk Turtle detract from its popularity in the aquarium. In spite of all this, it makes a hardy, easily fed, and rather unusual pet which will take food from one's fingers and even mate in crowded quarters. (See the section on longevity above.)

An aquarium kept at room temperature with straight sides and cork islands or any other small out-of-water rest is suitable; a dark place in which the turtle can hide is very advisable.

It should be fed on items selected from those named above

in the discussion of food. Chopped raw meat or fish may be used as a convenient supplement and earthworms are especially relished. The voracious habits of these turtles in captivity are well described by Newman:

" Their appetite is insatiable and indiscriminate. On one occasion I put a living rat in an aquarium containing several musk tortoises. Almost immediately three of them seized it by the feet and pulled it under, thus drowning it. Before it had ceased to struggle they proceeded to disembowel it and succeeded in making a fairly good skeleton of it in a few hours."

ECONOMIC VALUE. Little praise and less blame can be laid at the door of the Common Musk Turtle. Some benefit is probably derived from its feeding habits, but the flesh is useless. The few fish and fish eggs consumed are of no consequence.

Disgrace is brought upon it by anglers annoyed when it mistakes their bait for legitimate food. The habit of cleaning the hook without jerking is described as especially exasperating.

SOUTHERN MUSK TURTLE

Sternotherus minor (Agassiz)

[PLATES 8 AND 9]

IDENTIFICATION. Three distinct keels extend along the back, a well-developed gular shield is always present, and the shields of the carapace are overlapping. No yellow stripes are evident on the head, which has dark stripes and spots. The carapace is yellowish brown or olive, each shield more or less distinctly marked with dark spots or radiating lines.

SIZE. Measurements of an adult male are given by Rust as follows:

	Inches	Millimetres
Length of carapace	4.33	110
Width of carapace	2.99	76
Length of plastron	3.11	79
Width of front lobe of plastron	1.65	42
Height of shell	1.61	41

YOUNG. The carapace of a young male is only slightly longer than wide (41 × 34 mm.), and wider behind than in front of its middle line. In the adult the greater width is in front of this line.

THE SEXES. The tail of the male is long and ends in a spine. Two patches of horny scales are present on the inner side of each hind limb in this sex.

DISTRIBUTION. Northern Florida and southern Georgia westward into southern Alabama; Roane County, eastern Tennessee. The exact limits of the range are not well known because this species has been confused with the Keeled Musk Turtle.

Agassiz described this turtle from specimens labelled Columbus, Georgia; Mobile, Alabama; and New Orleans, Louisiana. The New Orleans specimens had undoubtedly been transported to that city from some more eastern point.

This species is typically an inhabitant of rivers flowing into the Atlantic and the extreme eastern part of the Gulf of Mexico. What, then, is it doing in the Emory River of eastern Tennessee, a secondary affluent of the Tennessee River and part of the Mississippi River system? Stejneger offers an explanation based on the history of these rivers: During the Miocene Period, which began about twenty million years ago, the Tennessee River was captured by the Mississippi system, whereas it had previously belonged to the Alabama River drainage. The turtle in question must, therefore, have attained the old Tennessee River when it flowed into the Gulf of Mexico through Alabama. Even though this explanation cred-

its the Southern Musk Turtle with a surprisingly long existence, it must stand until replaced by a better one. Unfortunately, almost nothing is known of the fossil history of the
Kinosternidæ in North America. The only fossil form known,
Kinosternon arizonense, was, as the name implies, found in
Arizona. It probably lived in the Pliocene, which ended only
about a million years ago.

HABITAT. The Southern Musk Turtle is typically an inhabitant of Coastal Plain rivers such as the Santa Fe of northern
Florida. It has, however, been taken at an altitude of 1,200
feet where the Emory River of eastern Tennessee flows
through rugged foothills. These foothills were well wooded
when the turtle was collected in them in 1895. The presence
of this species in Tennessee is discussed above in the section on
distribution.

CAPTIVITY. Rust found that captive specimens behave like
those of the Common Musk Turtle. Probably the two species
should be treated alike and given similar food.

KEELED MUSK TURTLE

Sternotherus carinatus (Gray)

IDENTIFICATION. A sharp keel extends along the middle of
the back, and from this keel the nearly flat sides of the carapace slope evenly to the marginals. The gular shield is nearly
always lacking; when discernible, it is very small. The shields
of the carapace are overlapping. No yellow stripes are present
on the head, which has dark spots and flecks. The carapace is
olive, each shield more or less distinctly marked with dark
spots or radiating lines.

SIZE. This turtle attains a carapace length of about five

inches. Ditmars gives the following measurements of a smaller specimen:

	Inches	Millimetres
Length of carapace	3.50	89
Width of carapace	2.37	60
Length of plastron	2.50	63
Width of front lobe of plastron at hinge	1.37	35

YOUNG. The carapace is almost as wide as long (30 × 27 mm. in one case) and usually has three keels.

THE SEXES. The tail of the male is longer and thicker, the transverse brown stripes on its jaws are usually much more intense, and two patches of horny scales are present on the inner side of each hind limb. Also in this sex the shields of the plastron are more widely separated by a continuous area of soft skin which is especially evident along the middle line. Consequently the plastral shields of the male are smaller than those of the female.

DISTRIBUTION. Lower Mississippi drainage as far north as central Arkansas and westward to the southeastern tip of Oklahoma. It also ranges over the lowlands of eastern Texas. In the southern part of this state it has been found as far west as the region of San Antonio. The limits of its range east of the Mississippi are uncertain because of its frequent confusion with the Southern Musk Turtle.

HABITAT. Bayous, swamps, lakes, and rivers.

CAPTIVITY. Rust recommends keeping this species in a shoreless aquarium with islands. The proper temperature is from about 72° to 77° F. and the food should be similar to that given the Common Musk Turtle.

A dark place in which to hide should also be provided.

STRIPED MUD TURTLE

Kinosternon baurii Garman

[PLATES 10 AND 11]

IDENTIFICATION. The ninth marginal shield (on the rear border of the carapace) is not noticeably higher than the eighth. Three dull yellow longitudinal stripes extend down the olive or reddish-brown carapace, and two yellow stripes are present on either side of the head.

The limited range of this species will help in its identification.

SIZE. The Striped Mud Turtle attains a carapace length of 4.72 inches. A female with a carapace 3.62 inches long and 2.44 wide had a shell 1.53 inches high.

YOUNG. Keels are present under the three stripes along the carapace from the time of hatching until the individual is about half grown. The colours of the young are brighter and more strongly contrasted than those of the adult.

THE SEXES. The tail of the male ends in a strong spine, and the inner side of each hind limb has two patches of horny scales. The female tail does not end in such a spine, and her hind limbs do not have the patches of horny scales. The plastron in the female is longer, and Siebenrock has mentioned, but not clearly explained, other sexual differences in this part of the shell.

LONGEVITY. A female of this species has lived in captivity since September 7, 1913, when it was taken at South Jacksonville, Florida. Its owner, Dr. W. T. Davis, informs me, in a letter dated June 16, 1938, that this individual was fully grown when caught and that it is still thriving. (See Plate 11.)

DISTRIBUTION. Peninsular Florida.

HABITAT. Van Hyning found this species common in both

large and small bodies of water in Alachua County, Florida, and others have also reported it from a variety of aquatic situations: river, brook, swamp, canal, and even mud-hole. It thrives in coastal brackish water, a fact that must account for its presence on the Florida keys.

CAPTIVITY. The female owned by Dr. Davis and referred to above under Longevity has lived for approximately twenty-five years in a large bowl with shallow water and a stone upon which she can climb to dry off. She has been fed on raw meat and may have secured a few fallen insects besides.

Rust recommends a shoreless aquarium with cork islands and temperature of about 70° to 75° F. The water can be either fresh or brackish, and, for food, snails, earthworms, tadpoles, salamanders, and raw meat or fish are preferable. A dark place in which to hide should also be provided.

YELLOW MUD TURTLE

Kinosternon flavescens flavescens (Agassiz)

IDENTIFICATION. The ninth marginal shield (at the rear border of the carapace) is roughly triangular in shape and distinctly higher than the eighth. The carapace has neither three light stripes nor three keels extending along it. Nearly all accounts describe some part or parts of the lateral or ventral aspect of the head and neck as bright immaculate yellow but there is little agreement as to the exact extent and distribution of this colour.

SIZE. The Yellow Mud Turtle attains a carapace length of 5.75 inches. Dimensions of a male specimen from Illinois as recorded by Cahn follow:

	Inches	Millimetres
Length of carapace	5.04	128
Width of carapace	3.54	90
Length of plastron	4.25	108
Width of plastron	2.95	75
Height of shell	1.65	42
Weight	13.8 ounces	

YOUNG. The carapace of very young individuals is nearly as wide as long (32.5 × 30 mm. in one case); it has an indistinct median keel, and its shields lack the dark margins of the adult. The ninth marginal shield is not yet enlarged and triangular in shape, and the vertebrals and costals have, according to Cahn, a broad band impressed along their front and side margins. Dark spots on the plastron form a more or less regular figure.

THE SEXES. Two patches of horny scales are present on the inner side of each hind limb of the male only. This sex has a longer tail and its upper jaw is more strongly hooked in front. The largest of the few females on record has a carapace only 4.41 inches long, whereas males are known to attain a much greater size.

EGG. The elliptical eggs measure 25 or 26 × 16 millimetres and have a hard white shell.

DISTRIBUTION. This species is found from extreme southern Nebraska southward through the western half of Kansas, all of Oklahoma but its southeastern section, and all of Texas except its eastern lowlands. There are good records for the southeastern corner of Colorado.

To the west the limits of its range are uncertain because it has been confused with the Sonoran Mud Turtle. Scattered records exist for New Mexico, extreme southern Utah, and southern Arizona. Oddly enough, it also occurs along the Illinois River from Meredosia Bay to Peoria, Illinois.

In northern Mexico it intergrades with the recently described *Kinosternon flavescens stejnegeri* Hartweg.

HABITAT. The Yellow Mud Turtle is an astonishingly successful species, as shown by its wide range, general abundance, and the following list of aquatic situations in which it has been taken: river, creek, stream, lake, pond, pool, prairie sink, flooded depression, and slough; in addition it makes use of such artificial bodies of water as a cattle tank, reservoir, cistern, and even a ditch or sewer drain holding water! In regions where it is most at home great numbers live even in uninviting places. For example, Ortenburger and Freeman write that it is perhaps the commonest turtle in Oklahoma wherever water is available, and in Harmon County roadside ditches only two to four feet wide and commonly less than one foot deep usually harbour at least one individual for every one or two hundred feet of length.

It occurs at an altitude of 5,000 feet in parts of its range.

HABITS. It is not surprising to find that a species which is able to thrive in such small bodies of water often takes to land to rest, bask, or even forage. In this respect it is an exceptional member of its thoroughly aquatic group. Presumably the Yellow Mud Turtle migrates overland when forced to do so by the drying up of a body of water. In fact, Cope long ago observed a migrating individual in northwestern Texas.

REPRODUCTION. No one has studied the reproductive habits of the Yellow Mud Turtle in a natural state, but at least one captive female has been observed to lay two eggs in August. Dissection of another female revealed as many well-developed ovarian eggs. Here is an indication of the number of eggs laid at a time.

Taylor described as follows the actions of some individuals that had been kept since October 2 in a large tank with more than a hundred and forty other American turtles of various species:

"On October 29 a pair of *Kinosternon* were observed in copulation, and two other pairs were observed clasping and

apparently tapping their bodies together. Here the semipre-
hensile tail with its spine-like tip serves as a very efficient grasping organ. When clasping, the male holds the female's shell by
all four of his feet and his tail. In copulation the hold of the
front feet is loosened, and the male stands erect."

The unusual date may be unnatural and consequently of
doubtful interest, but the observation on the astonishing ability
of the male to hold on to the shell of the female and stand
erect is of special value in view of the fact that the male has
the two horny patches of scales on its hind limbs referred to
above in the discussion of the sexes. These scales are probably
efficient grasping organs rather than " stridulating " or sound-
producing ones as believed by some reptile-men.

FOOD. Hooks baited with meat are readily taken. The only
stomach that has been examined held a quantity of grass or
semi-aquatic plant leaves. (See the remarks on food in the discussion of captivity below.)

DEFENCE. The strong odour, undoubtedly of great defensive
value, has won for this turtle the name of " stink pot."

CAPTIVITY. Texas specimens kept by Strecker preferred insects and small mollusks to meat; one killed a small snake and
devoured part of it.

Rust recommends a shoreless aquarium with cork islands and
temperature from 68° to 75° F.; tadpoles, earthworms, salamanders, snails, raw meat, and fish for food.

SONORAN MUD TURTLE

Kinosternon sonoriense Le Conte

IDENTIFICATION. The ninth marginal shield (on the rear
border of the carapace) is not noticeably higher than the

eighth. The carapace is without three longitudinal light stripes, but has at least traces of three longitudinal keels. The lateral and ventral aspects of the head and neck are mottled, not immaculate yellow, and the side of the head does not have a pair of yellow stripes.

SIZE. The largest specimen that I find on record has a carapace 5.67 inches long and 3.98 wide. Its plastron measures 5.27 × 3.11 inches. Ditmars, however, makes the general statement that this turtle attains a carapace length of six inches.

YOUNG. The carapace in the very young is only a little longer than wide (28.5 × 24.5 mm. in one case), and the tenth marginal is not noticeably larger than the ninth. Dark spots on the plastron form a more or less regular figure.

THE SEXES. Two patches of horny scales are present on the inner side of each hind limb of the male only, and the terminal nail of the tail is more strongly developed in this sex. Siebenrock states that the front lobe of the plastron is shorter than the hind one in the female, whereas in the male the lobes are of equal length. He gives other sexual differences in the shell which probably need confirmation since he apparently had only three specimens before him.

DISTRIBUTION. Central and southern Arizona and the extreme southeastern tip of California along the banks of the Colorado River in Imperial Valley; Sonora and Chihuahua, Mexico.

Scattered records extend the range of this turtle across New Mexico into western Texas, but until its relationship with the Yellow Mud Turtle is cleared up, the validity of these records is open to question.

HABITAT. The Sonoran Mud Turtle inhabits rivers and streams, ascending along the latter in Arizona to altitudes of more than 5,000 feet. Being thoroughly aquatic, its distribution is somewhat dependent on the season: during the dry part of the year it congregates in permanent water-holes of canyon streams, but becomes more generally distributed again after the rains return.

HABITS. This species sometimes leaves the water to bask. It readily takes a hook baited with meat.

CAPTIVITY. A specimen lived for more than five years and three months in the National Zoological Park, Washington. It will eat meat under water in captivity.

COMMON MUD TURTLE

Kinosternon subrubrum subrubrum (Lacépède)

[PLATES 12 AND 13]

IDENTIFICATION. The ninth marginal shield (on the rear border of the carapace) is not noticeably higher than the eighth, and the carapace has neither three light stripes nor (in the adult) three keels extending along it. The side of the head is spotted with yellow, the spots more or less arranged in two rows. The bridge width is at least two-thirds the length of the suture between the abdominal shields.

SIZE. The greatest carapace length attained by this turtle is 4.13 inches. Ditmars gives the following dimensions of a specimen of average size:

	Inches	Millimetres
Length of carapace	3.50	89
Width of carapace	2.50	63
Length of plastron	3.12	79
Width of front lobe of plastron at hinge	1.50	38
Width of rear lobe of plastron at hinge	1.50	38

YOUNG. The carapace of the very young has three indistinct keels. Its shape is apparently variable. In Agassiz's figure the carapace measures 21 × 16.5 millimetres and Siebenrock gives the dimensions of a juvenile as 25 × 22 millimetres. On the other hand, Grant states that an Indiana specimen measured 24 × 10.5 millimetres. Presumably he refers to the length and width of the carapace, even though he does not say so. If the 10.5 millimetres refers to the height of shell instead, the great discrepancy is removed, since the shell of Siebenrock's specimen was 12 millimetres high. Dark spots on the plastron form a more or less regular figure. (See Plate 13.)

THE SEXES. Sexual characters in the Common Mud Turtle have been studied by Grant. The most important differences noted by him are:

The longer thicker tail of the male ends in a blunt nail, that of the female in a slender pointed one. Two patches of horny scales are present on the inner side of each hind limb of the former sex. The jaws of the male are heavier and its head larger, and, correlated with these differences, the male carapace is lobed and more highly arched in front. (See Plate 12.) The rear end of the plastron is notched between the anal shields in the male, this notch being replaced by a seam in the female. As a rule the lower jaws in the latter sex are horn yellow, those of the male usually spotted or striped with dark brown.

Grant states that the male has the longer plastron, whereas Siebenrock credited the female with the longer one.

EGG. The elliptical eggs vary in size (23 to 29 × 14 to 17 mm.) and shape, but they ordinarily measure about 27.5 × 15 millimetres and have blunt ends. The white shell is hard, thick, and brittle.

LONGEVITY. A female Common Mud Turtle, which was fully adult when received, lived thirty-eight years in the possession of Dr. Franz Werner of Vienna and even laid eggs several times.

DISTRIBUTION. The Common Mud Turtle ranges from Long

12. Common Mud Turtles (*Kinosternon subrubrum subrubrum*) with carapaces 4.25 and 3.19 inches long. The male is the larger. (*Courtesy Zoological Society of Philadelphia, photograph by Mark Mooney, Jr.*)

13. Young Common Mud Turtle (*Kinosternon subrubrum subrubrum*) with a carapace 25 millimetres long. "For his size he was very tough, he would bite at anything," is the photographer's report. This species is often very good-natured, however. (*Courtesy Zoological Society of Philadelphia, photograph by Mark Mooney, Jr.*)

14. Steindachner's Mud Turtle (*Kinosternon subrubrum steindachneri*) from Gainesville, Florida, with a carapace 4.50 inches long. It is a male. (*Courtesy Zoological Society of Philadelphia, photograph by Mark Mooney, Jr.*)

15. Steindachner's Mud Turtle (*Kinosternon subrubrum steindachneri*) from Gainesville, Florida, with a carapace 4.50 inches long. It is a male. (*Courtesy Zoological Society of Philadelphia, photograph by Mark Mooney, Jr.*)

Island, central New Jersey, and extreme southeastern Pennsylvania southward throughout the Coastal Plain and into the Piedmont Plateau section of the south Atlantic states to southern Georgia and Alabama. Just where in the Alabama-Mississippi area it intergrades with the Mississippi Mud Turtle is not known.

To the northeast of the region outlined above, this species has been recorded from Stratford, Connecticut (an old record), and from Schenectady, New York. Its occurrence north of central New Jersey and Long Island is exceedingly sporadic.

To the west of the region first designated, it has been found in southwestern Pennsylvania, central Kentucky, the western third of Indiana, extreme southeastern Illinois, and southeastern as well as northwestern Tennessee. In western Tennessee the question of intergradation with the Mississippi Mud Turtle arises, so the status of specimens from there is uncertain.

HABITAT. There are more records of the occurrence of this turtle in ponds than anywhere else, but muddy streams, ditches and canals, marshes and swamps are also favourite haunts. Brackish marshes are not avoided.

HABITS. The Common Mud Turtle is decidedly less aquatic than the Common Musk Turtle and therefore frequents shallower water, from which it often wanders away. Neither can the former thrive in a straight-sided aquarium affording no out-of-water rest. Both of these species are bottom crawlers.

At times surprisingly agile on land, the Common Mud Turtle is also a good swimmer.

There is great difference of opinion as to the temperament of this reptile, some contending that it hisses and not infrequently bites when annoyed, others insisting that it cannot be persuaded to bite or defend itself in any way. Grant denies that it even emits an odour, but Werner's female referred to above in the section on longevity remained fierce through decades of captivity. (See Plate 13.) One cannot doubt that this species is decidedly more of a pacifist than its odoriferous relative, the Common Musk Turtle.

HIBERNATION. The only concrete clue to the wintering habits of this turtle is the discovery by Wetmore and Harper of an individual two miles from Alexandria, Virginia, near a hole in which it evidently had hibernated. This hole was nine and a half inches deep and descended at a slant through sandy loam to pasty mud. The entrance was well protected by some smilax growing fifty yards from a marsh in a broomsedge field with scattered shrubs and low trees. The date was March 25.

REPRODUCTION. Astonishingly little is known about the reproductive habits of the Common Mud Turtle. A pair was once seen mating while " walking on the bottom of a shallow pond." This and another mated couple were observed in northern Indiana, on May 9 and 11, respectively. The number of eggs laid by a female at one time varies from two to five.

Wright and Funkhouser give the only account of laying activities. They saw many females in the Okefinokee Swamp, Georgia, where the higher wooded parts of the swamp are the nesting grounds, and write as follows:

" The time during which the specimens were collected (May and June) seemed to be the egg-laying season. A fine large female was taken on the nest in the act of egg-laying, June 11, 1912, and three eggs were found with the specimen. The nest was in rotten wood by the side of a dead log and the eggs were deposited at a depth of three inches below the surface of the decayed wood. In the stomach of a king snake taken on Billy's Island, June 11, 1912, was found one egg."

The patches of horny scales on the inner side of each hind limb are probably, as suggested by Risley, grasping devices used during copulation and not " stridulating " organs rubbed together to make a shrill sound as contended by De Sola.

FOOD. The food is stated to be fish, insects, and worms although no one seems to have made any serious effort to determine what this form of turtle eats. Cahn did, however, examine one stomach and found remains of earthworms and beetles in it. The Common Mud Turtle annoys fishermen by taking their bait.

ENEMIES. As proved by the quotation in the section on reproduction, king snakes eat the eggs of this subspecies and indeed it seems that they even wait on the breeding grounds while the females lay. Various mammals certainly devour the eggs, although no definite proof is available.

There is some evidence that crows eat the adults and rodents gnaw on their shells. An encounter between a blue crab and a Common Mud Turtle has been witnessed with odds going decidedly against the reptile. It is doubtful if the turtle's musky odour is strong enough to discourage many enemies.

The terrestrial wanderings help to free the body of leeches, which so badly infect the highly aquatic Common Musk Turtle. Here is an advantage of being less dependent upon life in the water.

CAPTIVITY. Other specimens than the one mentioned above under the section on longevity have lived a long time in confinement, one thirteen and four others more than five years each. Secretive habits detract from the value of this form as a pet.

It should be treated in general like the Common Musk Turtle, but with due consideration of its terrestrial tendencies. Males kept together have been observed to fight among themselves.

Chopped fish and raw meat, earthworms, snails, tadpoles, and insect larvæ can be used as food. It will sometimes eat out of water.

MISSISSIPPI MUD TURTLE

Kinosternon subrubrum hippocrepis Gray

IDENTIFICATION. This subspecies of the Common Mud Turtle may be recognized by the two yellow lines on the side of the head, which are the fused spots of its near ally. In fact the two are so closely related that they may be distinguished on the basis of distribution alone.

DISTRIBUTION. This, the western form of the Common Mud Turtle, is found from the southeastern corner of Missouri southward through Arkansas and Louisiana and westward throughout the lowlands of eastern Texas to Austin and Dallas. It has been taken in Tulsa County, northeastern Oklahoma. The question of its intergradation with the Common Mud Turtle is discussed under that form.

MIGRATION. An exceptionally interesting observation made by Strecker helps to explain how shallow-water species are able to survive when their homes dry out. The " Dry Pond " of the following account was, before being drained, a good-sized grassy lagoon near Waco, Texas:

" In 1893 I witnessed a migration of these turtles at Dry Pond. The marsh was rapidly drying up, and as I walked along the levee I counted 45 specimens all headed in the same direction. At first I thought that they were merely changing their quarters to the ditch along the railroad track only about 200 yards away, but found that there was very little water there, and that turtles were scattered all over the damp meadow on the other side. I followed the line of march and discovered that they were headed for a large tank over half a mile from Dry Pond."

There is nothing in the meagre references to this subspecies indicating marked differences in habits between it and the

Common Mud Turtle. The lagoons, bayous, and extensive swamps prevalent over much of its range afford excellent habitats, which it by no means overlooks.

Captive specimens are fond of snails.

STEINDACHNER'S MUD TURTLE

Kinosternon subrubrum steindachneri Siebenrock

[PLATES 14 AND 15]

IDENTIFICATION. A relatively narrow bridge width of only about one-third to one-half the length of the suture between the abdominal shields characterizes this subspecies of the Common Mud Turtle. The two may be distinguished on the basis of distribution alone. In Steindachner's Mud Turtle the side of the head does not have a pair of stripes.

SIZE. This form attains a carapace length of 4.72 inches. The carapace of one of the cotypes, a male, measures 3.98 inches long by 2.52 wide, and the shell is 1.65 inches high. The corresponding measurements for the other cotype, a female with fully developed eggs, are 3.42, 2.24, and 1.85 inches.

THE SEXES. The head of the male is bigger and the markings on the jaws more intense. The longer tail of the male ends in a strong spine, whereas the short tail of the other sex either lacks a spine or has a very small one. The inner side of each hind limb of the male has two patches of horny scales that are not found in the female.

Other differences are mentioned, but not clearly explained, by Siebenrock, chief among them being relative size and shape of the plastron. Judging by his few measurements, the male is somewhat the larger.

DISTRIBUTION. Central to northern peninsular Florida, presumably intergrading with the Common Mud Turtle in the region where Georgia and Florida meet.

HABITAT. This turtle is moderately common in rivers and springs of Alachua County, Florida. It has also been recorded from small lakes.

CAPTIVITY. Rust recommends a shoreless aquarium with cork islands and temperature from 68° to 77° F.; for food, snails, earthworms, tadpoles, salamanders, raw meat or fish. A dark place in which to hide should also be provided.

CHAPTER III

THE SNAPPING TURTLES

Family CHELYDRIDÆ

Genera *MACROCHELYS* and *CHELYDRA*

The family Chelydridæ includes only three genera, each genus having but a single species. The species not treated in this book lives in the Fly River, New Guinea.

This widely scattered distribution is explained by the fossil record which shows that about ten to fifteen million years ago, during the Miocene Period and before the advent of man, the turtles of this group were numerous and well spread over the northern continents. The three remaining kinds are but remnants of a glorious and no doubt ferocious past.

The Alligator Snapper has no close relative. The genus *Chelydra* seems to have a single species divisible into two forms, the one with an extensive range, the other found only in Central America and southern Mexico.

IDENTIFICATION

The summary of major differences given under the Alligator Snapping Turtle and the photographs make determinations simple.

ALLIGATOR SNAPPING TURTLE

Macrochelys temminckii (Troost)

[PLATES 16 AND 17]

IDENTIFICATION. This species can be confused only with the Common Snapping Turtle, which it resembles in general appearance. The following characters will serve to distinguish the two:

The head of the Alligator Snapper is covered with smooth symmetrical plates, that of the other species with soft skin.

The under side of the tail in the Alligator Snapper is covered with numerous rounded scales, that of the common species with large plates more or less set in a double row (see Plate 20).

Only the Alligator Snapper has an extra row of three or four (or five) plates (the supramarginals) between the marginals and the costals in the region of the bridge.

The three dorsal keels so well developed in juveniles of both species remain conspicuous throughout life only in the Alligator Snapper.

SIZE. This, the largest non-marine turtle of the United States, is said to attain a weight of two hundred and nineteen pounds, but detailed dimensions of such giants are not available. Cahn gives the measurements of a large specimen of more usual size from Metropolis, Illinois, and states that it seemed to exert almost no extra effort when walking around with a one hundred and sixty-five pound man on its back. In these measurements, which in part follow, the enormous width of the head should be noted:

	Inches	Millimetres
Length of carapace	24.02	610
Width of carapace	18.19	462

	Inches	Millimetres
Length of plastron	15.75	400
Width of plastron	15.27	388
Width of head	7.87	200
Length of tail	13.11	333
Total length	51.30	1303
Weight	103 pounds	

YOUNG. Hatchlings strongly resemble the adult in form, but differ in being ornamented to an astonishing degree with corrugations and wart- and papilla-like protuberances. (See Plate 17.)

EGG. Spherical, about 36 millimetres in diameter, and with a white shell.

LONGEVITY. One of these turtles survived forty-two years in the Brighton Aquarium (Flower, 1925) and another has lived forty-seven in the Philadelphia Zoological Garden. The latter was well grown on arrival at the zoo, so it is considerably over fifty years old (see Plate 16).

DISTRIBUTION. From southeastern Georgia and northern Florida westward through the Coastal Plain to Austin and San Antonio, Texas. Up the Mississippi Valley this species ranges as far as Quincy, Illinois, and it occurs along the Ohio to the lower Wabash River between Illinois and Indiana. It has been found as far up the Arkansas River as the western border of Arkansas and there are records for the extreme southeastern corner of Oklahoma.

The Alligator Snapper is an old-timer in Texas, where it has a fossil record. This is proved by Pleistocene remains from the Brazos River a short distance above Navasota.

HABITAT. This thoroughly aquatic giant among American fresh-water turtles is primarily an inhabitant of large rivers, but it also frequents bayous, lagoons, canals, and swampy lakes and ponds. It prefers muddy bottoms affording ample retreat in the form of dark cavities and areas overgrown with rank aquatic vegetation.

MIGRATION. The movements of a specimen inhabiting an Oklahoma river were observed over a period of three years, during which time, according to Wickam, it migrated upstream an average of six miles per year.

FEEDING METHOD. Ditmars was apparently the first to describe the odd structure on the tongue of the Alligator Snapping Turtle. This structure, worm-like in shape, lies along the middle of the tongue, to which it is largely attached, only the ends being free. Whenever the mouth is held wide open the structure is set into motion, causing it to resemble a squirming worm. Being pink or red in colour, and strongly set off against the lining of the mouth, which closely resembles the dark colour of the jaws and head, this " worm " is generally conceded to be a lure. Even though no one has been fortunate enough to see a turtle actually attract prey by it, there is little doubt that its use has been correctly surmised. More than one observer has seen a captive individual set its " worm " in motion, but the field observation by Haltom is most convincing. His attention was first attracted to a moving object on a muddy bottom and only at second glance was he able to make out there the neatly camouflaged form of a turtle.

FOOD. There is astonishingly little scientific information on the food of this species. It is generally considered, however, to be carnivorous, with a preference for fish. Almost all other small animals that frequent its habitat probably fall prey to it sooner or later. It would be gratifying to have the results of the examination of a few score stomachs.

PARASITES. According to Cahn, leeches are common on the Alligator Snapper, and nematodes swarm inside it, as many as two hundred and fifty specimens of the same species having been taken from a single large intestine. A linguatulid, or degenerate spider relative, and various trematodes have also been found to infest it.

DEFENCE AND DISPOSITION. Great size, a thick shell, and prodigious strength render the adult Alligator Snapper all but invincible to non-human enemies. A big specimen can easily carry a large man on its back, bite a broom handle in two, or crush mussel shells. In fact, observers have been more concerned over its ability to break broom handles and bite through inch boards than anything else it can or does do.

Besides all this the species concerned is a master at the art of camouflage. Its general appearance, especially when the carapace is covered with a thick growth of algæ, and a habit of remaining motionless, combine to give it this ability which undoubtedly is useful to the big, heavily armoured adult in procuring food and necessary to the soft-bodied hatchling and yearling in eluding enemies.

A very young individual in my possession demonstrates this defensive inactivity to perfection. No amount of annoyance will make it do more than open its mouth to an astonishing width and turn its head in the direction of danger — no kicking or struggling, but merely an all but motionless defensive attitude.

In spite of this habit of " freezing," a stranded specimen, once enraged, strikes out so ferociously that it may even be raised from the ground and carried forward by the jerk of the massive head if the mark is missed. Enough has already been said to prove that caution in the proximity of an enraged individual is highly expedient.

A rather surprising degree of intelligent wariness was shown by an individual reported to Agassiz by its owner, the Reverend Edward Fontaine, who relates the whole incident thus:

" I kept two for several years in my fish-pond. They became very tame, but finding they were eating my fish I shot one, and wounded the other with a fish-gig; but his sagacity prevented my capturing him. I fed the perch and minnows with bread, which the alligator turtle devoured greedily. One day, after he had eaten, he remained upon the rock where I had fed him, and which was only about a foot beneath the surface, where it shelved over water ten feet deep. A swarm of minnows and perch were picking up crumbs around him, apparently unconscious of his presence. His head and feet were drawn sufficiently within his shell to be concealed. His mossy shell could not well be distinguished from the projections of the rock, on which he was lying in ambush. Several large bass were gliding around him, occasionally darting at the minnows. One of these, about fourteen inches in length, came within striking distance of his head, which he suddenly thrust out and fastened upon him, fixing his aquiline bill deeply into his side and belly. He immediately drew the fish under him, and, holding him down firmly to the rock with his forefeet, ate him greedily, very much as a hawk devours its prey. I drew out a large line and hook and baited it with a minnow, and threw it to him, determined to get rid of this skilful angler. He seized it; I gave a sharp jerk, and fastened it in his lower jaw. Finding him too heavy to lift by the hook upon a rock six feet perpendicular, I led him around to the lower end of the pool, where the bank was low, and the water shallow. But, after getting him within a few feet of the edge of the water, he anchored himself by stretching forward his forefeet, and resisted all my efforts to get him nearer. He seemed to be in a furious rage, and, after several sharp snaps at the line, he broke the hook and retreated into the deepest part of the pool. I never could get him to bite at any thing afterwards; and, finding I had a design upon his life, he became very shy. I afterwards discovered him in deep water, eating the bread which fell from the shelving rock, on which he had fed for several years, but upon which he never ventured afterwards when I was near. I threw a gig at him, and fastened it in his neck; but, by a violent effort with one of his forefeet, he tore it loose and ran under the rock. I frequently saw him after his escape, but always in the act of retreating to his hiding-place, which was entirely inaccessible. I intended sinking a steel-trap, baited with beef, to secure this sagacious old fellow, but my removal to the city side of the Colorado probably saved his life; and I have but little doubt he yet lives and thrives upon the numerous fishes I left with him."

CAPTIVITY. Properly cared-for specimens have been known to live in confinement for long periods. (See under Longevity above.)

The tank in which individuals of this highly aquatic turtle are kept should be provided with ample dark retreats. Fish is probably the best food, but it is said to like raw hamburger and bread as well.

RELATION TO MAN. Reports agree that southern markets regularly handle this turtle, whose flesh is fairly palatable. Clark and Southall state that, at certain seasons, an active fishery is carried on in the Louisiana swamps, where specimens are prepared for shipment by stringing wires through holes in the shells to imprison the feet and head.

The eggs are sometimes eaten.

Fish-eating habits and the fact that it probably destroys waterfowl make this turtle unpopular in many places. In addition to those sent to markets, great numbers are killed and left to rot by annoyed fishermen, so undoubtedly man is the greatest and perhaps the only significant non-parasitic enemy that the adult turtle has to fear.

COMMON SNAPPING TURTLE

Chelydra serpentina serpentina (Linnæus)

[PLATES 18, 19, 20, 21, 22, AND 23]

IDENTIFICATION. The plastron is narrow and cross-shaped, leaving the fleshy under parts largely exposed; the long tail has a conspicuous median dorsal crest of narrow plates; the head is large, with hooked jaws; and the carapace is serrated behind.

These characters, together with its large size and bad disposition, should serve to identify adults of this familiar reptile. Care must be taken, however, to distinguish it from the Alligator Snapping Turtle of the Mississippi and southern lowlands.

SIZE. The weight of this turtle has attracted much attention. Babcock has a record of one fattened in a swill barrel to eighty-six pounds. Such giants are certainly rare. Adults usually weigh from fifteen to thirty pounds, depending on the amount of persecution the population to which they belong has been subjected.

Measurements of a sixteen-pound specimen from Lake Maxinkuckee, Indiana, recorded by Evermann and Clark, follow:

	Inches	*Millimetres*
Length of carapace	13.25	337
Width of carapace	14.25	362
Length of plastron	9.12	232
Width of plastron	5	127
Length of head and neck	11	279
Length of tail	12	305

YOUNG. Very rough above, with three tuberculate ridges or keels along the carapace. The colour pattern is more vividly contrasted in early life. In hatchlings the tail is at least as long as the carapace. (See Plate 21.)

THE SEXES. The dearth of information on differences between the sexes is astonishing. The female is said to attain a larger size than the male, and the anus of the latter is described as nearer to the tip of the tail.

EGG. Spherical, averaging a little more than an inch in diameter, and with a white shell so tough that the egg may be bounced on a hard surface without breaking. Ovate eggs have been recorded. (See Plate 22.)

LONGEVITY. Individuals of the Common Snapping Turtle have been kept alive in European institutions 20, 18, 17, 13, 12, and 11 years, respectively, so the species probably has a potential longevity of considerably over a quarter-century.

Agassiz's casual mention of a specimen alleged to have lived forty-five years and probably much longer can scarcely be taken as scientific evidence.

DISTRIBUTION. From southeastern Canada southward through the eastern half of the United States, eastern Mexico, and parts of Central America to Ecuador. The relationship between this and *Chelydra rossignonii rossignonii* (Bocourt) of Central America and southern Mexico has never been elucidated. Presumably they are subspecies of a single form.

More specifically it is found in the north from Maine westward through the region of the Great Lakes to southeastern Manitoba. In the south it occurs westward through the eastern two-thirds of Texas; farther north, to the Oklahoma Panhandle and the Denver-Boulder region of Colorado.

Fossil remains of this species from the Pleistocene of Maryland are evidence that it has inhabited the eastern seaboard of the United States for at least tens of thousands of years.

HABITAT. This ubiquitous reptile may be looked for in any body of water large and permanent enough to support an association of aquatic plants. There are numerous records for ponds, lakes, rivers, streams of all sizes, swamps, and salt marshes. Although it exhibits a decided preference for quiet or sluggish water with a mucky, plant-grown bottom, clear lakes and deeps of clear swift streams are not avoided.

Altitudes exceeding three and five thousand feet are attained in the eastern and western states, respectively. Lack of suitable habitats seems to be the only factor limiting its ascent into mountains.

HABITS. The most outstanding habit of the Snapper is its willingness when on land not only to defend itself but even to attack its annoyer (see Plate 19). Contrasting with this is an apparent harmlessness when in its native element. I have picked up an enraged female soon after removal from her nest and held her in the water by the tail. The minute she was submerged all her idea of biting left her and she only struggled violently to escape. Mr. John T. Nichols first pointed out to me this remarkable difference in temperament between stranded and submerged Snappers. Whether the emission of the musky secretion from the subcutaneous glands has protective value in water, as it presumably does on land, is not known.

The defensive tactics call for only brief description because they have already been emphasized too much. Holding itself high above the ground, the enraged turtle opens the jaws and thrusts the head forward too quickly for the eye to follow. Once the jaws close on an object, they are reluctant to release their vice-like grip, a fact no doubt responsible for the superstition that a victim will not be freed until the sun goes down or thunder rolls. The force of the strokes are at times so great that complete misses carry the turtle off the ground, with subsequent loss of balance and a general appearance of impotent rage. Once warmed up, it deliberately advances to the attack like a true warrior. Even hatchlings still encumbered with egg membranes and yolk are quite ready to assert their place in the sun by viciously biting. The only safe way to hold a large

Snapper is by the tail with plenty of space between turtle and human legs!

A walking Snapper viewed from the side reminds one of prehistoric creatures with flat armoured backs. The body is held well off the ground, and the shell affords efficient protection only from above, leaving the sides and under parts largely exposed. The end of the long tail makes an undulating track between the marks of the feet; the gait is awkward, but not very slow. Walking on pond or river bottom is a common practice, as swimming ability is but poorly developed.

The aggressiveness of this reptile is apparently compensation for an incomplete shell. On land it is conspicuous and needs double protection, but in water its form, colour, deliberate movements, and sluggishness, especially when the shell is camouflaged with plant growth, combine to render it surprisingly inconspicuous, as Hurter found out when he inadvertently made a stepping-stone out of an algae-covered thirty-pounder!

All the reasons that the Snapper has for going on land are not clear, since both sexes are said to do so frequently in the spring. Seton once found in the latter part of August six good-sized specimens on a pile of sand that had been dumped only the day before about one hundred feet from a Connecticut lake. Nests were not evident, so an explanation of this gathering is no easy matter. Leaving the water to sun is seldom reported, but basking in the warmth of shallows and floating near the surface are well-established habits.

That this species is light-shy has been proved by direct observation and confirmed through anatomical studies of the eye. Walls found that cones as well as a good many rods are present in the retina.

HIBERNATION. The Common Snapping Turtle buries itself in mud or retreats into holes in banks to spend the winter. Large numbers have been taken by fishermen from muskrat holes or from mud under submerged logs. Temporarily aroused individuals are occasionally seen in the water through the ice during warm spells.

Spring emergence takes place in March or later in the northeastern states and autumn disappearance is usually well under way in early October.

Æstivation has been hinted at, but, to my knowledge, never proved.

MIGRATION. The presence of individuals in small isolated ponds leads one to believe them capable of making long overland journeys, and indeed there are many hints that such an ability is well developed. No one has made a study of their migrations, so for the present this aspect of Snapper behaviour must remain in a problematic state. In this species the movements of the adults as well as those of the hatchlings should be made the subject of careful experimentation.

Snappers living in watercourses are said to move upstream in the spring and downstream in the autumn, but no scientific evidence supporting this belief has been published.

MATING. A captive male and a female Snapper in shallow water have been seen with heads close together gulping water and forcing it out through the nostrils violently enough to cause a " boiling " at the surface. Taylor, who witnessed this procedure on November 11, could not determine whether it was a form of courtship. Actual copulation is described by Conant as follows:

" Captive snapping turtles were seen mating under water a number of times. When in coitus the plastrons of both male and female were in parallel planes, with the plastron of the male pressed tightly against the carapace of the female. The male grasped his mate by hooking the claws of all four feet under the edge of her carapace and his tail was curled under hers in such a manner that his anal opening was turned upward to meet hers. He also pressed upon her snout with his chin so that it was necessary for her to keep her head withdrawn. In every case the actions and attitudes were very much the same. Sometimes in struggling, both sexes were seen to bite ineffectually at each other's forelegs. Males occasionally grasped males and one was observed to seize another male rear end foremost. The dates of mating records of these captive specimens include all the months from April to October and no season of particular activity was noted."

NESTING. The laying period coincides well with the month of June in the northeastern states. The females come out to look for a site early in the morning, but may be met with at any hour before noon because much time is consumed by the nesting process or even by the search for a site.

The few data available indicate that in this same part of the country the young escape from the nests in September or early October. There are records of August hatching in Kansas, whereas in Ontario the eggs may carry over the winter, the young emerging during the spring. Even in one locality there is considerable variation in the time of hatching, due to different seasonal conditions and varying nest temperature.

A female lays from twenty to about forty eggs at one time. Higher numbers (even up to seventy) are often given, but they probably are either sheer estimates or counts made in compound nests.

A species that frequents such a variety of aquatic situations must necessarily be satisfied with almost any sort of a nesting site. Field observations support this generalization by proving that nests are made in many kinds of soil on bank or hillside, in field or meadow, the chief requirements being some moisture and an open sunny area. Muskrat houses are not infrequently used. That the female does try to make the most of her opportunity is shown by the way she often wanders distances even up to half a mile from water in search of a spot that suits her fancy.

The considerable differences in details between accounts of nest construction mean either that the habits of this turtle are not uniform or else that the females are often prevented from making a good nest by hardness or dryness of the only available soil.

The best nest is a fairly creditable flask-shaped cavity dug by alternate strokes of the hind feet which loosen the dirt and lift it out. After a slanting hole not more than a foot wide at the bottom and several inches deep has been made, the eggs are laid at approximately minute intervals, each one being directed into the bottom of the nest by a hind foot. The feet are used alternately for this and the rear end of the body elevated before the ejection of each egg. Finally the nest is filled in and its site carefully concealed by alternate raking movements of the hind limbs, any loose material available being used.

Agassiz believed that the female purposely made her nest chamber asymmetrical, but more likely any irregularity in shape results from interference by root, stone, or similar object. It has been stated that the carapace becomes covered with earth which falls into and fills the nest as the female crawls out to depart without showing further interest in or attempting to hide her handiwork. This gravity filling would happen only under special conditions. Its limiting effect on the behaviour of the female is a matter of some interest.

Disturbed while nesting, a Snapper either refuses to be interrupted or halts operations to await passage of danger. Her behaviour at such times may depend on the stage she was in when approached. On being removed from her nest, however, she immediately becomes vicious and ferociously strikes at everything within reach of her jaws.

I am indebted to Mr. C. F. Kauffeld for several details in the foregoing generalized account of nest construction.

BEHAVIOUR OF HATCHLING. A good deal of work has been done to determine how hatchling turtles manage to make their way to water. The baby turtles are so small and the distance of their nest from suitable water is often so great that some sense or senses other than direct sight of the water at least sometimes must guide them. Noble and Breslau give a good account of a a lot of newly emerged Snappers that they studied:

" On September 28, 1935, we found twenty-two recently hatched snapping turtles, Chelydra serpentina (Linné), crawling east along a path leading to Carman's River, Long Island. The distance between the first and last turtle of the series was ninety-eight feet. Twenty of the twenty-two turtles were headed down the path which was flanked on either side by grass approximately a foot in height. Parallel with the path was a drainage ditch only four to five feet from the turtles' route of travel and well grown with aquatic vegetation. The path descended a low bank and then extended across a grassy flat. Most of the turtles were on the nearly horizontal flat section of the path. Twenty feet west of the beginning of the path and approximately forty feet from the first turtle a small hole and an empty egg shell of a snapping turtle were found. Immediately below the surface surrounding the hole, over twenty other shells were found. This was in all probability the nest from which the snapping turtles had emerged. No other evidence of nests was seen but two other recently hatched snapping turtles were found in a shallow bay 100 yards to the north of the path. These turtles were very lethargic, in striking contrast to migrating individuals. It seemed very likely that they had emerged from another nest."

From these field observations and subsequent laboratory experiments, they were able to conclude that the course of the Long Island migration was in the direction of the most open horizon, humidity gradients and the position of the sun being without effect. The laboratory tests, however, convinced them that under other conditions both humidity and position of the sun may influence the direction of migration.

FOOD AND FEEDING. This species is almost entirely carnivorous although there is indisputable evidence of occasional lapses into vegetarianism. This is especially interesting because studies of the alimentary enzymes prove that the digestive system is well able to assimilate plant foods.

The prey is about equally divided between vertebrates and invertebrates. Among the latter, crayfish and snails are most commonly eaten, but adult and larval insects are not neglected, young turtles being especially fond of the soft larvæ. Among the vertebrates fish and frogs undoubtedly suffer most with birds, salamanders, reptiles, and even mammals coming last. No one has determined how much damage is done to young ducks and other waterfowl, but the chances are that in certain environments and seasons a good many birds are dragged down by the legs to be swallowed at leisure.

Scavenger tendencies have been observed many times.

A unique observation on the use of the tongue was made by Newman and is included in his account of the methods used in the capture of prey:

" Chelydra either stalks its prey or lies in wait for it. In the former case it approaches a resting tadpole or frog with movements so slow as to be almost imperceptible. The head is thrust out stiff and is kept very steady and when within easy reach of its prey the fierce jaws are suddenly opened and closed with a snap that leaves no hope of escape for the victim. In the latter case it lies buried in the mud at the bottom, allowing only the head to protrude. The long wormlike tongue is thrust out, probably as a lure for unwary fish. When the prey comes within reach it is suddenly snapped up."

By means of a balloon inserted in the stomach of *Chelydra serpentina*, Patterson found that its hunger contractions more closely resemble those of man than they do those of the frog. During the early stages of starvation the contractions occur at intervals of three to three and a half minutes and last about one minute; later, contractions double their time of duration and come three and a third to four minutes apart.

ENEMIES. Man is the chief enemy of the Snapper, destroying eggs as well as adults and young. Many individuals are killed by automobiles. Besides man, the large turtles seem to have no other non-parasitic enemy, but the young are eaten by crows, hawks, various mammals, and even large fishes. Needless to add, the eggs are dug up by skunks, raccoons, and other furred animals.

The average Snapper is virtually a culture medium for parasites. Leeches are frequently present in great numbers, especially about the anus and eye sockets and in the angles under the limbs. As many as fifty often infest one turtle at a time. Internal parasites are legion. A kind of amœba has been located in the intestine. Harwood found nematodes infesting the rectum of all nine specimens examined and trematodes and other nematodes were evident in various parts of the alimentary canal. Trematodes were also identified by him in the bladder and heart.

CAPTIVITY. An ungainly appearance and vicious temperament will prevent many persons from making a pet out of this species. In spite of these bad points, a striking appearance, willingness to eat, and general hardiness combine to recommend it as a welcome inmate of any large reptile collection.

Naturally it should not be indiscriminately confined with smaller animals unless they are intended to satisfy its broad appetite.

The fact that captives have been known to eat cherries and other fruit, lettuce, cheese, toads, salamander larvæ, crayfish, meat scraps, dead birds, and mice is a recommendation in itself, proving as it does that satisfying a hungry Snapper is a simple matter. The information in the section on food and feeding above should of course be considered in making out a balanced diet. Underwater swallowing is a natural habit and the Snapper is quite capable of rending rather large objects with claw and jaw. In spite of nocturnal tendencies, daytime activity in subdued light can be induced.

A shoreless aquarium largely protected from bright light and kept in room temperature is suitable. The bottom should be covered with sand or other material affording occupants ample opportunity to indulge in their favourite pastime of lying completely buried. In default of this, good hiding-places should be provided.

Captives remain sullen, but soon give up the idea of biting at everything within reach. The young are generally more tractable. Patience and gentle treatment will even make them more or less indifferent to handling if not actually tame.

ECONOMIC VALUE. The relation of the Snapper to man is perhaps more complex than that between man and any other turtle, terrapin, or tortoise. Serving him well as a source of food, a scavenger and destroyer of noxious invertebrates, this reptile wreaks vengeance, as it were, for being eaten by devouring considerable numbers of waterfowl and some valuable fish. There are almost no exact data on the amount of damage done, but a number of general statements to the effect that great numbers of aquatic birds are eaten. Actually, the whole question probably depends on the type of environment inhabited by the turtle and the season, many individuals perhaps never or rarely being so fortunate as to secure a meal of waterfowl; witness the fact that only one stomach among nineteen examined by Surface contained bird remains and several dissected at Lake Maxinkuckee, Indiana, held only evidence of a snail diet.

As an article of food the Snapper is widely used, even reaching the markets of large cities (see Plate 23). It is caught in a

16. Alligator Snapping Turtle (*Macrochelys temminckii*), the oldest guest in the Philadelphia Zoological Garden. It now weighs 52 pounds. See the section on longevity. Three shields, the supramarginals, can barely be made out lying just below the costals and appearing as the upper halves of three bisected marginals. (*Courtesy Zoological Society of Philadelphia, photograph by Mark Mooney, Jr.*)

17. Young Alligator Snapper (*Macrochelys temminckii*) with a carapace 53 millimetres long. (*Courtesy New York Aquarium, photograph by Mark Mooney, Jr.*)

18. Common Snapping Turtle (*Chelydra serpentina serpentina*) from the region of Philadelphia. It weighs 4.50 pounds. (*Courtesy Zoological Society of Philadelphia, photograph by Mark Mooney, Jr.*)

19. This Common Snapping Turtle (*Chelydra serpentina serpentina*), disturbed while digging her nest in Morris County, New Jersey, at 8.30 a.m., June 2, 1938, struck viciously at my boot. She has a carapace 11.75 inches long. (*Photograph by Douglas Cullen.*)

20. Common Snapping Turtle (*Chelydra serpentina serpentina*) from Morris County, New Jersey. This female has a carapace 11.75 inches long. (*Photograph by Douglas Cullen.*)

21. Young Common Snapping Turtle (*Chelydra serpentina serpentina*) from Florida with a carapace 53 millimetres long. (*Courtesy Zoological Society of Philadelphia, photograph by Mark Mooney, Jr.*)

22. Eggs of the Common Snapping Turtle from Burlington County, New Jersey. Diameters in millimetres: 26 to 28. The shells are stained from the material in which they were placed. (*Courtesy Zoological Society of Philadelphia, photograph by Mark Mooney, Jr.*)

23. The Common Snapping Turtle's last stop before the restaurant kitchen and dining-table. This one only awaits a Philadelphia retail buyer. (*Courtesy Milden and White, photograph by Mark Mooney, Jr.*)

variety of ways, such as with hook and line or harpoon. The latter method is used with efficiency only during the winter when numbers are hibernating together. Individuals are even fattened in farm swill barrels. The flesh of old specimens is said to be tough and rank.

The eggs are also eaten, but must be fried because they will not boil hard. Snapper oil is a primitive remedy supposed to cure pain when rubbed on the skin. An oil extracted from the liver is described in a German book on animal fat and oil by L. E. Andès which I have been unable to secure.

Writing about this species in Illinois, Cahn states that the dressed meat brings some twenty-five cents a pound and that one can count on getting an amount of meat equal to about half the total weight of the turtle. Eight pages are devoted to the Snapper in Clark and Southall's 1920 report on our native turtles as a source of meat supply.

SPOTTED, WOOD, PACIFIC POND, *and* MUHLENBERG'S TURTLES

Family TESTUDINIDÆ)

Genus *CLEMMYS*

This genus is especially interesting because of its extensive distribution in time and space. In North America it is known as far back as the Eocene Period, which ended some thirty-five million years ago. Today the ten known species occur in northern Africa, southern Europe and adjacent western Asia, eastern Asia, and eastern and western North America.

Only one of the four American species is thoroughly aquatic, the other three exhibiting aquatic habits tempered by various degrees of terrestrialism. The poorly developed webbing of the feet also indicates lack of thorough adaptation to life in water.

The two common eastern species, the Wood and Spotted Turtles, are among the most familiar and attractive chelonians of the northeastern states, and the Pacific Pond Turtle is the only fresh-water species with an extensive range on the Pacific Slope.

IDENTIFICATION

A simple key used together with the illustrations makes recognition of these turtles an easy matter. It must not be forgotten, however, that juveniles are astonishingly different from adults, and in identifying the young the section under each species devoted to them should be read.

KEY TO THE AMERICAN SPECIES OF *Clemmys*

A1: Found in eastern and central states; carapace with or without median keel.

  B1: Each shield of black carapace with one to several yellow or orange spots; carapace without median keel. SPOTTED TURTLE

  B2: Carapace without yellow spots and with median keel.

  C1: Skin salmon red; no orange blotch on temple. WOOD TURTLE

  C2: Skin not salmon red; conspicuous orange blotch on temple. MUHLENBERG'S TURTLE

A2: Found on Pacific Slope; carapace without median keel. PACIFIC POND TURTLE

SPOTTED TURTLE

Clemmys guttata (Schneider)

[PLATES 24, 25, AND 26]

IDENTIFICATION. The carapace is black, with numerous small round yellow or orange spots. Each of the large shields has from one to several of these spots; the marginals ordinarily have one spot apiece. The plastron is yellow or orange, with large black blotches, usually on the outer parts of the shields; occasionally it is almost entirely black.

SIZE. The maximum carapace length is generally stated to be four and a half inches. Measurements of a large male from northern New Jersey follow:

	Inches	Millimetres
Length of carapace	4.55	115.5
Width of carapace	3.38	86
Length of plastron	3.94	100
Width of plastron	2.38	60.5
Height of shell	1.30	33

YOUNG. When hatched, this species has one spot on each shield of the carapace (an occasional marginal lacks the spot) (see Plate 25), but as growth proceeds many additional spots appear on the vertebrals and costals. These spots are in reality tiny window-like areas in the shields which allow yellow pigment in the outer layer of the underlying bony plates to show through.

Yellow spots also develop with age on the legs and tail.

The entire centre of the plastron is black at hatching, but the black colour migrates radially to leave the yellow centre of the adult plastron.

The shell of newly hatched specimens is nearly circular.

Still other juvenile characters have been described.

THE SEXES. The most noticeable differences are to be found about the head and throat as enumerated:

Male: Eye dark brown; horny portion of both jaws always dusky; yellow stripe along lower jaw nearly or quite lacking; throat black, finely speckled with orange or yellow; head relatively wide and deep.

Female: Eye bright orange; horny portion of both jaws always pale yellow; yellow stripe along lower jaw always conspicuous; throat spotted and streaked with yellow; head not so wide and deep.

In addition, the male plastron is concave, that of the female flat or somewhat convex, and the slightly longer plastron of the latter sex more nearly approaches the hind edge of the carapace. When the tail is extended the anus lies some five millimetres beyond the hind edge of the carapace in the male, at or before it in the female.

Both Grant and Blake have made a special study of the sexes in this species. Some minor differences have been omitted here.

EGG. Elliptical (about 30 × 17 mm.) and with a white shell. (See Plate 26.)

LONGEVITY. The Spotted Turtle, according to Flower, has lived forty-two years in captivity.

DISTRIBUTION. This turtle is found in the northeastern and eastern United States and extreme southern Ontario.

In the north it is distributed from southwestern Maine westward to the southern shore of Lake Ontario, thence through the Lake Erie region, across the southern half of the lower peninsula of Michigan, to Lake Michigan. Farther south it ranges from the Atlantic coast through Pennsylvania, northern Maryland, the northern two-thirds and half of Ohio and Indiana, respectively. In the south Atlantic states it occurs in northern and eastern Virginia and eastern North Carolina. In eastern South Carolina and Georgia it is apparently but rarely seen.

Its reported presence in the southeastern corner of Wisconsin and extreme northeastern Illinois requires confirmation.

HABITAT. The Spotted Turtle is most at home in ponds, ditches and streams with muddy bottoms, swamps, bogs, or marshes. In short, it desires a combination of quiet or sluggish water, mud, and low vegetation. It is not averse to wandering away from water or living in wet woods and meadows that get fairly dry at certain seasons. There are also records for unusual habitats such as mountain streams, rivers, canals, and lakes, but the existence of the species in such places usually indicates the prevalence of local swampy or marshy areas along their courses, banks, or shores. Brackish marshes are frequented. Individuals living in such marshes have rougher shells than those occurring elsewhere.

HABITS. The extreme wariness of the Spotted Turtle is shown by its quickness to leave a basking site at the approach of danger. Numbers of individuals are frequently seen basking together, but upon the slightest alarm they scramble into the water to bury themselves in bottom mud or vegetation or hide under a bank. Surprised on land, they simply withdraw into the shell. No amount of handling will induce them to snap or show aggressiveness in any other way.

Cahn gives additional information on the habits of the Spotted Turtle:

"Experiments carried out by the writer years ago with this species in Massachusetts, showed that individuals have certain favorite perches and that they tend to return to the same sunning place day after day throughout the season, indicating at the same time that while in the water they are not given particularly to wandering far from their favorite spot. On land, however, the turtle is quite solitary in its habits, and seldom is more than a single individual found. The impulse which sets them wandering seems to destroy at the same time the gregarious instinct, and their rambles on shore are quite solitary."

A study of "space reactions" by Yerkes proved that this partly aquatic species exercises some judgment about walking off of an elevated surface. At heights of about one foot and one yard there was a certain amount of hesitation, whereas at approximately six feet the drop was not attempted. The thoroughly aquatic Painted Turtle showed only a little reluctance at any of these heights but the terrestrial Common Box Turtle hesitated on the average even more than the Spotted Turtle. The conclusion is that a correlation exists between the degree of aquatic adaptation and the fear of falling off an elevated surface, the water species being accustomed to making harmless drops into pond or river from a sunning site.

Yerkes also tested the intelligence of this species by using two mazes, one with four culs-de-sac, the other with six as well as a section of pathways leading up and down an incline. The victim had to learn by trial and error how to reach the goal, which in both cases was a dark " comfortable " place. The hunger "drive " in reptiles is relatively weak and therefore was not used as " motivation " in this experiment. The running time for the first trial in the simple maze was thirty-five minutes, but after twenty attempts it was reduced to less than a minute; in learning the complicated maze, the ninety minutes for the first run was reduced to some three or four after the twentieth. The accomplishment of this turtle is not unlike that of the rat in somewhat similar problems, the chief difference being that the turtle cannot run as fast even after it has learned perfectly.

HIBERNATION. Common as this species is, no one has published any detailed information on its hibernation. A few bare statements have been made that it winters in mud or in mud under water; and Netting has published a brief account of an apparent migration from an upland situation, where the cold months had presumably been spent, toward a swamp. More definite than this is an oral account given me by Asa Pittman of discovering in the winter about a dozen submerged individuals grouped under a bank at the source of a southern New Jersey spring, where they were obviously depending on the uniform temperature of the spring water to keep them from freezing.

The first appearance of the year of this turtle in New York, Massachusetts, and Indiana has been found to occur from March 2 to April 14, the early March record being for the southeastern corner of New York. November is the last month to find them abroad. Such records must not be taken too seriously, because of their dependence upon seasonal conditions and the vigilance of the observers.

REPRODUCTION. The bits of information extant on this part of the life history may be pieced together to make the following account:

The males are most evident in the spring during the mating season, which takes place from April 19 to May 1 in northern Indiana. The males chase the females about before mounting them to copulate. Courtship and mating may take place either in or out of the water.

In the latitude of southern New England the laying season covers the last two-thirds of June. In the late afternoon or evening the female digs a flask-shaped hole in earth of fine texture near the water with her hind feet, deposits two or three, occasionally one or four eggs, and buries them so carefully that little sign of her activity remains. If disturbed she withdraws into her shell to await the passing of danger but seldom deserts a hole she has begun. Eggs buried in sand by Babcock did not hatch until eighty-two days had elapsed (June 16 to September 6). Just how near to natural conditions these eggs were incubated is not stated.

The exact cause of a contest witnessed in Connecticut and described below is not evident, but almost certainly this fight had sexual significance. Babbitt's account follows:

"Two male Spotted Turtles, *Clemmys guttata*, staged another interesting contest. This fight took place in the late afternoon at the margin of a brook in the woods. In spite of the tormenting mosquitoes, I stood still, watching carefully. One was biting at the head and forefeet of the other, and by twisting one foot of its adversary one turtle turned the other upon its back, mounted upon its plastron and bit savagely as before. Then the apparently defeated one succeeded in righting itself and took up the attack in its turn, knocking its opponent over three times and biting at the exposed, soft parts. The shells and heads of both reptiles were marked by scratches, but, as far as I could see, no blood was drawn. The contest continued for half an hour when the gathering darkness forced me to leave unaware of the outcome."

FOOD AND FEEDING. Examination of twenty-seven stomachs by Surface indicated chiefly insectivorous feeding since every stomach contained at least some insect remains, mostly beetles, flies, and dragonflies. A few had eaten worms, snails and slugs, crustaceans and spiders; one had even downed a myriapod. Three had consumed at least some vegetable matter, but only in small amounts.

Tadpoles as well as frogs are nearly always listed as prey. In fact, Spotted Turtles have been seen to pursue small frogs. Soft-bodied insect larvæ are relished. Scavenger tendencies were once observed in a Long Island individual which helped other species eat a dead heron.

The question of how much food is eaten in and how much out of water has not been answered. Certainly there is a strong preference for swallowing under water, but flying insects found in the stomachs, and terrestrial tendencies, raise the question. It is possible that the insects had fallen on the water's surface, however.

ENEMIES. In northern Indiana, Grant found specimens with shells gnawed by rodents; others had been mutilated or killed by an unknown enemy which eats the legs or head.

Frequent excursions on land help it to get rid of leeches.

CAPTIVITY. Hardy and gentle as a pet, this species will thrive in a vivarium having a water as well as a land section. Room temperature is suitable.

Raw chopped meat and fish, mussel meat, crayfish, mealworms, tender water plants, and lettuce may be used to supplement the diet indicated in the section on food and feeding. Opportunity to swallow under water should be afforded.

It is remarkable that the first individual received by the London Zoological Gardens was presented just one hundred years ago, in 1839.

Several points of interest are brought out by Mertens in his account of the behaviour of a pair kept by him in Germany. A translation follows:

" Since the spring of 1935 when they awoke from hibernation, these animals have stayed together nearly always. On land their accustomed retreat is a shallow cavity under a large flagstone which lies on some smaller rocks. When the animals are not swimming in the pond, one can, in all probability, find both of them there. If these turtles remain in the water, the male almost always swims behind the female. This association appears to depend upon a permanent readiness for copulation by the male; moreover, it is astonishing how the male is always sure — I believe with the help of smell — to find his female again among dozens of other turtles as soon as he becomes separated from her. A true mating of these animals was observed only once; oddly enough it took place on land during the first days of September."

ECONOMIC VALUE. The feeding habits of the Spotted Turtle probably make it slightly beneficial and, having no harmful habits, it should be protected.

WOOD TURTLE

Clemmys insculpta (Le Conte)

[PLATES 27, 28, 29, AND 30]

IDENTIFICATION. The soft parts are largely salmon red, and a conspicuous black blotch covers the outer hind section of each of the large shields of the otherwise yellow plastron. The rough, " sculptured " carapace is another character by which this turtle can be readily distinguished. Each of the costal shields is built into a low, strongly eccentric pyramid whose sides are formed by concentric ridges and grooves. The keel along the back more or less divides the pyramids of the middle row of shields. Even the small marginals have a similar sculptured structure.

SIZE. The maximum length of the carapace is slightly less than nine inches, although giants of such dimensions are rare. A specimen 9.12 inches long *measured along the curve* is on record, but this individual would be less than nine inches long if measured in the ordinary way. The usual size is shown by the following data taken from a New Jersey female:

	Inches	Millimetres
Length of carapace	6.73	171
Width of carapace	4.90	124.5
Length of plastron	6.34	161
Width of plastron	3.68	93.5
Height of shell	2.64	67

YOUNG. In recently hatched specimens the tail is almost as long as the carapace, and the carapace is either longer than broad or broader than long (32 × 30, 33 × 35, and 31.5 × 34.5 mm. in three cases, the length being given first in each case). The greatly sculptured appearance of the adult develops only with successive periods of growth. The straight-sided notch of the adult plastron is replaced by a rounded emargination. In two living individuals in my possession, the soft parts lack the salmon red of the adult, the skin being a uniform buff like the carapace. The plastron is dark except for a narrow light margin and a little faint light mottling.

THE SEXES. The male has a concave, the female a slightly convex plastron, and the plastron of the female is longer, its rear edge extending almost as far as the hind edge of the carapace. The male has longer and thicker claws and more prominent scales on the front surface of the legs, especially the forelimbs. When the tail is extended the anus of the male lies beyond the hind edge of the carapace, that of the female at or before this edge. In other words, the part of the tail before the anus is about twice as long in the male as in the female.

EGG. Freshly laid eggs seen by Green were elliptical (38 × 26 mm.). The parchment-like shell is white.

DISTRIBUTION. From northern Maine southward through the other New England states, New York (except Long Island), Pennsylvania, northern and central New Jersey, northern Maryland to Fairfax County on the Virginia side of the Potomac River, and Monongalia County in northern West Virginia.

In the west it is found over the northern two-thirds of the southern peninsula of Michigan, the eastern part of its northern peninsula, and all of Wisconsin but the extreme southern section.

In addition there is a record for central Iowa and one for Searchmont, Ontario. Searchmont is just northeast of Sault Ste. Marie.

Pleistocene fossil remains of the Wood Turtle prove that it has inhabited Pennsylvania for at least tens of thousands of years.

HABITAT. The Wood Turtle is both aquatic and terrestrial, the general consensus of opinion being that it spends the midsummer months in dry meadow or woodland, but frequents the vicinity of pond, brook, or swamp during autumn and spring, often entering the water. Probably general conditions of humidity also influence its movements, dry spells sending it toward water even in midsummer. It is, therefore, found at one time or another in almost every type of country, open or wooded, but most of the records are for damp to wet or actually aquatic situations.

HABITS. This species is active on land and in water, where it swims well. It is also an astonishingly good climber, one individual having surprised its owner by getting over the

24. Spotted Turtles (*Clemmys guttata*) from the region of Philadelphia with carapaces 3.87 and 3.69 inches long. The lower and smaller one is a male, the other a female. Both have unusually few spots for such large individuals. (*Courtesy Zoological Society of Philadelphia, photograph by Mark Mooney, Jr.*)

25 [RIGHT]. Young Spotted Turtles (*Clemmys guttata*). The very small one, from Burlington County, New Jersey, is but recently hatched, its carapace measuring only 28 millimetres long. (*Courtesy Zoological Society of Philadelphia, photograph by Mark Mooney, Jr.*)

26 [BELOW]. Egg of the Spotted Turtle from Burlington County, New Jersey. This egg measures 30 x 16 millimetres. (*Courtesy Zoological Society of Philadelphia, photograph by Mark Mooney, Jr.*)

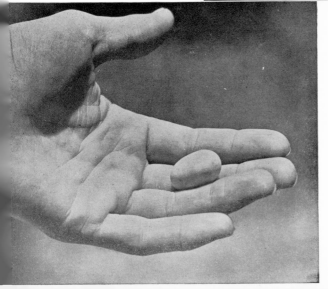

27. Wood Turtle (*Clemmys insculpta*) from the region of Philadelphia with a carapace 7.20 inches long. It is a female. (*Courtesy Zoological Society of Philadelphia, photograph by Mark Mooney, Jr.*)

28. Wood Turtle (*Clemmys insculpta*) from New Jersey with a carapace 6.69 inches long. It is a female. (*Photograph by Douglas Cullen.*)

chicken-wire fence of a rabbit pen, another by escaping from a wastebasket with bulging sides and a height of more than thirty inches. Specimens put in a shallow box climb over its sides with ease, as shown in Plate 29.

Although by no means vicious, this turtle will occasionally bite when annoyed.

" Space reactions " as studied by Yerkes indicate stronger terrestrial tendencies in this than in the Spotted Turtle. See the fuller discussion in the section on habits under the latter species.

The intelligence of a Wood Turtle that had become quite tame was tested in a maze with a compartment containing food as the goal. In order to reach the latter, three correct turns at ends of passages had to be made and one blind alley passed by. The seven runs took 15, 9, 10, 9, 6, 5.5, and 5.5 minutes after leaving the starting box, with 4, 3, 2, 2, 0, 0, and 0 errors per run, respectively. Tinklepaugh, the experimenter, concluded that " the learning of the turtle equalled the expected accomplishment of a rat in the same maze under ordinary experimental conditions." He also emphasized the fact that the reptile seemed to depend largely on sight in its choice of the path to be followed because at each turn it protruded its head and looked all about before making a decision.

HIBERNATION. The weight of evidence points to aquatic hibernation, either in bottom mud or in holes in banks. Surface, however, definitely states that it has been found wintering in decaying vegetation of comparatively dry woods.

The best account of the discovery of hibernating sites is given by Bishop and Schoonmacher, who investigated two streams in Rensselaer County, New York. One of these was spring-fed and in it two specimens were seen on October 12 beneath about eighteen inches of water, one resting on the other. It is possible that they were copulating rather than hibernating. (See the remarks on autumn mating under the section on reproduction.) The other stream, described as small, was investigated first on December 12, when several submerged Wood Turtles were taken from abandoned musk-rat holes in its side. About a month later further search of the same stream revealed one turtle in the mud of its bottom about eighteen inches below the surface of the water. The method used in making such investigations well illustrates one type of physical hardship that herpetologists may at times be called upon to endure:

"The equipment needed for turtle hunting in winter is simple, — an axe, a bath towel, a Farm Bureau Manager with a Ford Car and a strong constitution being the chief requisites. With the axe the ice was cut from the edge of the stream to permit exploration of the muskrat holes and shallow, water excavated cavities underneath the bank. Stout sticks were used for prodding until something hard was encountered; investigations were then continued by lying prone on the bank and thrusting the arm to the shoulder, in the icy water. The bath towel functioned after each bit of exploration."

The first spring appearance in New York and Massachusetts has been found over a period of years to occur from March 20 to May 14, with the third week of April as the average time.

Gathering in streams preparatory to retiring for the winter usually takes place in New York between September 20 and October 15.

REPRODUCTION. Spring mating takes place in New York and New Jersey during May or the latter part of April, and the occurrence of a second mating season has been proved by the discovery of a pair copulating on October 1 in New York. In fact the only detailed account of this act is based on an autumn observation by Wright:

"This fall on October 1, I chanced on what I mistook for a dead wood turtle in the dammed up stretch of a woodland stream, which was 4 feet wide and 1 or 2 feet deep. The head was hanging perpendicularly downward as if it were caught or held by something. Upon endeavor to move it the turtle seemed very heavy and soon to my surprise it proved the male of a mated pair. The head looked to be hooked between the edge of the carapace and plastron of the female turtle. Apparently this was not for purposes of holding the female but like the action of the whistling male previously recorded. The female's head looked to be retracted and the male's head had followed to the withdrawn head of the female. After these turtles were taken from the water the writer could not verify the actual head relations nor see the actual cloacal contact. For several minutes the male however maintained its grasp. With the prominent fore-claws the male held on the edge of the female's carapace near the suture between the first and second cephalic plates. The space between these two feet was barely the width of the male's head. The hind claws similarly held the next to the last pair of caudal marginals."

The reference to whistling in this description is of special interest because the male Wood Turtle is known to make a " distinct yet subdued note not unlike that of a tea-kettle " and audible at thirty or forty feet; even the female can give a low whistle. It was Wright himself who kept a male which repeatedly whistled at a female, so presumably the whistling has sexual significance. The under-water mating of this species indicates, however, that the whistle is the by-product of a courtship gesture rather than an overt effort to produce a sound for the edification of a mate.

No one seems to have recorded the date of laying under natural conditions, but the little available evidence points to the middle two weeks of June as the nesting season in New England. Mid-afternoon has been given as the time of laying, and sandy places near water as well as more upland situations as the sites.

The eggs are buried by the female and left-to be hatched by the heat of the sun. Half of a lot of eight eggs deposited on May 26 in a Philadelphia yard by a female that had been taken three days before in southeastern Pennsylvania hatched about October 1; three had been opened for examination and one was bad. Information on the number of eggs per clutch is as scanty as that on the nesting habits, but apparently seven to twelve eggs are produced by a female at one time.

FOOD AND FEEDING. Although omnivorous in feeding habits, this species is said to exhibit a strong preference for vegetable matter such as fruits, berries, and the tender leaves of plants. Listing of names is pointless because no preference for any particular type or group has been detected. Mushrooms are relished.

In spite of a general and doubtless correct opinion that herbivorous tendencies predominate, Surface found animal matter in twenty-one out of twenty-six food-containing stomachs, plant remains in only twenty. The animal matter consisted chiefly of insects, but included a good share of snails and myriapods, with a scattering of earthworms, slugs, and crustaceans. Bird remains in two stomachs indicate scavenger tendencies, since the capture of a bird by a turtle is hard to picture.

Without doubt the choice of food depends largely on the habitat, which in turn varies from season to season. A turtle living in the fields and woods with plants growing on every hand would hardly be expected to waste much effort pursuing insects. In a stream, on the other hand, aquatic animals probably would be the more readily available food.

The legs are used as aids in feeding to a greater extent than in most chelonians. One captive was described as holding strawberries with the forefeet while biting and tearing them apart, and Allard's account of a specimen watched by him one afternoon for many hours offers confirmation:

" When several feet away, its keen eye spied some large, red wild strawberries on a certain bank. It was interesting to see how eagerly and hurriedly it scrambled toward these berries. It spent considerable time among them, reaching up and clawing down the plants in order to reach the berries which it raked off awkwardly, together with the leaves, into its jaws."

ENEMIES. Thoreau saw a skunk robbing the nest of a Wood Turtle, and a very small specimen was once taken from the stomach of a large-mouthed black bass.

CAPTIVITY. Perhaps no turtle can be more highly recommended as a pet where space is not too limited than this alert intelligent creature. It is often shy, however, when first confined. Getting tame individuals to eat from one's hand is easy and more than one owner has reported being followed by his pet. Shufeldt even describes one that would beg for food by waving a leg, or walking around in a circle a few feet in diameter. Mating in captivity is also on record.

A sunny vivarium about equally divided between land and water is most suitable. A hiding-place should be provided. Good temperatures are from 68° to 75° F. Earthworms, chopped meat, and fish or almost any tender fruit, berry, or vegetable will do for food. Additional items mentioned in the discussion of food and feeding may of course be put on the menu.

The Wood Turtle is an old boarder in the London Zoological Gardens, which received its first specimen just one hundred years ago, in 1839. An individual lived in the National Zoological Park, Washington, five years and ten months.

ECONOMIC VALUE. Although without real market value as a food, this turtle is sometimes eaten locally. It is a harmless animal that should be protected by law, as indeed it is in some states.

PACIFIC POND TURTLE

Clemmys marmorata (Baird and Girard)

[PLATE 31]

IDENTIFICATION. The carapace is olive to black, each shield marked with numerous yellow-brown or black dots or dashes which may be scarcely discernible. Black or brown blotches or dark posterior shield margins are more or less in evidence on the yellow plastron.

The extreme western distribution of this species should serve to identify specimens of known origin.

SIZE. The measurements of a rather large individual as given by Van Denburgh follow:

	Inches	Millimetres
Length of carapace	6.46	164
Width of carapace	5.12	130
Length of plastron	6.02	153
Width of plastron	4.13	105
Length of tail	2.56	65

The largest of fifty specimens measured by Storer was a male with a carapace 7.20 inches long and a weight of thirty-three ounces.

YOUNG. The carapace is more nearly round than in the adult.

THE SEXES. The adult male is readily identified by its concave plastron. In this sex the anus in the extended tail is at or beyond the hind edge of the carapace, whereas in the female it is usually in front of this edge. The terminal portion of the female's tail is more slender and her shell is on the average higher.

EGG. The shell is white and hard and the elliptical eggs vary in length from 32.8 to 40.6 millimetres, in width from 19.7 to 22.6 millimetres.

GROWTH. There is no detailed information on the growth rate of this turtle, but measurements indicate that it may be expected to attain a carapace length of about five and a half inches in ten years.

DISTRIBUTION. The Pacific drainage from 31° N. Latitude in Lower California to the Rogue and Umpqua River valleys of Oregon.

In northern California and extreme southern Oregon it penetrates eastward along the Klamath River as far as Lower Klamath Lake in Siskiyou County, California, and Fall River Mills on the Pit River, Shasta County, California. Farther south it reaches Coulterville in Mariposa County. In the Sierra Nevadas this species attains an altitude of 3,500 feet.

Just how far to the north of the Umpqua River the Pacific Pond Turtle occurs is still problematical. Storer considers Fort Steilacoom, Washington, to be the only authentic locality record north of this river, but Cowan records a specimen collected in Vancouver in 1933. All older records for Canada have been unanimously eliminated.

HABITAT. Ponds and streams are the favourite haunts of this thoroughly aquatic turtle, but rivers, lakes, marshes, sloughs, and reservoirs are also frequented. A preference for quiet water is shown by its abundance in streams with numerous deep quiet pools. Along the coast it enters brackish water, and Charles M. Bogert has even seen it at the edge of the sea far from the mouth of creek or river.

HABITS. This shy species is fond of sunning itself over the water or at its edge, but dives and swims to the bottom at the least disturbance. As many as two dozen are sometimes found in a single pool no larger than twenty by thirty-five feet. During the middle of the day those not basking remain quietly on the bottom of pools, but in the early morning and evening they may be seen moving up or down stream from one pool to another.

HIBERNATION. Toward the end of September this turtle hibernates in the bottom of the pond or stream in which it lives, and it comes out in late March or early April of the following year. Needless to say, the exact extent of the hibernation period varies with season, altitude, and latitude, so it is not surprising to find a record of its appearance on March 1 in southern California (San Bernardino County).

A turtle-trapper consulted by Storer made artificial hibernating quarters for his specimens by spreading three inches of mud over them and covering the mud with eight inches of leaves. Each turtle made a breathing-hole up through the mud.

REPRODUCTION. From the middle of June to the middle of July is the period during which most of the eggs are deposited, but the laying season really begins about the first of June and may even extend into August. Here again season, latitude, and altitude exert an influence. Judging by the few available records, a female normally lays from five to eleven eggs at a time.

The nesting site may be either in an open field or on a bare sandy bank adjacent to the water in which the turtles live, or in a sunny field or on a hillside as much as two or three hundred feet above and hundreds of yards from the stream or pond. When the borders of a stream or pond are heavily shaded, the turtles' choice of a distant sunny site is not hard to explain, but the actions of females that cross warm sandy banks to climb laboriously to a less inviting spot are puzzling.

FOOD AND FEEDING. One individual was once found eating the larva of a neuropteroid insect, and aquatic beetles were found in the stomach of another. Specimens are attracted by hooks baited with earthworms, dead minnows, grasshoppers, or pieces of liver.

ECONOMIC VALUE. This species has long been caught in traps

29. Wood Turtles (*Clemmys insculpta*) from New Jersey climbing out of a box 7.50 inches deep. (*Photograph by Douglas Cullen.*)

30. Young Wood Turtle (*Clemmys insculpta*) from Sussex County, New Jersey, with a carapace 52 millimetres long. At hatching, the carapace is about as broad as long. (*Courtesy Zoological Society of Philadelphia, photograph by Mark Mooney, Jr.*)

31. Pacific Pond Turtle (*Clemmys marmorata*) with a carapace 5.75 inches long. No pattern is evident on the carapace of this male. (*Courtesy Zoological Society of Philadelphia, photograph by Mark Mooney, Jr.*)

32. Muhlenberg's Turtles (*Clemmys muhlenbergii*) from Berks County, Pennsylvania. The male is at once recognized by its larger tail. Its carapace is 3.79, that of the female 3.27 inches long. (*Courtesy Zoological Society of Philadelphia, photograph by Mark Mooney, Jr.*)

made of fish-nets, baited with meat or fish and set so that the trapped individuals are free to rise for air; if imprisoned under water the turtles drown in three hours. In San Francisco during the decade from 1920 to 1930 the turtles sold as an article of food for three to six dollars per dozen.

Storer's excellent account of the Pacific Pond Turtle has been largely drawn upon.

MUHLENBERG'S TURTLE

Clemmys muhlenbergii (Schoepff)

[PLATE 32]

IDENTIFICATION. The conspicuous orange blotch on each temple is the standard character used in recognizing this turtle. The carapace is dull brown or black, with more or less distinct yellow or red markings in the centre of each large shield. These markings may even be entirely lacking. The plastron is black, irregularly marked with yellow (or red).

SIZE. The dimensions of a male specimen of usual size from Chatham, New Jersey, follow:

	Inches	Millimetres
Length of carapace	3.46	88
Width of carapace	2.44	62
Length of plastron	3.03	77
Width of plastron	1.71	43.5
Height of shell	1.42	36

The species is generally given credit for attaining a carapace length of about four and a half inches, but 3.88 inches is the largest measurement that I find based on a preserved specimen.

YOUNG. The carapace of a newly hatched young Muhlenberg's Turtle measured 34 × 29 millimetres. Hatchlings are apparently wider in proportion to their length than adults.

THE SEXES. The tail of the adult male is thicker and longer than that of the female so that the anus lies about five millimetres beyond the hind edge of the carapace when the tail is extended (see Plate 32). The plastron in this sex is distinctly concave in contrast to the flat plastron of the female — which, on the other hand, has a proportionately wider and higher shell. The male has heavier claws on the forelimb, a deeper and wider head and longer snout. Wright has pointed out additional sexual differences, and in a New Jersey pair in my possession the two outer claws of the forelimb are turned abruptly outward in the male, whereas in the female all the claws are straight.

EGG. Elliptical in shape, measuring about 30 × 16 millimetres.

DISTRIBUTION. This turtle has a continuous range from the southeastern corner of Pennsylvania through southern, central, and northeastern New Jersey to the southeastern tip of New York (exclusive of Long Island and Staten Island).

In addition, it is known to occur as follows: New York, from the region just south of Lake Ontario eastward to Albany County and Lake George; Rhode Island, Newport (an old record); Crawford and Mercer Counties, northwestern Pennsylvania; Fairfax County, northeastern Virginia; western North Carolina (Statesville is the easternmost record for this state).

HABITAT. In central and western New York and northwestern Pennsylvania, Muhlenberg's Turtle is found almost entirely near if not actually in sphagnum bogs and swamps. Elsewhere it frequents clear meadow streams and flooded ditches or even wet grassy areas as well as bogs and swamps. No other American turtle is so dependent on a definite type of plant association and it is indeed probable that this species was originally confined to tamarack-sphagnum bogs and swamps (Netting).

This species is known to occur from sea-level to an altitude of about 1,000 feet in the northeastern states and from 2,100 to at least 4,200 feet in western North Carolina. This difference between altitude preference in the north and the south merely shows that it is a northern turtle which survives only at high altitudes in the south where climatic conditions approximate those prevalent at lower elevations in the north.

HABITS. Although found only in aquatic or at least wet environments, this turtle is about as much at home on land as in the water. It is often described as terrestrial.

The Spotted Turtle is commonly found with it.

REPRODUCTION. Next to nothing is known about the reproductive habits of Muhlenberg's Turtle. Wright relates that a female taken in New York state on June 15 laid an egg five days later and still another on July 30, at which time a third was in her oviduct ready to be laid.

FOOD. Surface found berries and fragments of insects in one stomach and concluded that its owner had eaten on land rather than in water. Some information on the feeding of confined specimens is given below in the treatment of captivity.

CAPTIVITY. Muhlenberg's Turtle does well in captivity and will eat raw meat, earthworms, mealworms, lettuce, and berries. Rust recommends giving it the same food as that fed to the Wood Turtle and carefully keeping it at 68° to 75° F., as it is sensitive to cold. Its aquarium should have a large land section.

Food is readily eaten either in or out of water. However, a specimen in my possession overcame and swallowed earthworms much more easily in than out of water.

Rare as this species is supposed to be, it was exhibited in the London Zoological Gardens as long ago as 1839.

CHAPTER V

BLANDING'S TURTLE *and* THE BOX TURTLES

Family TESTUDINIDÆ

Genera *EMYS* and *TERRAPENE*

Although forming but a small part of their large family, the species of *Emys* and *Terrapene* are conveniently grouped together because of a common ability to close the shell up. Blanding's Turtle, however, cannot do this nearly so well as can the box turtles.

The genus *Emys* is interesting in having a rather long fossil history, carrying it back more than thirty-five million years from the present into the Eocene of the Old World. Today only two species exist, one in Europe, western Asia, and northern Africa, the other in the United States and Canada.

Five species of box turtles of the genus *Terrapene* are known to live today, two in this country and three in Mexico. Fossil remains of extinct kinds have been found in Maryland, Pennsylvania, Georgia, Florida, Texas, and Kansas. The majority of these apparently lived in the United States some tens of thousands of years ago during Pleistocene times, but the most ancient of all carries the genus back well over a million years into the Pliocene of Kansas.

Box turtles deserve a place in the turtle hall of fame as having perfected the ability to protect their vulnerable parts by

33.   Blanding's Turtle (*Emys blandingii*) from Lucas County, Ohio, with a carapace 6.06 inches long. The notch in the front of the upper jaw of this male is readily seen. (*Courtesy Zoological Society of Philadelphia, photograph by Mark Mooney, Jr.*)

34.   Common Box Turtle (*Terrapene carolina carolina*) from the region of Philadelphia. This male with a carapace 5.59 inches long is turning over. (*Courtesy Zoological Society of Philadelphia, photograph by Mark Mooney, Jr.*)

35. Common Box Turtles (*Terrapene carolina carolina*) from northern New Jersey, illustrating the great range of variation in pattern of the carapace. (*Photograph by Douglas Cullen.*)

36. Common Box Turtles (*Terrapene carolina carolina*) from northern New Jersey, illustrating the degree of variation in the amount of dark colour on the plastron. (*Photograph by Douglas Cullen.*)

sealing these within the shell. So well is this done that in some kinds a thin blade cannot be inserted between plastron and carapace. Although other groups have developed hinges in the plastron and, in one case, even in the carapace, none has really rivalled the American box turtles in their perfection of this particular protective device.

IDENTIFICATION

The hooked beak of the box turtles immediately distinguishes them from Blanding's Turtle, which has a deeply notched upper jaw devoid of all signs of a hook (see Plate 33). The shell of the former is highly arched, that of the latter depressed.

The recognition of kinds of *Terrapene* in the northern and central states, where only one or two species occur, is a simple matter that will trouble few, but in the extreme southeastern part of this country the situation is different. Here the Ornate Box Turtle does not occur but *T. carolina* splits up into subspecies that make a quagmire in which many a competent herpetologist has floundered and amateurs have expired with scarcely a struggle. The difficulty was merely this: an attempt was usually made to separate as distinct entities (full species) four freely intergrading subspecies whose ranges meet chiefly in the region from northern Florida to Tennessee, the result being that the same individuals were being identified first as this by one worker and then as that by another. The addition of many grey hairs to the heads of all human beings concerned was but a minor result.

At the advice of Dr. Archie F. Carr, Jr., who has studied these reptiles in the field with a modern conception of relationships, I am treating all these alleged southeastern "species" as geographical subspecies of the widely distributed *T. carolina*, thus making practical their identification on the basis of distribution alone. Any puzzling individual from an area intermediate between two or even three ranges can be conveniently set aside as an " intergrade."

Dr. Carr has also given me diagnostic characters that will enable anyone to recognize fairly typical representatives of the subspecies involved, but the importance of ranges must always be kept in mind and specimens identified largely on the basis of them alone.

The crucial step in naming any *Terrapene* of this country is to determine whether it represents the Ornate Box Turtle or one of the subspecies of *T. carolina* of which only the eastern Common Box Turtle and the southern and western Three-toed one are found north of Florida and the Gulf Coastal Plain. In the Ornate Box Turtle the carapace is somewhat flattened on top and lacks a distinct longitudinal median keel; the plastron has the characteristic pattern as described below and illustrated. If these points taken together with the place of origin do not seem to settle the matter, it will be necessary to read the identification sections of the Common and Ornate Box Turtles for fuller comparison. Curiously enough, the shell pattern of the Florida Box Turtle sometimes strongly suggests that of *T. ornata*.

Lack of a hinged plastron in quite immature individuals, together with other juvenile characters, make identification of very young specimens difficult unless the sections devoted to them are carefully read.

BLANDING'S TURTLE

Emys blandingii (Holbrook)

[PLATE 33]

IDENTIFICATION. The lower jaw and throat are uniform bright yellow and the upper jaw is without a beak and notched in front. The carapace is black, with hundreds of pale yellow round or oblong spots. The yellow plastron is notched at the hind end and hinged near its middle; each of its large shields has a dark blotch in its outer, rear section.

SIZE. The usual adult carapace length is seven to eight inches. Measurements of a very large female from Illinois follow:

	Inches	Millimetres
Length of carapace	9.45	240
Width of carapace	6.46	164
Length of plastron	8.66	220
Width of plastron	4.57	116
Height of shell	3.27	83

A living Michigan specimen with a carapace 9.05 inches long weighed five pounds.

YOUNG. An Indiana specimen collected by Grant and obviously very young had a mottled brown carapace measuring 35 × 30 millimetres. Its plastron was dark brown, with a narrow yellow border. The future hinge was represented only by a double line or crease. The lack of spots on the carapace is a point of special importance.

THE SEXES. This species seems to be peculiarly lacking in sexual differences. The tail of the male is the longer, its length being a third or more of that of the carapace, whereas the tail of the female is a quarter the length of the carapace.

EGG. Elliptical (about 36 × 25 mm.), with a white shell.

LONGEVITY. Oddly enough, there are no records of this turtle having lived more than three years either in or out of confinement even though its close European relative, *Emys orbicularis*, is famous for its survival of long periods of captivity. Flower gives this European turtle's known length of life as "70, probably 120 years." It is reasonable to assume that

Blanding's Turtle lives approximately as long as its Old World cousin.

DISTRIBUTION. This turtle has a continuous distribution over the territory comprising the northernmost strips of Ohio and Indiana, the northern third of Illinois, about all of Wisconsin, the southern peninsula of Michigan, and the tip of Ontario between Lake Erie and Lake St. Clair. Surrounding this area there are more or less isolated records for northeastern Nebraska, northwestern Iowa, central Illinois, central Ohio, the northwestern tip of Pennsylvania, Port Maitland, Ontario (near the northeastern end of Lake Erie), and the northern peninsula of Michigan (Marquette County).

East of the territory already outlined, Blanding's Turtle has two small areas of distribution: one (in which the species is not rare) in eastern Ontario along the lower St. Lawrence and the country bordering the eastern end of Lake Ontario; the other (in which it is rare) in eastern Massachusetts and the southeastern corner of New Hampshire. Bordering on the latter area one finds a recent reliable record for central Connecticut; a sight identification for the southwestern part of the same state; a reliable record for the Lewisburg region, eastern Pennsylvania; a highly questionable one for central New Jersey, and one for Long Island that is little better. There is in addition an old indefinite record for Rhode Island.

It is possible that some of these peripheral records are based on escaped specimens; on the other hand the fact that this turtle has a habit of turning up rarely in widely separated places argues against such an explanation. Netting offers five possible explanations of the spotty Pennsylvania distribution, which, though interesting, are too detailed to be taken up here.

HABITAT. Blanding's Turtle is a lover of shallow plant-grown water of lake or river bays, ponds, marshes, swamps, sloughs, ditches, sluggish creeks, or low fields. Not infrequently it is referred to as a terrestrial species; just how extensively it may live on land has not, however, been definitely determined. Some reports of terrestrialism have no doubt been based on females in search of a nesting site, but it is entirely possible that at certain seasons or during rainy or extremely humid spells this turtle wanders from its native element. Schmidt and Necker state for the Chicago region that Blanding's Turtle is hard to find during the summer and autumn, "when it does not seem averse to a land existence."

HABITS. When surprised on land, this shy species hisses and seeks protection by drawing into and closing its shell, but when individuals are alarmed while sunning over the water or at its edge, they quickly dive and swim with agility to the bottom, where the pattern of their carapace blends with the bubble-filled algal growth or other aquatic vegetation. Basking in the sun is a favourite occupation, especially in the spring.

March 29 is the earliest date that I find for the spring appearance of this turtle in northern Indiana, but several records exist to prove its activity there during the first ten days of April. In the same region it has been found abroad as late as November 4. These dates give at least a clue to the time of its annual appearance and retreat; due allowance must of course be made for latitude and early and late seasons. Cahn states that hibernating specimens have been taken from underwater muskrat runways and the mud of spring-fed ditches. Probes with steel points are used in locating the torpid turtles.

In the Toledo Zoological Park many individuals hibernated beneath masses of soggy leaves, their bodies being at least partly submerged, but two specimens spent the winter several feet from water under wet leaves.

REPRODUCTION. Besides one complete and one incomplete account of the nesting of Blanding's Turtle, extremely little has been written about the reproduction of this species. May 22 and October 11 have been recorded as mating dates for the Chicago area, but confirmation of the latter date would be very valuable because so little is known about autumn copulation in turtles.

A newly hatched infant was found in northern Ohio on September 3.

MATING. As observed by Conant, the mating of Blanding's Turtles closely resembled that of Common Snapping Turtles living in similar confinement. He describes this act as performed by the Snappers under water thus:

" When in coitu the plastrons of both male and female were in parallel planes, with the plastron of the male pressed tightly against the carapace of the female. The male grasped his mate by hooking the claws of all four feet under the edge of her carapace and his tail was curled under hers in such a manner that his anal opening was turned upward to meet hers. He also pressed upon her snout with his chin so that it was necessary for her to keep her head withdrawn. In every case the actions and attitudes were very much the same. Sometimes in struggling, both sexes were seen to bite ineffectually at each other's forelegs."

NESTING. J. R. Brown has given us the only complete description of nest construction. His account is so good that I quote him almost in full:

" On the evening of July seventeenth at Camp Teetonkah, Port Maitland, Ontario, a Blanding's Turtle (*Emys blandingii*) began at seven thirty p.m. preparations for laying its eggs. It chose a sand hill about ten feet above the level of the Feeder to the old Welland Canal which is inhabited by turtles of this species. The hill was about a half mile from the Feeder.

" It planted its fore feet in the sand and with its hind feet, using them alternately, gradually hollowed out a hole. The hole at first was only the width of its foot, about an inch wide. It would put its left foot in, scrape around the inside of the hole, then lift out the sand turning its foot sideways in the form of a scoop. Now it would put its right foot in and repeat the action. Counting slowly, it took between twelve and fifteen counts from the time it placed its foot in the hole until it took it out again. The hole gradually became bigger until it measured five inches in depth, two inches wide at the top and four inches wide at the bottom.

" The turtle didn't seem to mind company. From the time it began to dig until it finished laying its eggs there was an average of ten boys watching the performance. The boys, including myself, were lying face down within a foot of the turtle's tail.

" While digging the last part of its hole it put so much energy into the work that its jaws clicked under the strain.

" At eight twenty p.m. it stopped digging and rested with its right foot in the hole."

Next comes a minute-by-minute record of the laying of the eleven eggs which began at eight twenty-six and ended twenty-eight and a quarter minutes later; seven of the ten intervals between appearance of the eggs were from one and a half to two minutes long, the remaining three from three and a half to six and three-quarters. The right hind foot was kept in the hole to arrange the first five eggs, the left hind foot the next five, whereas the last egg was placed with the right hind one.

Brown continues:

" After taking a rest of three-quarters of a minute it began to slowly scrape sand from the inside of the hole on to the eggs, using its hind feet alternately. Then it took both feet out of the hole and began scraping sand into it with them, alternately. When it had got some in, it would pack it down and then put more in and pack that down until it finally had the hole filled up and the sand well packed. The last egg was three inches below the surface of the sand. The turtle required one hour and thirty-nine minutes to satisfy itself that the eggs were safely stowed away. It very very slowly moved away from the nest, packing the sand as it moved.

" At ten twenty-three p.m. it crawled away toward the Feeder.

"During the whole process it never once saw the hole it dug nor the eggs it laid.

" It rested five times while packing the eggs."

So much for Brown's observations. At about six in the afternoon of June 22 a female was seen at Point Pelee, Ontario, digging a nest in sand, but the approach of the observer frightened her away. However, in the same area half an hour later L. L. Snyder saw two other females preparing their nests and watched one until she had finished digging and begun to lay. The cavity was estimated to be seven inches deep, three and a half to four across the mouth, and seven in diameter below. About forty-five minutes were required for its completion. Eleven eggs were later removed from this nest and buried in a box full of sand. On August 26 an accident broke them, to reveal near hatchlings. This indicates an incubation period of a little more than two months. The conditions of course were not natural.

These observations, chiefly by Brown and Snyder, agree in most details and from them certain interesting comparisons and conclusions may be drawn:

The southern Ontario laying season extends at least from June 22 through July 17. Nests are dug in the late afternoon by alternate strokes of the hind limbs. Snyder states that the sand is carried out on the upturned sole of the hind foot, whereas Brown writes that the foot is turned sideways " in the form of a scoop." There was little difference in the time required to dig the two cavities and one was slightly larger than the other. (Nest size probably depends entirely on the leg length of the digger.) Eleven eggs were deposited in each case. Agassiz's dissections indicate that seven to nine eggs form a clutch and Cahn gives six to ten as the range in number.

Once well started on her task, the female is not disturbed by the presence of a human being. Would she be as indifferent to the approach of some turtle- or egg-eating mammal? The whole nesting process is so automatic and mechanical that the female does not even need her sense of sight, nor does curiosity prompt her to cast even a farewell glance at the result of her astonishing handiwork.

FOOD AND FEEDING. According to Cahn, on land Blanding's Turtle eats leaves, grasses, berries, and other succulent vegetation, slugs, grubs, larvæ of insects, and earthworms; in water, tadpoles, frogs, crayfish, minnows, and larvæ of aquatic insects. Conant has seen them devour snails and carrion such as dead fish and turtles. Food is swallowed either under water or out of it.

ENEMIES. The shells of several specimens collected by Grant in northern Indiana had been badly gnawed by some rodent.

CAPTIVITY. Earthworms, insects, tadpoles, young frogs, small fish, chopped raw meat or fish, berries, lettuce, and other tender plant parts as available may be given to specimens kept as pets. The aquarium should be sunny, have a hiding-place and a large land section; temperatures from 68° to 75° F. are recommended by Rust. Conant found that specimens did well in shallow outdoor pools with gently sloping sides, badly in fairly steep tanks even though these were provided with ample resting-places.

Some individuals show no signs of fear after a few days of confinement, when handling will not even make them draw into their shells. Usually no amount of teasing will cause even wild specimens to bite.

COMMON BOX TURTLE

Terrapene carolina carolina (Linnæus)

[PLATES 34, 35, 36, 37, AND 38]

IDENTIFICATION. The carapace is dome-shaped (not flattened on top), its highest point in the middle, and its posterior margin not noticeably flaring. It always has a median keel and is generally slightly longer than the plastron. Usually there are four claws on each hind foot, and the sides of the head are not striped. The pattern of the shell is astonishingly variable, but in most specimens each large shield of the carapace has conspicuous yellow spots, stripes or blotches on a dark brown ground colour, these markings often radiating from the growth centres. Conspicuous but highly variable brown to black markings are generally present on the plastron, which is only rarely immaculate yellow.

SIZE. The most detailed information on the maximum size of the Common Box Turtle has been accumulated by John T. Nichols, who marked and measured no fewer than 843 Long Island individuals over a period of many years. Because juvenile box turtles are seldom found, the vast majority of the 843 were adult, 696 of them having plastrons at least 4.50 inches long. Only seven were 6 or more inches in length; the two largest measured 6.25 inches. Also:

52	specimens	had	plastrons	5.62	inches	long
98	”	”	”	5.50	”	”
101	”	”	”	5.37	”	”
129	”	”	”	5.25	”	”
90	”	”	”	5.12	”	”
68	”	”	”	5.00	”	”

Measurements were taken to 0.125 of an inch.

A Long Island male with a plastron 6.50 inches long is on record.

Dimensions of a female of average size from northern New Jersey follow:

	Inches	Millimetres
Length of carapace	5.37	136
Width of carapace	4.12	105
Length of plastron	5.25	133
Width of front lobe of plastron	2.81	71
Width of rear lobe of plastron	3.25	83
Height of shell	2.69	68

YOUNG. The carapace of very young specimens has a prominent median keel, the highest parts of which are yellow. The plastral hinge is not developed. There is a more or less distinct yellow spot about in the centre of each costal shield, and the outer borders of the marginals are yellow. The head largely or entirely lacks the conspicuous yellow or orange markings usually seen in the adult, and the yellowish edges of the plastron surround a big dark central area. (See Plate 37.)

The carapace of the hatchling is more nearly round (28 × 22 mm. in one case) than that of the adult. In fact, in Agassiz's figure the length and width are equal (29 × 29 mm.).

THE SEXES. Strange as it may be, no one has ever made a thorough study of sexual differences in this common turtle. The following characters have been pointed out, but some of them require further investigation:

When the tail is extended, the anus of the male lies well beyond, that of the female under or scarcely beyond, the edge of the carapace.

In the male there is a marked concavity in the hind lobe of the plastron, whereas the plastron of the female is flat.

The carapace of the female is more convex on top, therefore

the height of this sex is greater in proportion to the length.
The nuchal notch is said to be more marked in the male, and
its carapace has a greater tendency to flare at the posterior
corners.

The claws of the hind foot are shorter and thicker in the
male.

The eye of the male is usually pink or bright red, that of
the female dark red, reddish brown, purple or grey. There is
considerable variation, however, in the eye colour of both
sexes.

The male attains the greater average size. Mr. Nichols concluded that on Long Island most adult specimens with plastrons less than 5.12 inches long are females, whereas most
specimens with plastrons more than 5.50 inches in length are
males.

EGG. The elliptical eggs have a thin, flexible white shell.
Cahn gives the " average size of a typical egg " as 33.2 × 19.5
millimetres. The largest of the fifty-four eggs measured by
him was 35 × 19, the smallest 30.5 × 18.5 millimetres. However, according to Allard, the greater diameter may be as
much as 38, the lesser 22 millimetres. Eggs of such exceptional
size are generally found in small clutches of large females.

LONGEVITY. The habit of carving initials on the plastron of
box turtles has given rise to a quantity of more or less reliable
information as to its length of life. After going over a great
deal of this information Flower (1937) concludes that the evidence suggests, without proving, that individuals of this species may still be alive at ages of 45, 50, 55, 75, 85, 115, 116, and
even 123 years. He allows five years for adolescence.

Some of the eight hundred and forty-three Common Box
Turtles marked by Mr. Nichols on Long Island were, he believes, sixty to eighty years old. He is also convinced that individuals only exceptionally live much more than eighty years.

Although the type of evidence for the long life of this turtle is not really scientific, its cumulative weight convinces me. In all probability, then, individuals of this subspecies, like man, occasionally pass the hundred-year mark.

GROWTH. Growth from hatching to an age of five years has been observed by three workers. In a case reported by Ditmars, a Connecticut specimen attained a carapace length of about five inches in slightly more than five years. In Pennsylvania Rosenberger kept two females and a male from their hatching in the late summer of 1929 to the autumn of 1933, when he saw the male try to mount one of the females. The following summer prolonged amatory activities by the male were observed. The plastron of this specimen then measured four and three-quarters inches, those of the females four inches. Unfortunately the exact conditions under which the specimens lived were not reported by Ditmars and Rosenberger, so we do not know whether the turtles remained active throughout the year. Frothingham relates how a captive Massachusetts individual, hatched in October 1930, attained a plastron length of 3.31 inches by May 1935. This turtle was kept in an unheated room during the winters and feeding was then suspended.

Mr. Nichols's study indicates that age can be accurately determined by growth-ring counts up through five or six years; from seven to fifteen years with a fair degree of accuracy; above fifteen years with little certainty. In the larger number of specimens retaken by him after a lapse of two or more years (all of which were probably at least five years old), fewer rings were added than years elapsed, the difference being only one in six of the ten cases.

DISTRIBUTION. From western Georgia, extreme northeastern Florida, and parts of Tennessee northwestward through the southern halves of Illinois and the lower peninsula of Michigan; northward through most of Ohio; northeastward through the Atlantic states, all of Pennsylvania and Massachusetts, and southeastern New York as far north as Albany.

In New England this turtle is usually recorded for Vermont, New Hampshire, and Maine, but I find definite records only for the southeastern tip of New Hampshire. Since, according to Babcock, it is rare even in Massachusetts except on Cape Cod, two of the three northern New England states are probably not a part of its range. But one reliable record for Wisconsin has been published since 1890, for Waukesha County, in the southeastern corner of the state. Its present existence in Wisconsin is thus seen to be problematical.

Intergradation between the Common and Three-toed Box Turtles presumably takes place in Tennessee and adjacent territory.

Fossil remains of this turtle have been found in the Pleistocene of Indiana and Pennsylvania, so its existence in these states dates back probably some tens of thousands of years.

HABITAT. The Common Box Turtle is essentially a woodland species, there being about five times as many records of it in woods as in all other types of country together, such as meadows, fields, and open areas adjacent to woods. In rolling or hilly regions it prefers hillsides and other upland situations, but the species is often abundant in perfectly flat country. An altitude of 2,500 feet is attained in North Carolina.

Although frequently found in dry woods, it craves a certain degree of moisture when the temperature is high. This is shown by the way great numbers seek large mud-holes, bogs, swamps, shallow ponds, and even the edges of deeper (fresh or salt) water during hot dry spells of midsummer. The aquatic inclinations are treated in greater detail below under æstivation.

The swimming ability of Long Island individuals has been described too often to be doubted. Overton, for example, writes:

" Specimens are frequently seen swimming in the water, or

resting in the shallows with only the head protruding above the surface. When alarmed, the turtles often leave the land and enter the water voluntarily. They usually swim beneath the surface, but come up readily to breathe and to take observations. They seem to be familiar with the water, and in their ease and rapidity of swimming they compare favorably with the pond turtle (*Chrysemys picta*)."

Others describe its movements in the water as slow and laborious. Perhaps turtles living in a relatively aquatic environment demonstrate the axiom that practice makes perfect.

HABITS. This interesting reptile is diurnal and solitary, its movements slow and deliberate. When approached, it either tightly closes itself up with a hiss, remains motionless but on the alert, or attempts to escape through flight. The first type of behaviour is most common, the last very unusual. When actually picked up, an occasional individual is bold enough to keep the limbs out and kick by way of protest. John T. Nichols found that only two among twenty-four marked specimens failed to behave in the same general way when recaptured after a lapse of one to fifteen years. One, a male, had changed from " retiring " to " bold " at the end of seven years; the other, a female, had, in five years, become " bold and somewhat restless " instead of " retiring." Whether seasonal sexual urge had anything to do with these changes cannot be said.

Although the disposition is good in the vast majority of specimens, rarely one is found that bites and snaps until accustomed to its new surroundings. The bite, of course, is not severe enough to inflict injury on anyone but a very small child. Fights that seem to lack a sexual motive are on record. The best account of such a battle is quoted from Allard, who kept large numbers in confinement under fairly natural conditions:

" The box turtles usually live peacefully together in their enclosure, but they can become very vicious fighters. In one instance two turtles eating from the same dish suddenly became enraged. Both quickly adopted a characteristic fighting attitude as they faced each other. Each lifted a front foot from the ground, and held himself as high as possible in a rearing position on the remaining three legs. At the same time they engaged in a peculiar teetering motion. With the quickness of lightning, one suddenly struck savagely at the other's head, its powerful jaws catching its adversary's beak. The turtle attacked retracted its head instantly into its shell, breaking the hold with a loud snap. The big aggressive fellow now stood high upon three legs over its enemy, one front foot uplifted, its reptile-like neck out-stretched, waiting motionless with savage ferocity in its expression for it to protrude its head again. This turtle seemed well aware of danger, and merely waited until its vicious enemy tired of the fray and repaired to the food again."

The same author, although not the only one to record the surprising degree of " associative memory " displayed by this reptile, has given the best evidence. For example, he frequently dug earthworms in the enclosure or shook caterpillars from a tree growing in it and found that the turtles soon learned to associate either action with food, and approached in numbers to feast. Even his appearance in the pen at feeding time would awaken the inmates to activity.

The " space reactions " experiments by Yerkes involve this form and are summarized under the corresponding section for the Spotted Turtle.

Sleep is indulged in not only at night but through the day during the heat of midsummer. Such daytime slumber probably approaches the state of æstivation discussed below. A sleeping individual often seems to be quite surprised and disturbed to awaken and find itself in one's hand; a protest is registered by violent efforts to escape.

There is good evidence that very young box turtles have distinct aquatic proclivities, and such a leaning may in part ac-

37. Young Common Box Turtles (*Terrapene carolina carolina*) with carapaces 33 and 34 millimetres long. Both individuals were hatched in the Philadelphia Zoological Garden, and their parents came from the region of Philadelphia. (*Courtesy Zoological Society of Philadelphia, photograph by Mark Mooney, Jr.*)

38. Common Box Turtle (*Terrapene carolina carolina*) digging her nest in a pen at Swarthmore, Pennsylvania, on July 1, 1933. The photograph was taken at 8.05 p.m. (*Photograph by Francis Harper.*)

39. Three-toed Box Turtle (*Terrapene carolina triunguis*) with a carapace 4.87 inches long. The pattern of the much worn carapace is obscure. The hind foot has three claws. (*Courtesy Zoological Society of Philadelphia, photograph by Mark Mooney, Jr.*)

40. Gulf Coast Box Turtle (*Terrapene carolina major*) from Bay County, Florida, with a carapace 3.44 inches long. The fourth claw on the hind foot is barely visible. (*Courtesy Zoological Society of Philadelphia, photograph by Mark Mooney, Jr.*)

count for their astonishingly infrequent discovery. They are, moreover, masters at the art of concealment. The rather complex relationship of the adult to water is treated under the section on habitat above and that on æstivation and aquatic tendencies below. An inclination to be abroad during or after warm rains is but another aspect of its craving for a degree of moisture.

HIBERNATION. North of Maryland hibernation usually begins in November and ends in April or early May; farther south it is of course somewhat shortened. Actual dates mean little unless based on observations covering a great many years, and, unfortunately, no one has ever kept such a continuous record for any single locality. Warm spells of mild winters occasionally bring hardy individuals out even in the northern states.

Hibernation is entered by degrees, the turtles at first burying themselves late each day when the temperature falls, to remain in shallow burrows and emerge the next day when the sun has again warmed earth and air. As the season advances, they penetrate deeper and deeper. Cahn found that one kept under observation outdoors in Illinois was two inches deep on October 21, five on November 4, eleven two weeks later, and nineteen on December 5 and February 9. The final depth varies a great deal. In the latitude of Washington, D.C., Allard gives it as three to eight inches, whereas Cahn, presumably referring to Illinois, puts the depth as one to two feet. In the Washington region, barely covered individuals have been known to survive even a severe winter, snow apparently making up for lack of depth. Such individuals are, nevertheless, *above* the frost line. In spite of this hardiness some undoubtedly are frozen to death.

Loose soil mixed with or covered by dead or decayed vegetable matter such as fallen leaves is the favourite hibernation site, but the turtles dig with their forelimbs into whatever soft material is available; Latham found specimens that had been washed out of beach sand by a record flood. Hibernation under water has been reported once in nature by Davis, observed by Cahn in an Illinois pen enclosing ample, readily available land sites, and by Conant in the Toledo Zoological Park. In the case described by Davis a turtle, discovered on February 22, had apparently buried itself under a few inches of leaves in a dry depression which had later become filled with water and covered by ice. Although it is impossible to say how long this individual had been submerged, the voluntary entering of water by Cahn's and Conant's specimens makes all subaqueous hibernation interesting. The Illinois turtles spent the winter in a pool supplied with water from a pipe. The temperature of the turtles remained about 1.8° F. below that of the water, which stayed well above the freezing-point.

ÆSTIVATION AND AQUATIC TENDENCIES. The Common Box Turtle was once described as strictly terrestrial, but now we know better. Hot, dry spells of midsummer send them scurrying to all muddy or watery places, and where the turtle population is large, and wet places are far apart, great numbers congregate in every suitable spot. They either soak in water or bury themselves several inches in mud and, if adverse conditions persist, fall into a deep sleep, which seems to be a form of æstivation.

It is only fair to add, however, that Allard detected no " definite midsummer period of inactivity " or lapse of appetite among some seventy-five individuals kept by him under nearly natural conditions. His turtles did, nevertheless, constantly tunnel deeply into a huge pile of damp ground débris raked together for them. Not only nights but summer days were often spent in sound sleep in the depths of their tunnels.

INDIVIDUAL RANGE AND HOMING. The habit of carving initials on turtles has produced information not only on the maximum age attained by the individual but also on its tendency to remain in a restricted area. The information on the latter subject secured thus is of course unsatisfactory because of its hit or miss nature, but the results strongly suggest that a Common Box Turtle has a home territory in which it probably spends much if not all of its life.

John T. Nichols's work on Long Island turtles, referred to more than once above, throws much light on this territorial habit and also on the ability to return to the home ground. His studies cover a span of about twenty years, during which time sixty-two turtles were marked, each being recaptured from two to seven times after lapses of one to fifteen years (only three months in one case). His conclusions follow:

The normal home territory of most specimens has a diameter of two hundred and fifty yards or less; more than half a mile in very exceptional cases. With the passage of time the territory may be shifted somewhat.

About ninety per cent of adult turtles exhibited some homing tendencies; exceptional ones definitely did not.

All of the eleven grown turtles that were moved more than one-half to approximately three-fourths of a mile, went back toward where they were found, returning distances of one thousand to fourteen hundred yards.

Young turtles with plastrons four and a half inches long or less showed relatively little homing tendency, only three out of seven making returns. The greatest distance retraced was seven hundred yards.

Two adults brought from afar remained near where they were released without attempting to return.

An attack on this same subject was made some years ago by Ruth Breder, who used the unique method of securing a spool of thread to the rear of the carapace, thus making the turtle leave a trail of thread. Only four individuals were used and the results are therefore not too impressive. However, they give additional evidence of a territorial habit and indicate that

the Comon Box Turtle "has a well developed sense of direction" and "takes the most direct route in regard to both the
horizontal angle and the vertical and uses discrimination in a
choice of paths in avoiding obstacles while attempting to reach
a desired location." A surprising result was the discovery that
these spooled subjects, after digging into soft soil for the night,
emerged the following morning by pushing on through, always completing the tunnel; in no case did one reach the surface by retracing its steps.

MATING. Soon after emergence from hibernation the males
most actively seek the females, but less frequent matings occur
throughout the summer and, from Maryland southward, even
into early October. Just how often late summer and autumn
copulations occur is not known, but Ewing mentions a minor
pre-hibernation peak and gives evidence that autumn matings
produce fertile eggs. In this connection it is worth remarking
that his females that were kept away from males for an entire
season reproduced as usual, laying a high percentage of fertile eggs.

When ready to mate, the male follows the female about,
pushing or lunging against her, viciously biting at her shell
and soft parts, and trying to get his feet between her carapace and plastron. She may resist and, if he has already
mounted her, render him temporarily helpless by closing her
shell on his beak and feet. After sufficiently subduing his mate,
the male, from his mounted position, succeeds in thrusting his
hind legs into the cavities between the inner rear lateral parts
of her carapace and thighs. She in turn firmly grips his legs
from the outside with hers. This position brings the tails together but the male cannot affect union without assuming a
verticle position and placing the cloacæ in actual contact, one
tail being turned to the right, the other to the left. Thus the
pair remain for periods varying in length from several minutes
to an hour or even longer. Cahn and Conder have given the

only full description of copulation, the details of which, however, have been well corroborated by subsequent observers.

In confinement, at least, males sometimes mount males, a procedure that may result in fights since the bottom male usually closes his shell upon the feet of his rider, which in turn retaliates by biting at the head of his adversary.

The not infrequent contests witnessed between Common Box Turtles can be explained in various ways: they may be struggles for the possession of a female, misinterpreted courtship, frustrated attempts at mating between the same or opposite sexes, territorial battles, or the result of pure " cussedness," as the one described above in the section on habits certainly was. This whole field lies wide open for investigation.

NESTING. Considerable data accumulated by Allard and Ewing for the region of Washington, D.C., show that the eggs are laid from May 28 to July 14. Only one female laid in May, however. The season is presumably a little later in the northeastern states.

The number of eggs per clutch for sixty layings was found by Allard to vary from two to seven and average 4.2. Only one turtle deposited the maximum number and more than half laid either four or five eggs. Data from various other sources agree well with those secured by Allard except that batches of seven are not so exceptional and there are one or two records of eight.

There is surprisingly little definite information on the type of nesting site chosen by this species, as most observers have neglected to give adequate descriptions of the sites discovered by them. Loose, preferably sandy soil of open cultivated or grassy areas seems to be hunted for by the expectant layer, and there is one statement that a southern exposure is usually selected. I say " hunted for " advisedly since, as brought out above in the treatment of habitat, the Common Box Turtle is a lover of shaded woodlands where, one assumes, the ground would not be sufficiently warmed by a direct sun to promote rapid development.

The superb account of nest construction by Allard is quoted in full below because I know of no better evidence supporting the belief that each species of turtle follows a characteristic complex pattern of behaviour in depositing its eggs. Once the trigger is sprung, the animal machine must go through the entire process to the bitter end, unmodified by either vision or mental activity remotely approaching reason. For example, the possession of only one hind foot by a confined female did not modify her behaviour during nest construction, the stump being moved alternately with the good leg, but an asymmetrical nest resulted. In this connection it is also interesting to note that the hind limbs are used during nest construction, the forelimbs when digging for any other purpose.

This is Allard's account:

" The box turtle attends to the deposition of her eggs with meticulous care. When a suitable spot is found, the female near sunset begins the laborious work of digging the egg-bed. Once the fore feet have been placed and digging has begun, these are never moved and the position of the body with respect to the eggs is not changed until the eggs are covered. The operation of digging is done entirely with the hind feet, and these are invariably alternated in the digging performance. The egg-bed or egg-cavity when completed is somewhat flask-shaped with a relatively narrow neck widening into the cavity proper which has been cut beneath the surface-layer. The soil is lifted and pushed upward and backward. The diameter and the depth of the cavity are limited by the length of the leg, and digging appears to continue until the feet can reach no farther in the deepening and lateral cutting operations.

" The time required to complete the egg-cavity depends largely upon the character and firmness of the soil. In hard-packed soil, digging may require several hours of patient labor.

In the writer's enclosure, digging has sometimes persisted between three and four hours before egg-laying began. Oftentimes pebbles and bits of soil are actually grasped by the toes to be lifted out of the cavity and placed to the rear. As the loose soil is removed and accumulates in a ridge behind, the turtle from time to time pushes it backward with the big, powerful hind feet.

" When digging begins, the place is rarely changed or abandoned until the hole is completed. Three females only, of twenty-five observed digging, abandoned the work, one after a good-sized depression had been made; two very soon after beginning. There seemed to be no good reason to explain these behaviors. Pebbles and roots are very disconcerting to the creatures, for every effort seems to be made to excavate a clean-cut egg-bed. In one instance the writer found a female with her egg-cavity completed, but a round pebble remained within which she could feel and push about with her feet but could not remove. She made repeated efforts with the usual alternations of the feet to grasp or to push the pebble out, but without success. The writer finally came to her assistance and when her leg was withdrawn, he removed the troublesome pebble with a stick, and perhaps obviated her abandonment of the hole after hours of hard labor; however, she was never aware of the beneficent deed.

" Of sixty females observed, eggs were found at the point of the operation of covering in all but two instances. Whether the turtles never laid eggs, or whether they laid elsewhere, became frightened, left and lost their original orientation with respect to the true egg-activity will never be known.

" So far as observed the egg-cavity has always been begun on rainless evenings. Light showers have intervened later, however, but the operation of digging, laying and covering did not cease. Whether a heavy downpour would cause the turtle to abandon her work is not known.

" When the hole has been deepened as far as the feet can reach, the eggs one by one are dropped into the cavity. In one instance four eggs were dropped within 25 minutes; in another 6 eggs were dropped within 10 minutes; a third female dropped three eggs within five minutes. After each egg is dropped, a hind foot is inserted into the cavity and swept around as if to feel if all is well, and to place the egg as far forward as possible. If some minutes elapse before the second egg is dropped, the hind feet alternate in these movements, as in the digging operations. When the last egg has been dropped, there usually follows a brief interval of rest, with the hind foot which had been used to push and place the eggs around oftentimes left dangling into the cavity. It has been stated in the literature that the eggs are covered separately, but this procedure has not been followed in any instance in the writer's experience.

" Almost invariably the first covering operation is a widely executed lateral sweep of the extended hind leg toward the hole to bring in earth. The other hind leg is then used in a similar manner. From time to time a hind foot may be inserted into the cavity to push the·earth over the eggs more efficiently. From time to time wide lateral sweeps are made always with one leg to bring in the soil. Now and then, the two hind legs are extended flat and at full length backward with the toes close together, and then brought forward to the hole to sweep in earth straight from the rear where it had been pushed. It is a movement in every way comparable to that of a person crouched on the earth who would sweep in the loose sand from in front with his hands open and his fingers together. When considerable earth has been brought in upon the eggs so that to the observer they are no longer visible, or they can no longer be felt by the feet of the turtle, treading and tramping operations take place. This is always an extremely interesting and painstaking procedure and involves many nice variations in the skilful use of the toes, feet, knees and plastron in the final tamping of the soil over the eggs.

" The two feet are often used in a peculiar treading operation, the knees almost or quite touching the ground. The feet are brought very close together so that the heels touch. The feet are now lifted alternately, the treading being performed practically on the tip of the toes, for the heels remain elevated. So closely are the feet brought together that she frequently steps upon her own heels, extricating her feet for each alternating tread with some difficulty. In this operation a distinct rotary motion of the feet sometimes takes place. At other times a position is taken upon the knees, so that toes, heels and knees can be combined in the treading tamping operations. At such times with the plastron held above the soil a jerky lowering of the body may be noted, as if the creature were utilizing the weight momentum of its body to supplement the simple pressing operations of the feet.

" The actual covering is a long and methodically performed operation, but when it is completed there is little trace of the location of the egg-bed. In some instances the actual covering has required nearly two hours before the creature was ready to walk away. The entire operation of digging the egg-bed, laying the eggs and subsequent covering has sometimes required four to five hours. In one instance, digging was performed from 6 to 9 p.m., a period of three hours; 6 eggs were laid from 9.10 to 9.20, a period of 10 minutes; covering was extended until 11.15, a period of 55 minutes.

" The egg-cavity is about two and one-half inches in width and nearly two inches in depth. Neither the cavity nor the eggs are seen by the turtle, for these operations are usually performed in the darkness of night, and by the sense of touch of the hind feet alone. Under these circumstances the matter of proper orientation depends entirely upon keeping the position of the front legs rigidly fixed, and using these as pivots upon which to swing if need be, in making lateral reaches for soil with the hind legs. To demonstrate this point the writer inserted a stick very carefully under the plastron of a turtle which was covering and tamping the soil over its egg-bed, and gently swung it around into another position without disturbing it. The turtle continued its covering and treading operations, but over a spot now some distance from its egg-bed.

" It has been stated in the literature that the box turtle usually deposits its eggs during the day. This statement is completely at variance with all observations of the writer on this point. Of sixty laying females observed in 1932, 1933 and 1934, none began to dig the egg-cavity until late in the afternoon or near sunset, and with few exceptions the eggs were deposited near darkness or long after night had set in."

Allard makes no mention of any wetting down of the nest by water discharged from the cloaca, a process that has been observed by Conant to take place between excavation and laying.

INCUBATION AND HATCHING. The hatching season is even more extensive than the laying one because the development after laying is so greatly affected by differences in temperature and humidity. Allard shortened the period of incubation about forty-two days by keeping eggs in his office at high room temperature. In nature the young escape from the eggs in approximately three months, but incubation periods ranging in length from sixty-nine to one hundred and fourteen days are on record. Most of the hatchlings emerge in September, some in August or October, and a very few still later. Ewing seems to think that, even in the latitude of Washington, a small percentage may spend the winter in the nest.

Allard's account of hatching and hatchling cannot well be condensed:

" Although the baby turtles are equipped with a tiny egg tooth, it is doubtful if this plays any very great part in rupturing the eggs. At the time the eggs are ready to hatch, the shells appear thin and soft, and subject to easy rupturing. Oftentimes the fore legs are thrust through the shell before the head emerges, and usually the active exertions of the tiny, restless turtle develop a longitudinal rent, allowing it to emerge. The creature now digs its way to the surface, or in some instances remains for a day or two below the soil, with only its head projecting above the surface. In firm clay soil, the egg cavity may not be entirely filled in the covering process, so that the eggs sometimes repose in a very loosely filled cavity.

"All evidence at hand would indicate that the newly emerged turtles go into hibernation for their first winter usually without eating. As soon as they have been liberated in their enclosure they repair at once to the ground-cover of leaves and litter and remain concealed. Every effort to tempt them with tiny earthworms or grubs has given no response."

FOOD AND FEEDING. A great variety of food about equally divided between the animal and vegetable kingdoms is consumed by the Common Box Turtle. Among forty stomach contents, Surface found vegetable matter in twenty-five, animals or their remains in thirty-two. The favourite foods, named in approximate order of their importance, are mushrooms, insects and their larvæ, earthworms, slugs, snails, myriapods, dead animals, blackberries, strawberries, and various other fruits. This list could be greatly extended.

Seasonal preferences have been noted, indicating a desire for variety. Allard's turtles greedily consumed earthworms early in the summer, but refused them later; tomatoes, at first relished, were ultimately almost ignored in favour of blackberries and cantaloupe.

Once Scranton coal miners on strike were taken sick after a forced diet partly of turtle meat. The most reasonable explanation of their illness is that the turtles consumed had in turn fed on poisonous mushrooms. I am informed by Robert

Snedigar, who knows turtles as well as mushrooms, that the immunity of *Terrapene* to such deadly forms as the fly mushroom and destroying angel (*Amanita* species) is an established fact in spite of at least one report to the contrary.

Two observers have found very young captives reluctant to eat any vegetable food, a fact presumably correlated with the alleged juvenile aquatic habits. Certainly the type of animals preferred would be more readily found in aquatic situations than would suitable plant matter.

Common Box Turtles are fond of drinking, during which the head is kept in the water for minutes on end. A captive may drink several times a day. Such frequent drinks are by no means necessary, however, since individuals have been known to live for months without water. Ruth Breder took the trouble to test the capacity of two adults and found that the female usually consumed half, the male one-quarter of an ounce at a time, fifteen to twenty-five minutes generally being required, but the head was raised several times during each complete drink.

ENEMIES. The shell of the mature turtle ordinarily affords efficient protection against all predatory animals, but individuals too fat to close both ends of the plastron at once are open to attack by rats and other voracious creatures. The tender young are eaten by various mammals as well as by crows and probably other large birds. But undoubtedly more adults are destroyed by automobiles and forest or brush fires than in any other way.

The eggs are devoured by such egg-loving animals as skunks, dogs, and crows, even ants doing their bit.

Two external parasites attack this turtle, the common North American chigger, appropriately christened *Trombicula irritans* by science, and a bot-fly. The larva of the latter produces a swelling on the neck, but neither of these " guests " causes great discomfort or serious injury.

CAPTIVITY. Few turtles make better pets or are more easily kept in close confinement or under semi-natural conditions. Individuals will sometimes voluntarily remain many years in farm or even town yards.

In making living-quarters the following special requirements should be borne in mind: bushes, low trees, or tall grass affording ample dry shade; shallow pools of water for drinking and bathing; piles of loose damp dead leaves or other decaying vegetation for nocturnal retreats, æstivation, and hibernation; loose sandy soil exposed to direct sun for nesting; temperature of about 70° F. or higher; a varied diet. The food items named above in the treatment of food and feeding can be supplemented by such readily procured provisions as lettuce, bananas, and raw or cooked meat.

Common Box Turtles have lived periods of thirteen, twelve, and eleven years in the London Zoological Gardens, and Conant tells of one that spent twenty-three years in captivity. Others have reported survival of long periods of confinement.

ECONOMIC VALUE. Although without value as a food for man, this reptile serves him as a destroyer of noxious insects and therefore warrants protection.

THREE-TOED BOX TURTLE

Terrapene carolina triunguis (Agassiz)

[PLATE 39]

IDENTIFICATION. In this near ally of the Common Box Turtle, the keeled carapace is relatively elongate and narrow, its posterior margin somewhat flaring. Usually there are three claws on each hind foot. As a rule the sides of the head are spotted, often with orange, and spots of the same colour are generally evident on the front surface of each forelimb. The carapace pattern is much like that of the Common Box Turtle but the plastron is usually immaculate yellow.

EGG. Elliptical in shape, measuring 35 × 23 millimetres, according to Hurter. Agassiz, however, figures one 38.5 × 20 millimetres. The shell is white.

DISTRIBUTION. From western Georgia westward as far as Waco and Gainesville in northeastern Texas, with the exception of the Gulf Coastal Plain, which is the home of the Gulf Coast Box Turtle. Northward from northern Louisiana and northeastern Texas it ranges west of the Mississippi River through Arkansas, the eastern half of Oklahoma, and all of Missouri but approximately its northwestern sixth. A few records carry it into extreme eastern Kansas south of the Missouri River and into the southeastern corner of that state.

Intergradation with the Common Box Turtle apparently takes place in Tennessee and adjacent territory; north of Tennessee the Mississippi River itself seems to form a boundary between the two subspecies. This fact is of unusual interest because a river seldom forms such an effective barrier in reptile dispersal.

Nearly all of the relatively few references to this turtle give information only on its habitat preference which is much like that of the Common Box Turtle. Whether future studies will show that the habits of the Three-toed differ materially from those of the Common Box Turtle is a matter of conjecture, but the chances are that the two will prove to have much the same habits.

More than one observer has been impressed by the great numbers crushed under automobiles.

Harwood found a Texas series of fourteen well infested with nematodes of five species; each of three species of these parasitic worms belonging to as many genera were found in the intestines of ninety-two per cent of the turtles.

GULF COAST BOX TURTLE

Terrapene carolina major (Agassiz)

[PLATE 40]

IDENTIFICATION. In this second and largest near ally of the Common Box Turtle, the keeled carapace is relatively elongate, its highest point in the middle, and its posterior margin flaring. Usually there are four claws on each hind foot. The sides of the head are spotted or unmarked and the carapace is either without pattern (horn-coloured or nearly black) or with broad and broken radial lines.

SIZE. Generally conceded to be the largest *Terrapene* in the United States, this form attains a carapace length of seven inches. Oddly enough, no really detailed measurements are available. However, the carapaces of three of the cotypes from Florida measure 6.42 × 4.57, 6.02 × 4.33, and 5.43 × 4.09 inches.

DISTRIBUTION. The Gulf Coastal Plain from southwestern Georgia and northwestern Florida westward to Matagorda County, Texas.

There is an old record for San Antonio, and another for Val Verde County, still farther to the west in Texas, but these need confirmation. The same may be said for an old Nashville, Tennessee, record.

HABITAT. Reports on the habitat of this turtle are meagre, but indicate a preference for wooded swamps and pine forests.

HABITS. The even more meagre account of its habits indicate activity throughout the year in coastal Mississippi, where, without apparent injury, specimens have even survived being frozen solid in ice for twenty-four hours. In this same region captives kept by Allen thrived on a variety of animal and vegetable matter and mated throughout the year.

FOLK-LORE. Good evidence that this is the turtle which the Creek Indians believed capable of causing drought and flood was given by Strecker. Because of this, all specimens encountered by these Indians were quickly dashed to pieces.

FLORIDA BOX TURTLE

Terrapene carolina bauri Taylor

[PLATES 41 AND 42]

IDENTIFICATION. In this third and most handsome close ally of the Common Box Turtle, the keeled carapace is relatively narrow and elongate, the highest point as a rule noticeably behind the middle, and the posterior margin flaring. Usually there are three claws on each hind foot. The head markings tend to fall into two stripes, one below, the other running from the rear edge of the eye. In most specimens each costal shield is brightly decorated with narrow unbroken radial lines, although rarely a speckled carapace is seen.

EGG. Ewing published a picture of a single infertile egg laid in captivity by a female from Big Pine Key, Florida, with a carapace 5.29 inches long. In his illustration the egg is considerably longer but no wider than the Common Box Turtle egg photographed with it for comparison. Both eggs have a white shell.

DISTRIBUTION. Peninsular Florida. Intergradation with the Common Box Turtle and with the Gulf Coast Box Turtle takes place in northeastern and in northwestern Florida, respectively.

HABITAT. Wooded as well as open country is frequented by the Florida Box Turtle, which seems to have a preference for the vicinity of water.

41. Florida Box Turtle (*Terrapene carolina bauri*) from Gainesville, Florida. The carapace of this female is 4.50 inches long. (*Courtesy Zoological Society of Philadelphia, photograph by Mark Mooney, Jr.*)

42. Florida Box Turtle (*Terrapene carolina bauri*) from Gainesville, Florida, with a carapace 4.50 inches long. It is a female. (*Courtesy Zoological Society of Philadelphia, photograph by Mark Mooney, Jr.*)

43. Ornate Box Turtle (*Terrapene ornata*) from Reno County, Kansas, with a carapace 5 inches long. (*Courtesy Zoological Society of Philadelphia, photograph by Mark Mooney, Jr.*)

44. Ornate Box Turtle (*Terrapene ornata*) from Reno County, Kansas, with a carapace 5 inches long. (*Courtesy Zoological Society of Philadelphia, photograph by Mark Mooney, Jr.*)

REPRODUCTION. A female taken May 23 on Big Pine Key, Florida, and kept by Ewing in a Maryland garden, laid a single infertile egg on June 20 of the same year. She finished digging the nest soon after 9.21 p.m. of that day, laid the egg at 9.47, and by 10.11 had about filled the hole up. The nest was dug in the same way that the Common Box Turtle digs its nest. Under natural conditions eggs are said to hatch out in October.

CAPTIVITY. Rust recommends a slightly damp vivarium with a large water-container. He states that this turtle likes damp air kept at room temperature. It should be fed on earthworms, snails, raw meat, berries, and bananas, and will eat with the head under water. He adds that it still feeds when the thermometer stands at 41° F., which is a lower temperature than other reptiles take food at.

When the female written about in the section on reproduction attempted to hibernate in Ewing's Maryland garden, she failed to survive the very severe winter even though four Common Box Turtles successfully hibernated within less than three feet of her. The tops of the carapaces of all the turtles were about one and a half inches below the surface of the ground litter which, together with snow, afforded protection from cold. This is interesting though hardly surprising.

ORNATE BOX TURTLE

Terrapene ornata (Agassiz)

[PLATES 43 AND 44]

IDENTIFICATION. The carapace is flattened on top, as a rule slightly shorter than the plastron, and very rarely with a median keel. There are four claws on each hind foot. The carapace is usually chocolate to reddish brown, its large shields decorated with spots and stripes of bright yellow which tend to radiate from the growth centres. In most specimens the plastron is boldly decorated with numerous yellow lines of different lengths extending in various directions on the dark ground colour. The markings of this species are not nearly so variable as those of the Common Box Turtle.

SIZE. Cahn gives the following measurements of a good-sized Illinois female:

	Inches	Millimetres
Length of carapace	4.13	105
Width of carapace	3.50	89
Length of plastron	4.17	106
Width of plastron	2.68	68
Height of shell	2.01	51
Weight	11.3 ounces	

A specimen probably representing the maximum size has a plastron 5.31, a carapace 5.27 inches long. This is a western individual, almost certainly from Arizona. The plastron averages about four-fifths of an inch shorter in Indiana than in regions west of the Mississippi River.

YOUNG. The young have never been adequately described. Hurter mentions two having carapaces measuring 30 × 24 millimetres. There is difference of opinion as to the presence of a median keel, which probably means that a keel is either present or absent.

THE SEXES. When the tail is extended, the anus of the male lies beyond, that of the female under, the edge of the carapace, and the distance from anus to tip of tail is greater in the male. The first claw on the hind foot of males is turned abruptly forward.

EGG. No one has described eggs of the Ornate Box Turtle that were deposited in a wild state, but measurements of eggs laid by captive females and others taken from the oviducts indicate that the range in size is from 35 to 37 × 21 to 24 milli-metres. The shell is white and relatively thin.

DISTRIBUTION. From Texas and Oklahoma northward through Missouri, Iowa, Kansas, Nebraska, and eastern Colorado into southeastern Wyoming and southern South Dakota. An altitude of 6,000 feet is attained in Colorado.

In the southwest the Ornate Box Turtle ranges from southwestern Texas and northern Mexico through extreme southern New Mexico as far as Santa Cruz and eastern Pima Counties of the southeastern corner of Arizona; to the southeast it has been recorded once from southwestern Arkansas, but its occurrence in that state and in the lowlands of eastern Texas is very local; to the northeast and east it is found through Illinois into extreme southern Wisconsin, but is rare in northern Illinois, Wisconsin, and northern Iowa. The easternmost extension of its distribution takes it across Newton and Jasper Counties of northwestern Indiana to Lake Maxinkuckee in Marshall County of the same state.

HABITAT. The Ornate Box Turtle is typically an inhabitant of prairies but frequents open hilly country as well. It is decidedly partial to sandy, dry, or even semi-arid regions. Although sometimes found in light or open woodland, it shuns forests and other types of heavy cover. No aquatic tendencies have been noted; in this respect the Ornate and Common Box Turtles differ greatly.

Its astonishing abundance has opened the eyes of many an observer since Cragin made his extravagant statement that in some parts of southern Kansas it was so common " as to amount to a nuisance as a cumberer of the ground." Brennan reports the counting in Ellis County, Kansas, of thirty individuals in less than half an hour near a melon patch, and Ortenburger and Freeman record the collecting of nearly one hundred and fifty in Cimarron County, Oklahoma. More were not taken simply because there was no way of keeping them. Writing of Wilbarger County, Texas, Strecker leaves no doubt about the existence of this turtle there:

" One who has never visited these north Texas prairie counties can have any conception of the abundance of these box tortoises on the mesquite prairies. We literally saw hundreds of them. A count was kept of the number of living and dead examples observed on the road between Vernon and Wichita Falls. The total was forty-six."

HABITS. When not active this species rests in natural cavities, under objects, or in shallow burrows made by itself. The last are often barely as deep as the shell is high. When the sun is very hot, the turtle is most active in the early morning or late afternoon.

Ortenburger and Freeman report that all the specimens collected before 8.oo a.m. were found in the sun on the eastern side of tufts of high grass or sage. Presumably they take their sun baths before the heat gets too great.

Like other box turtles the species under discussion is incapable of inflicting more than a very slight injury on man in spite of the fact that some individuals hiss and open the mouth threateningly when annoyed. Two observers have independently remarked on the uniform docility of specimens from east of the Mississippi. We can only conclude that a geographical contrast in temperament exists. A difference in size between extreme eastern and other individuals has been mentioned above, so it seems that these " easterners " are smaller as well as more even-tempered!

HIBERNATION. At Urbana, Illinois, Cahn observed that the Ornate Box Turtle began to hibernate in late October two or more weeks in advance of the Common Box Turtle. The following spring found the former out a week or two later than the latter. This longer hibernation period was apparently correlated with a greater depth of penetration; the Ornate species descended to a depth of twenty-two and a half, the other to only nineteen inches. All the turtles concerned were confined in an outdoor pen and all went into hibernation by slowly increasing the depth of descent with the gradually falling temperature.

REPRODUCTION. The sole observation on the reproduction of this common turtle in a state of nature was made by Cope and published in 1892. In northwestern Texas he saw them mating in May. Recently, however, captive Kansas and Indiana individuals have been seen to attempt or accomplish copulation during the period from May 11 to 20 and a female from the former state laid eggs in confinement on August 2, 3, and 4, probably also a few days before.

Biting of the male by the female is a regular part of courtship, if Grant's observations of amorous activities of some captive specimens prove to be typical.

FOOD AND FEEDING. The few stomachs examined by various workers have contained insects (June and other beetles and ants) and vegetable matter; field studies have established earthworms, caterpillars, robber flies, lubber and other grasshoppers, and cantaloupe as included in its diet.

The Ornate Box Turtle feeds on grasshoppers to a considerable extent in certain regions and sometimes shows astonishing agility in catching them. Ortenburger and Freeman describe one that caught a large lubber grasshopper in flight by stretching the neck and actually jumping at it! A captive individual once even attacked and ate an adult six-lined racerunner. This last incident is put in to illustrate what an aggressive feeder this turtle is rather than to imply that it regularly eats lizards. An interesting account of the feeding of three tame individuals is given in the treatment of captivity below.

ENEMIES. Automobiles kill a great many of these turtles as they walk along or attempt to cross roads.

CAPTIVITY. Some Texas specimens kept by Strecker not only became extraordinarily tame but exhibited a certain degree of intelligence, as shown by his account:

" At one time I had three specimens of this species and made it a rule to feed them regularly at the same hour each day. Finally I turned them loose in my back yard and every evening about six o'clock they would come to me to be fed. It was laughable to watch them as they stood on their hind legs scratching at my shoes and the bottom of my trousers in their endeavor to attract my attention. I fed them on raw beef cut into strips, and as soon as their appetites were satisfied they would go back to their quarters under the coal shed and I would not see them again until about the same time the next evening."

The pen or vivarium in which specimens are kept should have a low water-container, soft sandy soil, a shady section, and a hiding-place. Temperature from 68° to 73° F. is suitable.

ECONOMIC VALUE. In regions where this species is abundant it certainly destroys large numbers of noxious insects. The meagreness of the data on its feeding habits is indicated above under the discussion of food and feeding. Further investigations are much needed.

When these turtles invade a cantaloupe patch in great numbers, they cause much damage by biting into the ends of the melons. No detailed information on this destructive habit is available, however.

In South Dakota, according to Over, Sioux Indians eat the Ornate Box Turtle.

ARTIFICIAL DISTRIBUTION. Putting it mildly, congested Michigan Avenue, Chicago, is not an ideal collecting site for Ornate Box Turtles. Nevertheless, no fewer than five hundred were caught there on November 4, 1930. This inundation presumably occurred when a turtle-racing promoter became insolvent and had to release his performers. Mr. Karl P.

Schmidt, of the Field Museum of Natural History, finally turned these unemployed loose in the sandy area around Waukegan (where the species does not occur), not, however, before marking them by drilling holes in the posterior margin of the carapace.

CHAPTER VI

DIAMOND-BACK TERRAPINS
Genus *MALACLEMYS*

MAP TURTLES
Genus *GRAPTEMYS*

PAINTED TURTLES
Genus *CHRYSEMYS*

PSEUDEMYD TURTLES
Genus *PSEUDEMYS*

CHICKEN TURTLE
Genus *DEIROCHELYS*

Family *TESTUDINIDÆ*

The genera treated in this chapter, although bound together by anatomical relationships, exclusively New World distributions, and aquatic habitat preferences, do not comprise a complete systematic group, though they are a good part of the water-loving contingent, forming about half, of the one large turtle family. Thus it is clear that the grouping is not entirely one of convenience.

Every large truly aquatic turtle of the United States and Canada belongs here and all the species in the group pass their lives in water.

Pseudemys alone has extra-limital species, those of the other genera being almost if not entirely confined to the United States and southern Canada.

Malaclemys seems to have no fossil history whatsoever, and that of the other genera is fragmentary; indeed, it is doubtful whether *Graptemys* is really known as a fossil even though remains from the Oligocene of South Dakota have been tentatively assigned to it. *Chrysemys picta*, and another species of this genus, have been found in the Pleistocene of Florida and Nebraska, respectively, whence a species assigned to *Deirochelys* has been taken. *Pseudemys* fossils are more numerous, with *P. floridana* and two other species recorded from the Pleistocene of Florida, and another from the Pliocene of Idaho, provisionally referred to this genus. On a basis of all these data we can conclude that probably turtles of some of these genera were common in the Florida region during the Pleistocene, which began about a million and ended some ten thousand years ago; during the early part of this period and at least some of the preceding Pliocene they must have been rather more widely distributed than at present.

IDENTIFICATION

Making sure that specimens belong in the present chapter is most easily accomplished by a process of elimination, because its species have no one outstanding character in common. The presence of many longitudinal yellow lines on head and neck is, however, a strong indication that a turtle does go here, especially if it has no unusual feature such as a shell that closes like a box, fewer than twelve (six contiguous pairs of) shields on the plastron, a soft flexible shell, flippers, or stump-shaped hind limbs.

Unfortunately all the real stumbling-blocks of identification are packed into this one chapter. In an effort to make the following inevitably difficult key as brief as possible I have omitted all descriptive references to subspecies, an expedient that greatly simplifies identification in the genus *Pseudemys*.

Since subspecies are strictly geographical units, their determination based on place of origin alone should suffice for ordinary purposes.

Probably the point in the key that will be most troublesome is the necessity of ascertaining the relative width of the crushing surface of the upper jaw, the B1–B2 alternative under A2. It should be noticed that this point involves the identity of only two species, the Chicken and Painted Turtles, so the easier way for many readers will be to turn to the treatment of these species and decide the matter there, coming back to continue with the key in case of a negative decision.

In regard to the last part of the key, the D1–D2–D3 choice, I can only say that the genus involved, *Pseudemys*, has been the major problem in the classification of American turtles, and failure to get satisfactory results should not be too discouraging. The fact, explained above, that only the characters for the species are included reduces this problem to the simplest possible terms.

The forms of *Pseudemys* have but recently been worked out by Dr. Archie F. Carr, Jr., of the University of Florida, to whom I am deeply indebted for personal advice and assistance, the use of manuscript in advance of publication, and living turtles to be examined and photographed. Dr. Carr's admirable arrangement of species and subspecies has been adopted in its entirety.

Persuading a living turtle to open its mouth widely enough to afford a good look at the crushing surface of the upper jaw is not usually very difficult. Pulling the legs, tapping on the tip of the snout with a pencil, gently poking under the rear of the carapace, blowing in the face (with due consideration for the reach of the jaws), or more ingenious forms of petty annoyance will often produce the required effect. A sharp stick or pencil point inserted in whatever crack appears will keep the jaws open long enough for the necessary look inside.

The usual warning must be given in regard to the identification of very young specimens, which unfortunately differ so astonishingly from their elders. The only safe course is to make full use of the section under each species devoted to its young. No one has ever written a key to juvenile American turtles.

KEY TO THE SPECIES OF *Malaclemys, Chrysemys, Deirochelys, Graptemys,* AND *Pseudemys* FOUND IN THE UNITED STATES

A1: Head and neck without longitudinal yellow stripes; shields of carapace usually with concentric ridges and grooves (see Pl. 45); salt-marsh habitat (*Malaclemys*).

  B1: Keels of vertebral shields never tuberculate; Atlantic coast. SOUTHERN and NORTHERN DIAMOND-BACK TERRAPINS

  B2: Keels of vertebral shields more or less tuberculate; Gulf coast. MISSISSIPPI, TEXAS, and FLORIDA DIAMOND-BACK TERRAPINS

A2: Head and neck usually with longitudinal yellow stripes; shields of carapace without concentric ridges and grooves; fresh-water habitats, generally not found in salt marshes.

  B1: Crushing surface of upper jaw narrow (*Chrysemys* and *Deirochelys*).

    C1: Carapace without network of yellow lines; widely distributed. EASTERN, CENTRAL, WESTERN, and SOUTHERN PAINTED TURTLES

    C2: Carapace with large-meshed network of fine yellow lines; Coastal Plain from North Carolina to Texas. CHICKEN TURTLE

  B2: Crushing surface of upper jaw broad.

C1: Crushing surface of upper jaw without a median ridge (*Graptemys*).

  D1: A triangular spot behind eye; hind edge of carapace feebly dentate; crushing surface of upper jaw greatly expanded.

                       COMMON MAP TURTLE

  D2: A crescent-shaped spot behind eye; hind edge of carapace strongly dentate; crushing surface of upper jaw moderately expanded.

             MISSISSIPPI, OCELLATED, and TEXAS MAP TURTLES

C2: Crushing surface of upper jaw with a median ridge (*Pseudemys*).

  D1: Median ridge of crushing surface of upper jaw high and strongly toothed (especially in the Texas Turtle); this jaw without teeth near tip (except in the Texas Turtle); a strong tooth at tip of lower jaw. FLORIDA, PENINSULAR, RIVER, MOBILE, SUWANNEE, HIEROGLYPHIC, and TEXAS TURTLES

  D2: Median ridge of crushing surface of upper jaw high and strongly toothed; this jaw with a prominent tooth on either side of notch at tip; lower jaw strongly serrate, with a prominent tooth on either side of long one at tip (see Pl. 75).

    E1: About four to six stripes along head counted from lower edge of one ear over head to lower edge of other.

      F1: Markings on lower parts of marginal shields usually concentric or light centred. RED-BELLIED and PLYMOUTH TURTLES

      F2: Markings on lower parts of marginals

        usually solid and smudge-like; peninsular
        Florida.   Florida Red-bellied Turtle

E2: About thirteen to seventeen stripes along
     head from edge to edge of ears; Gulf coast
     from northwestern Florida to Louisiana.

                                 Alabama Turtle

D3: Median ridge of crushing surface of upper jaw
     low and smooth or only slightly serrate; this
     jaw without teeth near tip; edges of both jaws
     smooth.   Yellow-bellied, Troost's,
                     and Rio Grande Turtles

SOUTHERN DIAMOND-BACK TERRAPIN

Malaclemys centrata centrata (Latreille)

IDENTIFICATION. The carapace usually has conspicuous concentric ridges and grooves, and the keels of the vertebral
shields are never tuberculate. The head is relatively large and
the sides of the carapace are about parallel. The coloration is
extremely variable in this as well as in the Northern Diamond-
back Terrapin.

Specimens of either the northern or the southern form with
known origin can often be identified by the narrow range and
restricted habitat of the species.

SIZE. The maximum plastron length of the female living in
a wild state is about seven and a half, of the male about four
and four-fifths inches. However, a female with a six-inch
plastron and a male with one four inches long may be regarded
as large representatives of their sexes. The plastral lengths
given are in this and other species of the genus taken from the
lowest point in front to the bottom of the posterior notch.
This is the measurement used in terrapin commerce.

YOUNG. In form, immature specimens strongly resemble the adult female except in having, when very small, a much more nearly circular carapace. The carapace above is light olive to dark brown, the plastron and soft parts light grey. All the shields of the shell are decorated with black lines running parallel to the shield margins, these lines being very conspicuous against the light ground colour of the shell viewed from below. The soft parts are marked with black lines and speckling. The young do not exhibit the great range of variation in colour seen in the adult.

The plastron is about 27 millimetres long at hatching.

(See the pictures of the young Northern Diamond-back, Plates 46 and 47.)

THE SEXES. Sexual differences are well developed and appear in the male when its plastron is 3.2 to 3.5 inches long. The female is much larger (as shown by the measurements given in the discussion of size), has a larger head and more rounded snout, deeper shell, and shorter tail. The outline of the male carapace as viewed from above is more triangular posteriorly, and its margins from a little in front of the bridge to the hind end are nearly always strongly turned up (Hay, 1905).

EGG. Elliptical in shape and with a white shell. Agassiz figures diamond-back eggs measuring 36 × 20 millimetres, but I cannot tell to which species or subspecies they belong.

LONGEVITY. A batch of confined individuals, hatched in 1910, still looked comparatively young in 1932, and Hildebrand has seen wild breeders alive seventeen years after they had all the appearance of great age. He believes that their span of life is much in excess of forty years. This information applies to the northern and southern forms of *M. centrata* taken together rather than to either one.

GROWTH. Seven years is the usual age at which the female reaches sexual maturity, four and nine years the extremes. Males probably become mature as early as females. Size is an even better criterion. Females seldom begin to lay before the plastron is 5.5 inches long, whereas males 3.2 to 3.5 inches in length are probably mature. These data are based on specimens raised in captivity and apply to both subspecies of *Malaclemys centrata*.

In regard to full growth, Hildebrand states that, in captive *M. centrata*, a few individuals are nearly or quite fully grown when eight or nine years old, whereas the majority require a much longer period of time, sometimes even as much as twelve to fifteen or more years. As far as known, the rate of growth in natural and under artificial conditions is about the same over a period of years.

DISTRIBUTION. South Atlantic coastal strip from Florida to the region of Cape Hatteras, North Carolina, where intergradation with the Northern Diamond-back Terrapin takes place.

HABITAT. Salt and brackish marshes and estuaries.

HABITS. It is not surprising that these thoroughly aquatic terrapins are good divers and swimmers. When not active, they bask in the sun or conceal themselves under débris or in soft mud. At high tide during daylight hours one may see them swimming about the marshes in search of food.

All accounts say that these terrapins hibernate in mud, but there is no general agreement as to what relation the mud chosen bears to water-level. The indications are, however, that a well-submerged site is usually selected.

REPRODUCTION. A good account of the nests of the Southern Diamond-back Terrapin in North Carolina is given by Coker as follows:

"The marshes of Beaufort Harbor and tributary rivers are usually very low and, except for the tops of the grass, completely submerged at high tide. In a very few spots the winds and waves have beaten up sandy lumps that have been rendered stable by grass roots and are exposed at all times except

during very high storm-tides. Such elevations on one of the
' Middle Marshes,' between the mouth of North River and
Shakleford Banks, seemed to offer very favorable places for
nesting; it was known, too, that new-born terrapins had been
found there once before. On the 21st and 22d of July the
writer made a search of two of the three lumps on this marsh.
The ground was dug up carefully, and, in 3 or 4 hours digging,
7 nests were discovered. On one lump 4 nests, containing 4, 5,
6 and 7 eggs respectively, were found at depths of 6 to 8 inches;
except that the nest with 4 eggs (the only one not on the highest part of the elevation) was only 3 inches below the surface.
This nest contained only small eggs. On the other lumps were
found 3 nests of about the same depths with 2, 5 and 8 eggs respectively. Perhaps not more than one-half of the ground was
dug, for it was not desired to disturb other nests. In each
lump the higher part was 20 to 30 feet long by about 6 feet
wide. With one exception, the nests were found on the highest
part, which could be submerged only by a very high storm-
tide. The third elevation was not so high, was shelly and less
promising in appearance, and was not examined for eggs. In
digging, occasional bits of egg-shell were found, vestiges of
former seasons. One old entire egg was found, through which
a blade of grass had grown, and one of the new eggs found had
met the same fate. Some of the eggs taken here and transplanted to Pivers Island had hatched by August 25th and 26th.
On August 22, 1902, a nest of 3 terrapins had been found here
by the collector, Mr. Guthrie. One of the terrapins, he stated,
was found emerging from the shell."

Nothing unusual as to the method of nest-making has been
described. The hind feet are used in digging and filling the
jug-shaped hole, and the site is concealed by the female crawling back and forth over it after filling and packing has been
accomplished.

In North Carolina the eggs are deposited from May 6 to

45. Northern Diamond-back Terrapins (*Malaclemys centrata concentrica*) from Accomac County, Virginia. These males have carapaces 4.75 and 5.19 inches long. (*Courtesy Zoological Society of Philadelphia, photograph by Mark Mooney, Jr.*)

46–47. Young Northern Diamond-back Terrapin (*Malaclemys centrata concentrica*) from Talbot County, Maryland, with a carapace 29 millimetres long. (*Courtesy Zoological Society of Philadelphia, photograph by Mark Mooney, Jr.*)

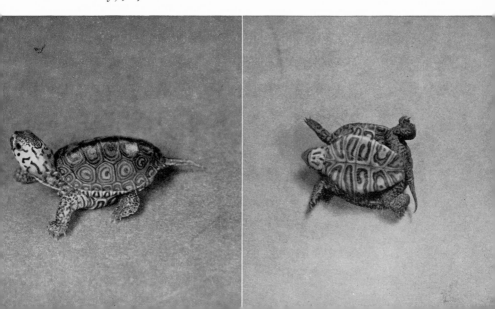

48. Common Map Turtle (*Graptemys geographica*) from Michigan. This female has a carapace 7.62 inches long. (*Courtesy Zoological Society of Philadelphia, photograph by Mark Mooney, Jr.*)

49. Common Map Turtle (*Graptemys geographica*). (*Courtesy Field Museum of Natural History, photograph by Douglas Cullen.*)

July 31. A female may lay from one to five times during a single season, but very few produce more than three clutches. The average incubation period is about ninety days, though this period varies considerably with temperature conditions.

The artificial propagation of Diamond-back Terrapins is dealt with at length below, but one unsuspected and exceedingly important discovery resulting from this propagation is properly treated here. This is the fact that a female may lay fertile eggs for years after a single period of mating. Hildebrand tells us what happened when ten old females were penned without males:

" During the first season following separation from males these 10 females laid 124 eggs, and only 1 failed to hatch; during the second summer 116 eggs were produced and 14 failed to hatch; during the third summer 130 eggs were laid and 91 failed to hatch; and during the fourth summer 108 eggs were produced and only 4 hatched. Thereupon, seven old males were introduced, and in the next season 145 eggs were laid, of which only 4 failed to hatch."

No one knows how long after a single mating period other kinds of turtles may lay eggs, but certainly here is a whole field of investigation lying wide open.

FOOD AND FEEDING. Fourteen stomachs of North Carolina terrapins examined by Coker contained chiefly fragments of a small snail exceedingly common on the blades of the marsh grass growing where the terrapins were caught. Small fiddler and other crabs and annelid worms were also found. The few shreds of marsh grass included might have been swallowed accidentally along with the animals. Hay and others, however, believe that vegetable matter such as tender shoots and rootlets is deliberately eaten.

Artificially propagated terrapins are fed chopped fish, oysters, clams, crabs, and the like. Insects are probably eaten by " cultivated " terrapins as well as by those in a state of nature.

A picture of feeding time in a turtle pen published by Hilde-brand and Hatsel shows several specimens returning to the water with food just picked up on land. This indicates a preference for under-water swallowing although Pearse, Lepkovsky, and Hintze definitely state that food is readily swallowed out of water. Emphasis is placed on this subject because there is a general belief, supported by numerous printed statements, that this and several species of aquatic tur-tles and terrapins are unable to get food down the throat until the head is submerged.

ENEMIES. Without doubt man is the great enemy of the adult terrapin. The eggs and soft-bodied hatchlings are de-stroyed by skunks, raccoons, other small mammals, and crows.

ARTIFICIAL PROPAGATION. One hundred and fifty years ago Diamond-back Terrapins were already well known in the mar-kets of Philadelphia and their use increased greatly throughout the nineteenth century. By the end of that period it was ob-vious that something would have to be done to save this van-ishing but important delicacy for future epicures.

In 1902 the United States Fish Commission began an investi-gation on Chesapeake Bay, the home of the famous "Chesa-peakes." At about the same time another investigation was instituted at Beaufort, North Carolina, by that state in co-operation with the Fish Commission. Although soon discon-tinued, these North Carolina researches were described by Coker in an interesting paper. In 1909 the Chesapeake Bay work was removed from Lloyds, Maryland, to Beaufort.

The Maryland and North Carolina researches prior to 1909 determined that adult terrapins would lay while confined in pens and that the eggs could be hatched in special boxes. The young, however, had not been successfully raised. Since that year terrapin propagation has been placed on a truly scientific basis as shown by the series of reports published by the Bureau of Fisheries, successor to the Fish Commission. Charles Hatsel, terrapin culturist, is largely responsible for the success of the work which has been supervised by Hildebrand and others.

The actual terrapin material has been from the start a mixture of Southern and Northern Diamond-backs. Although the latter were the original market " Chesapeakes," the former have long been sent to markets as well, and Hildebrand, after so many years of work with them, does not know whether the northern subspecies actually excels in flavour, as the dealers used to maintain.

Details of terrapin culture are far too numerous to be considered here, but in 1926 Hildebrand and Hatsel gave a description of pen construction which, with the deletion of two paragraphs, follows:

" The most desirable situation for a terrapin pen is on some well-protected, gently sloping shore of sand or mixed sand and clay, where the rise and fall of tides bring an abundant supply of clean, unpolluted, salt or brackish water. In such a place the inclosing wall need not be made unduly strong, and the clean bottom will make it easier to keep the place in sanitary condition. However, such a combination of conditions seldom is to be found, and probably it will be necessary to make the best of some bad points in almost any location.

" The pen should be built so that at extreme high tide most of the inclosure, with the exception of the sand beds provided for the eggs, is covered by water, while at low tide there should be water over a part of the area. In other words, some dry land for a part of the day and some water all day is desirable. By this arrangement the females are compelled to resort to the sand beds when in search of a suitable place to make their nests; there is opportunity for the animals to crawl about and sun themselves; there is a place in which to bathe; and a good hibernating bed is provided for the winter.

" It is advantageous to locate the outside or seaward wall of the pound slightly above mean low water in order that all the water may be drained from the pound when desired. Unless this is done the pens can not be cleaned properly and in time they will become insanitary. However, as stated above, it is desirable that some water be retained in the pound at low tide. This may be accomplished by building the wall underneath the gates to the desired level. A pipe about 2 inches in diameter should be inserted in the wall at the ground level and kept plugged. When it is desired to clean the pound (which should be done at least once a year), the plug is withdrawn at ebb tide, after the water has fallen below the level of the pipe, and the remaining water is allowed to drain from the pound. At Beaufort the filth and sediment are removed most readily by scraping it together in the lowest place in the pound and then bailing it out.

"The inclosed area should allow approximately 5 square feet for each adult terrapin to be impounded and about one-half square foot for each young one. A pen 60 feet square will accommodate comfortably 720 adult animals and several times that many young ones.

"The walls of the inclosure preferably should be built of concrete or masonry, for wooden walls are attacked readily by shipworms in the South and last only a short time. Terrapins always prowl around the walls of the inclosure, and if any avenue of escape is open they will be sure to find it. In a wall made of lumber a single board may get loose, worm-eaten, or broken, and many terrapins may be lost before the caretaker can discover the open place, which generally would be hidden in part by water. The risk of losing terrapins, therefore, is too great to make the use of lumber for the construction of the outside walls of a terrapin pound advisable. As partitions in the main pound, to separate the young from the adults, wooden walls may be used and probably are more economical than concrete or other material. They have the advantage that they may be moved readily if for any reason it may be desired to change the size of the pens within the permanent walls. The walls must be high enough and strong enough to overtop the highest tides by at least 3 feet and to resist any waves to which they may be exposed. . . .

" The seaward wall of the pound should have ' gates ' at intervals of about 20 feet to permit the change of water on the rise and fall of the tides. The gates should be about 3 feet wide and are made by leaving open places in the wall; that is, the base of the wall is built solid until a height is reached that will insure the retention of some water inside the pound at all times, and from that point to the top of the wall an opening 3 feet wide is left. To tie the upper sections of the wall together, and in order to strengthen them, one or more strong iron bars, such as railroad iron, should be laid in the concrete near the top of the gate. At Beaufort it has been found difficult to determine exactly how high to build the wall under the gates in order to retain the desired amount of water at low tide. However, if this wall is not made too high in the beginning additional concrete may be added after the rest of the pound has been completed until the desired level is reached. . . .

" The interior of the pen should be divided into two or preferably three parts — a large area for the adult terrapins and two much smaller ones for the young. One of the smaller compartments may serve as a pen for very small young and the other for larger ones. The partitions may be made of wood, but to minimize the attacks of wood borers they should be set, as far as possible, in shallow water and have sand or earth thrown against their bases. It has been the practice in recent years at Beaufort to treat the lower sections of the partitions with a coat of copper paint, which for a time prevents attacks of wood borers and preserves the wood much longer than when it is left untreated.

" In the inclosure for adults an egg bed should be built along the shoreward side. Its area should allow about 1 square foot

for each female terrapin. It should consist of clean sand leveled
off and well packed down, and its surface should stand about
1 foot above extreme high-tide level. In constructing the egg
bed it will be found most convenient to build a fence of boards
supported by posts along the outer edge and to fill in the sand
behind it. A slope of earth or other material should extend up
to the level of the egg bed so that the terrapins may easily
crawl up to the sand.

" The inclosure for the young should be partly dry at low
tide but should always contain some water. The fence surrounding it must be built so that the young ones can not make
their escape. As stated farther on, the young, up to an age of
2 or 3 years, are proficient climbers and will be certain to leave
their quarters if they possibly can do so. The inside of the wall
must have a board or sheet of metal set on the top of the wall
around the entire inclosure. The boards or metal should pro-
ject shelflike, from 3 to 4 inches, beyond the inner margins of
the walls, for the young terrapins can climb a straight wall but
they can not hold onto an overhanging surface.

" It is a matter of dispute among those who handle terrapins
whether fresh water is necessary to the animals, for they have
been kept for months without any other fresh water than that
supplied by the rain and dew and apparently suffered no ill
effects. However, when it is supplied they drink of it freely,
and after considerable experience we regard it as advantageous.
A large amount of fresh water is not needed, and where it is inconvenient to pipe it the water may be poured about once a
day into troughs provided for that purpose.

" It is possible that in some localities salt-water ponds of
suitable size and condition for propagating terrapins may exist,
although none has been observed by us. If a natural pond suitable for terrapin culture could be found, the cost of the plant
could be reduced greatly, for it would be necessary only to
surround the pond with a fence and to screen the inlet.

" Locations on high ground, remote from salt water and in places where there is no tidal flow, are entirely unsuited to terrapin culture on a commercial scale and are not recommended.

" No covering is required over any part of the pen, and no protection except the wall is needed along the outside. It must be remembered, however, that so valuable and easily marketed an animal as a diamond-back terrapin is a temptation that it is hard for a poacher to resist. It will be safest, therefore, to add a few strands of barbed wire to the top of the inclosing walls and to inclose the pen by a barbed-wire fence set back some 20 or 25 feet. The latter is particularly desirable, as it will not only make depredations difficult but will prevent inquisitive visitors from approaching the pen. The terrapins are timid and, especially during the laying season, should be disturbed as little as possible.

" In constructing a terrapin pen the possibility of muskrats digging under the fence and furnishing an avenue for the escape of the terrapins should be borne in mind. The common rat will eat the eggs and kill the young terrapins, and crows are said to do the same. Common rats at times have done much damage at Beaufort. Because of their depredations it is necessary daily to inspect the egg beds, as well as the pens containing the young. One rat may destroy a dozen or more young during a single night, for the rat often does not eat much of the animals killed but appears only to draw the blood from them. When any sign of a rat is noticed, every means should be used to catch it."

Hildebrand's 1929 summary of general results is quoted in part below:

" Egg production has fluctuated greatly from year to year within lots and within broods. The number of eggs produced by individual females of the same age is known to vary from 5 to 29 during a single season. Within a single lot, egg production has varied from 7.6 to 23.9 eggs per female. It is concluded that in general terrapin culture an average annual production of 12 eggs per female may be expected.

"The degree of fertility of the eggs, too, has fluctuated greatly, for which often no good reasons can be given. In general, the highest percentage of fertility has resulted in the lots having the largest proportionate number of males, although exceptions to this rule are noted. Data are presented that would indicate that with the proper sex ratio present, which appears to be about one male to five females, at least 90 per cent of the eggs laid should be fertile.

"Great fluctuations in the death rate have taken place among the young animals, both among the ones that were kept warm and fed during the winter as well as among the hibernating lots. The cause of the deaths in the hibernating lots is not known, but in the winter-fed lots the mortality has been due principally to two causes, namely, a disease causing sores and to 'soft shell.' The disease causing sores, which may be of bacterial origin, was not equally severe from year to year, and it, more than anything else, has caused fluctuations in the death rate of winter-fed animals. Soft shell is associated with a failure to eat, causing general emaciation and gradually the softening of the shell, frequently, although not always, followed by death. Soft shell also causes many deaths among terrapins after they emerge from hibernation, and it results in more deaths than all other losses combined in both groups of animals.

"The percentage of terrapins that were grown to maturity has been reduced materially in some of the lots on hand through depredations by rats while the animals were small, losses during storms, and apparently by escapes made by the terrapins because of their well-developed climbing propensities.

"Evidence is produced that would tend to show that about

60.7 per cent of the animals hatched may be grown to maturity and that winter feeding increases the rate of survival.

"Terrapins have an average length of about 27 millimeters at hatching. Young animals, when kept warm — that is, if placed in a brooder house — remain active during the winter, and the majority of them will begin to take food within a month or two after hatching. If the young are left out doors, they do not feed until they are 7 to 8 months old; that is, they go into hibernation soon after hatching or they remain in the nests in which they are hatched to hibernate, and they do not feed until the weather gets warm the following spring.

"Generally about 1 year's growth was gained during their first winter by the recently hatched young when placed in the brooder house, in which the temperature was kept as far as possible at 80° F. or higher; that is, an average gain of growth (for all lots that had been fed the first winter) of 4.7 millimeters was made. The advantage in growth attained through winter feeding usually was retained and, furthermore, the winter-fed animals produced eggs a year earlier than the hibernating lots.

"Winter feeding, aside from its advantages with respect to earlier maturity when animals are grown in captivity, has the advantage of carrying the animals through the critical stages of life at an earlier age. When terrapin culture is engaged in for the purpose of rebuilding or augmenting the supply in nature, the winter-fed animals apparently are able to take care of themselves and stand just as good a chance of survival at an age of about 8 months as the hibernating ones do a year later. The earlier liberation reduces the amount of care necessary and presumably hastens returns."

Time and again private individuals have attempted to raise Diamond-backs on "farms," but such enterprises usually have produced only pens or "crawls" in which the reptiles are held for a better market or fed to increase their size. The Beaufort Terrapin Farm, organized in 1913, was a notable exception, for within a few years this well-equipped plant, modelled after that of the Bureau of Fisheries, was hatching 15,000 to 20,000 eggs per annum. Its good progress was interrupted, however, by the curtailment of luxuries during the World War and also, it was believed, by the advent of prohibition. In view of the discouraging outlook the enterprise was virtually abandoned in 1918.

MARKET VALUE. The top market price for a Diamond-back with a plastron six to seven inches long is six to seven dollars, the value increasing sometimes as much as a dollar for every additional half-inch in length. The price is " straight " when the terrapins are sold by the dozen. Females measuring less than six inches and males sell for a much reduced figure, six inches being the " dead-line " from the buyer's point of view.

PROTECTION. The Diamond-back may not be caught or possessed between April 1 and October 31 in Maryland; between April 15 and July 31 in North Carolina. Both states prohibit taking, catching, or possessing any specimen with a plastron less than five inches long. Here at least are samples of the slight protection afforded turtles and terrapins by the law.

NORTHERN DIAMOND-BACK TERRAPIN

Malaclemys centrata concentrica (Shaw)

[PLATES 45, 46, AND 47]

IDENTIFICATION. This and the Southern Diamond-back Terrapin are subspecies of a single species and differ only in minor points. In the northern form, the head is smaller and the carapace widest posteriorly instead of having approximately parallel sides. For ordinary purposes the two subspecies can be considered the same or else any individual may be identified by its point of origin alone.

SIZE. Slightly larger than the Southern Diamond-back Terrapin.

DISTRIBUTION. North Atlantic coastal strip from Eastham on Cape Cod, Massachusetts, to the region of Cape Hatteras, North Carolina, where intergradation with the Southern Diamond-back Terrapin takes place.

For additional information see the account of the Southern Diamond-back Terrapin. No essential difference between the habits of the two subspecies has been pointed out.

Although there seems to be no record of the southern form beyond the limits of brackish water, the northern one has been taken as far up the Hudson as Newburgh, along the Potomac to within four miles of Washington, and in the York to West Point, Virginia. No record for a Diamond-back above the region of tidal influence exists.

MISSISSIPPI DIAMOND-BACK TERRAPIN

Malaclemys pileata pileata (Wied)

IDENTIFICATION. The uniform black or dark brown carapace usually has conspicuous concentric ridges and grooves, and the keels of the vertebral shields are more or less tuberculate. The top of the head and upper lip are dark.

Specimens of this, the Florida, and the Texas Diamond-back Terrapins of known origin can often be identified by the narrow ranges and restricted habitat of the subspecies.

THE SEXES. Sexual dimorphism has not been described in as

great detail for *Malaclemys pileata* as for *M. centrata,* but most if not all of the same differences undoubtedly occur. In addition, the keels of the vertebral shields of the former are said to be more knob-like in the male and there may be a constant difference in the colour of the upper lip.

DISTRIBUTION. Gulf coastal strip from southeastern Louisiana to western Florida, where intergradation with the Florida Diamond-back Terrapin occurs.

HABITAT. Salt and brackish marshes and estuaries.

Almost nothing has been recorded about the habits of this Gulf subspecies. Although sold in markets, its flesh is not so good as that of the Northern and Southern Diamond-backs.

TEXAS DIAMOND–BACK TERRAPIN

Malaclemys pileata littoralis (Hay)

IDENTIFICATION. This extreme western subspecies usually has a uniform light brown carapace. The upper lip is always white, the top of the head often so. In other respects it strongly resembles its closest relatives, the Florida and Mississippi Diamond-back Terrapins.

SIZE. It is somewhat larger than the Southern Diamond-back Terrapin, females apparently averaging about seven inches in length of plastron (measured from the lowest point in front to the bottom of the posterior notch).

YOUNG. Very small specimens have a keel on each vertebral shield ranging in form from a mere trace on the fifth or last and a broad low one on the first, to a button-like knob with constricted base on the fourth. The tops of these protuberances are smooth in contrast to the rough surface of the remainder of each shield.

The margins of the shields of the carapace are somewhat darkened. The hatchlings are about twice as bulky as those of the Southern Diamond-back Terrapin.

DISTRIBUTION. Gulf coastal strip and islands of Texas. This form probably ranges from Galveston southward into Mexico. Strauch recorded two Mexican specimens and Hay states that it is said to occur southward at least to Brownsville, Texas.

HABITAT AND HABITS. Salt and brackish marshes and estuaries. Few observations on the habits of the Texas Diamond-back have been made.

HYBRIDIZATION. The Texas Diamond-back Terrapin is larger than either the Northern or Southern Diamond-back of the Atlantic seaboard, but has a lower market value owing to its inferior flavour. Workers at the United States Fisheries Biological Station, Beaufort, North Carolina, hoped that a large, fast growing, delicious variety would result from a cross between Atlantic and Texas terrapins. Breeding experiments were begun in 1914, but bore only disappointing results. The hybrids had a tendency to grow slowly, mature late, and include a preponderance of males, the sex which has relatively little market value. The palatability of the flesh was not tested.

FLORIDA DIAMOND-BACK TERRAPIN

Malaclemys pileata macrospilota (Hay)

IDENTIFICATION. This terrapin is recognized by its conspicuous yellow or orange spots, one in the centre of each vertebral and costal shield. The ground colour of these shields is deep blue-black. Being a subspecies of the species to which the Texas and Mississippi Diamond-back Terrapins belong, the present form strongly resembles those two in other characteristics.

DISTRIBUTION. Gulf coastal strip of Florida northward from Cape Sable to the western part of the state, where intergradation with the Mississippi Diamond-back Terrapin occurs.

HABITAT. Salt and brackish marshes and estuaries.

This subspecies has remained almost without mention by reptile students. Hay remarks on its readiness to bite and ability to inflict a painful wound. It is eaten only locally if at all, the flesh being inferior.

COMMON MAP TURTLE

Graptemys geographica (Le Sueur)

[PLATES 48 AND 49]

IDENTIFICATION. No median ridge extends along the greatly expanded crushing surface of the upper jaw. An even to slightly tuberculate keel runs down the middle of the carapace, which has a feebly dentate hind edge. A more or less triangular spot is evident behind the eye, and the neck has numerous narrow longitudinal yellow stripes. The dull olive or brown carapace is devoid of concentric ridges and grooves and has a more or less conspicuous network of greenish-yellow lines.

SIZE. The Common Map Turtle is generally credited with an average adult carapace length of nine inches and a maximum one of twelve. However, among published measurements of fifty-nine individuals, the largest, an Indiana specimen, has a carapace only ten and three-quarters inches long and a weight of four and one-quarter pounds. Such dimensions must refer to females since males apparently do not exceed five and one-quarter inches in carapace length.

Measurements of an Illinois female follow:

	Inches	Millimetres
Length of carapace	7.99	203
Width of carapace	6.22	158
Length of plastron	7.20	183
Width of plastron	4.45	113
Height of shell	2.83	72

YOUNG. The dorsal keel is more strongly developed than in the adult, and the carapace is about as wide as long. The plastron has irregularly placed and highly variable black spots and blotches which disappear well before full growth is reached, and the reticulate pattern of the carapace is always conspicuous.

THE SEXES. The tail of the male is longer, whereas the female has a relatively larger head. In the female the carapace is more rounded behind, and the much greater size attained by this sex has been noted above. A study of the shields showed that abnormalities occur in their number and arrangement more frequently among females. Newman found the males to be not only weaker but more timid and retiring.

EGG. The elliptical eggs (about 35 × 22 mm.) have a soft, easily indented white shell.

GROWTH. The carapace of the smallest breeding female found by Newman was seven and a half inches long. Just what length of time it takes a female to attain such dimensions has not been determined.

MOULT. The horny shields are apparently cast off periodically and therefore concentric growth rings do not appear on the growing shell.

DISTRIBUTION. From Arkansas, northeastern Oklahoma, and extreme eastern Kansas northeastward through Missouri, western and northern Kentucky, Illinois and Indiana, western and southern Wisconsin, the southern third of the lower peninsula of Michigan, Ohio, and the Lake Erie-Ontario region.

It has also reached, apparently via the St. Lawrence, Lakes Champlain and George; the Ottawa River has been ascended as far as Norway Bay west of Ottawa.

In addition this turtle is known from the Austin and Waco regions of Texas, the Cumberland River valley in northern, and Blount County in eastern, Tennessee, extreme southwestern Virginia, and Allegheny and Armstrong Counties of southwestern Pennsylvania. Specimens have been recorded from unnamed localities of Louisiana and West Virginia.

HABITAT. A thoroughly aquatic inhabitant of substantial bodies of water, this species frequents rivers, large streams, and lakes. It abounds in marshes and shallow bays of big rivers and lakes, and river backwaters and overflow ponds. Plant-grown, soft bottoms are most attractive to it, whereas clear swiftly flowing streams are shunned.

HABITS. Seldom leaving the water except to lay, this turtle is a good swimmer and especially adept at concealing itself by burrowing into thick masses of aquatic vegetation. Progress on land is slow. When captured, it withdraws its head with a hiss, depending chiefly on the protection afforded by the shell. Although a finger thrust too close to the retracted head may receive a deliberate bite, advancing the jaws toward or snapping at an offending object is not a habit of this shy, inoffensive species.

HIBERNATION. Evermann and Clark as well as Newman made detailed studies of the Common Map Turtle in Lake Maxinkuckee, northern Indiana. The former concluded that many if not all of the population there did not hibernate during the winter of 1900–1. Throughout the cold months they were observed through clear ice walking slowly on the bottom of the lake. Newman, on the other hand, states that these turtles hibernate in soft bottom mud, especially that of the lagoons. Cahn mentions submerged muskrat runways and soft banks as hibernation sites in Illinois.

50. Mississippi Map Turtle (*Graptemys pseudogeographica pseudogeographica*) from Reelfoot Lake, Tennessee. This female has a carapace 7.75 inches long. "Le Sueur's Terrapin" is another common name of this species. (*Courtesy Zoological Society of Philadelphia, photograph by Mark Mooney, Jr.*)

51. Young Mississippi Map Turtle (*Graptemys pseudogeographica pseudogeographica*) with a carapace 3 inches long. (*Courtesy Zoological Society of Philadelphia, photograph by Mark Mooney, Jr.*)

52 [INSET]. Eastern Painted Turtle (*Chrysemys picta picta*) from Morris County, New Jersey, shedding. The old shields, two of which are seen lying near the turtle, have already come off of the light areas of the plastron. (*Photograph by Robert Devine.*)

53. Young Eastern Painted Turtle (*Chrysemys picta picta*) from Burlington County, New Jersey. (*Courtesy Zoological Society of Philadelphia, photograph by Mark Mooney, Jr.*)

It is generally agreed that the warmth of the shallow water of bays and lagoons attracts these turtles in the autumn, making them largely desert the deeper parts of large lakes or rivers.

In northern Indiana retirement for the winter takes place during early November although a few individuals may be seen basking somewhat later. Spring emergence begins any time after the first week of April, whereas in May great numbers are always active. Allowances must of course be made for unusual seasons.

GREGARIOUS SUNNING. Newman's account of groups basking in the sun at Lake Maxinkuckee, Indiana, could not easily be improved, so I am quoting it here:

" These tortoises are in evidence during the summer months to a greater extent than other native species. Basking seems to be their principal occupation. On warm days they literally line the shores of the lake at certain favorable places. Scarcely a floating board or pier lacks its quota of occupants. In some places where the trees overhang the water or have fallen in from lack of support, the smaller specimens of Graptemys mount among the branches to heights of six or seven feet.

" When basking they are decidedly gregarious, collecting in such numbers on certain sheltered ledges that it becomes necessary for them to pile up two or even three layers deep, the smaller ones perching high on the backs of the larger ones. Every member of these groups is on the alert and, at the slightest indication of danger, there is a general scramble for the water. The imitative instinct seems to be highly developed. If one animal scents danger and topples over into the water his neighbors quickly follow suit. I have seen all the tortoises within a hundred yards of shore line follow the lead of one that had become alarmed. So acute is their sense of danger that almost any slight divergence from normal conditions serves to give the alarm. A startled bird flying from the grass along the shore or a frog jumping into the water is sufficient cause for a general commotion among the basking tortoises.

" By concealing myself in the long grass across the lagoon from a favorite basking place, I was able to note their behavior. After the initial alarm caused by my approach, they regained confidence and cautiously came to the surface. After reconnoitering carefully and seeing nothing suspicious, they proceeded to crawl out upon the narrow ledge where they habitually congregated. One after another they crawled out, the last ones, for lack of room, upon the backs of the first occupants, until, on a ledge scarcely twenty feet long and averaging less than two feet in width, there were crowded over sixty tortoises. In a few minutes one of them took alarm at something that escaped my observation and slid precipitately into the water. All the others, with one exception, followed the lead and in about four seconds the ledge was in possession of one unusually large female, that, for some reason or other, whether from superior experience or unusual sluggishness, refused to leave the vantage ground. In a few minutes the ledge was again crowded and the previous performance was repeated. During the first forty-five minutes of observation the ledge was vacated seven times.

" As they lay basking they were continually snapping at passing insects and wriggling their feet, upon which flies and mosquitos were crawling, their actions reminding one of those of a dog tormented by flies. When undisturbed by pests, however, they stretch themselves out to the fullest extent, the hind legs being extended backward so that the soles of the feet are in contact. This love for warmth and relaxation seems to be one of the most pronounced traits of Graptemys and must be considered as one of the potent factors governing its behavior. Other species show the same traits to a less marked degree."

REPRODUCTION. In northern Indiana, apparently courting

individuals have been seen on April 27 and again in October. However, this indication of an autumn mating period calls for confirmation.

The laying period in Indiana and Illinois begins during late May and reaches its height in June. There seems to be a peak during the second and third weeks of this month followed by a prolongation of occasional deposition extending through July.

The eggs laid in June hatch through the last half of August and early September, but those deposited much later probably tide over the winter to release their contents the following spring or early summer; at least the May and June appearance of hatchlings can be explained in no other way.

A female ready to lay hunts early in the morning for a site, usually beyond the immediate shoreline or narrow beach of her haunt, sometimes even attaining a soft ploughed field or sandy stretch as much as a quarter of a mile inland. A hatchling could scarcely cover such a distance in less than two days of hard travel! The selection of an exact site is often a tedious task requiring hours of search. A chosen spot may be abandoned because of a buried root or stone, hard soil, sand that caves in too readily, or for some reason that defies detection by mere man.

Once a satisfactory spot has been selected and digging begun, the approach of a person may delay operations, but the digger is not easily frightened away. The flask-shaped cavity is dug with the hind feet and filled with two layers of eggs in the main cavity and two or three eggs in the neck. Over the latter the loose dirt is scraped. The site is then carefully concealed by the industrious female, who drags her plastron back and forth across the disturbed area.

The eggs laid at one time vary in number from ten to sixteen.

The above general account of reproduction has been pieced

together almost entirely from the details recorded by Newman, Cahn, and Evermann and Clark.

FOOD AND FEEDING. The broad crushing surface of its powerful jaws gives a clue to the mollusk-eating habits of the Common Map Turtle. Although the juveniles eat only thin-shelled species, the adults are able to crush the shells of tougher kinds. Snails form the greater part of the diet, but clams are also relished. After the shell has been crushed, the claws are used in getting rid of the larger fragments. When, as frequently happens, the victims are caught unawares with their soft parts extended, this necessity of crushing the shell is avoided.

Crayfish and a limited number of insects are also consumed. References to herbivorous tendencies require confirmation.

ENEMIES. No one has definitely determined the chief sources of danger, but numerous mutilated individuals have been observed in Ontario. The leech is also a potent enemy. Both eggs and hatchlings are undoubtedly destroyed by various mammals.

CAPTIVITY. The natural shyness of this species persists during confinement, and getting captives to feed is sometimes impossible. Newman flatly states that they do not eat, but wear deep paths along the edges of their enclosures in endless efforts to escape. Others have had better results and persuaded individuals to take snails and clams. Ditmars even lists chopped fish, meat, mealworms, soft-bodied grubs, earthworms, and lily pads as the diet consumed by them in the New York Zoological Park and adds that they always drag this food under the water before swallowing it.

The vivarium should include some land and be in a sunny place. A suitable temperature range is from 68° to 75° F.

ECONOMIC VALUE. Of distinctly second-rate value as a source of food, this turtle, nevertheless, sometimes finds its way to market. Eight among thirteen reports on its status say that it is used as food, three deny this, and two report very limited use. The flesh is palatable.

MISSISSIPPI MAP TURTLE

Graptemys pseudogeographica pseudogeographica (Gray)

[PLATES 50 AND 51]

IDENTIFICATION. No median ridge extends along the moderately expanded crushing surface of the upper jaw. A tuberculate keel runs down the middle of the carapace, which has a strongly dentate hind edge. A crescent-shaped spot is located behind the eye, and the neck has numerous narrow longitudinal yellow stripes. The olive or brownish carapace is devoid of concentric ridges and grooves. It has a more or less visible network of greenish or yellow lines. One to two dark blotches are present near the posterior edge of each vertebral and costal as well as many of the marginal shields.

SIZE. The female of this species is generally said to attain a carapace length of ten inches. Ditmars records a female nine and three-quarters inches long that weighed four pounds. The dimensions of a large male from Illinois follow:

	Inches	Millimetres
Length of carapace	7.99	203
Width of carapace	5.98	152
Length of plastron	7.28	185
Width of plastron	3.35	85
Height of shell	2.56	65

YOUNG. The dorsal keel is strongly developed on the first three vertebrals, producing a markedly saw-toothed or humped profile (see Plate 51). The carapace is about as wide as long, and its hind edge is even more noticeably dentate than in the adult. The colour of the shell above is bright green, with conspicuous yellow tracings; below, a complicated, dark, bilaterally symmetrical pattern is evident on a yellow ground colour. Cahn gives further details.

THE SEXES. The tail of the male is longer, the vent in the extended tail lying beyond the hind edge of the carapace. The head of the female is relatively large. Judging by the few available dimensions, the sexual difference in size is not nearly so great as in the Common Map Turtle. The measurements given above under the discussion of size illustrate this point.

EGG. The elliptical eggs have a soft white shell. The average dimensions of eggs of seven lots (seventy-one eggs) are given by Cahn as 32.7 × 22.5 millimetres, while the three or four eggs figured by Agassiz were 35–39 × 25 millimetres, the smallest of Agassiz's eggs being larger than the largest of eleven individual eggs measured by Cahn.

MOULT. The horny shields are apparently cast off periodically, and therefore concentric growth rings do not appear on the growing shell.

DISTRIBUTION. Numerous reports show that the range of this species extends from the eastern third of Kansas eastward across Missouri, southern Illinois, and the southern third of Indiana. It also follows the Mississippi into southwestern Wisconsin and ascends the Missouri to South Dakota. South of Missouri it enters extreme northeastern Oklahoma, northern Arkansas, and extreme western Tennessee, to intergrade with a southern form somewhere in the strip of country extending from southeastern Oklahoma eastward across the Mississippi Valley.

HABITAT. Streams, rivers, lakes, ponds, bayous, and sloughs are the haunts of this thoroughly aquatic turtle. Abundance of aquatic vegetation and lack of a strong current are two conditions most congenial to it.

HABITS. Nearly all observers are struck by the excessive shyness of the Mississippi Map Turtle. Its gregarious sunning habits have been repeatedly described; often more than a score of individuals are seen on a stranded log or similar object far from bank or shore.

HIBERNATION. According to Cahn, in northern Illinois hibernation is entered during October and emergence from it does not take place the following spring until after the disappearance of the ice. Muskrat houses under the water are favourite sites, but any submerged mud in which the turtles can bury themselves to a depth of four or more inches may be selected.

In the milder climate of southern Illinois a period of sluggish inactivity is substituted for hibernation, and on the mildest winter days colonies of basking individuals may be seen.

REPRODUCTION. In central Illinois this turtle lays from seven to thirteen eggs during July; very small specimens, probably near hatchlings, have been seen there in late August and early September.

Cahn, whom we must thank for all the information on the reproductive habits of the Mississippi Map Turtle, gives the following account of nest construction by a large Meredosia female observed on July 6 (time of day not recorded):

"The nesting site was in the middle of an old road, between the ruts made by the wagon wheels. The road runs about thirty feet from the river on one side and along a ditch about twenty feet away on the other. The soil is black and fairly solid. The turtle had a heavy growth of algæ on her shell, and may well have come out of the ditch which is full of algæ. She had apparently started digging but a few minutes before, judging from the rapidity with which the rest of the nest was dug. During the observed digging of the nest, which lasted five minutes (probably not over ten minutes was required for the entire excavation) the turtle worked with great rapidity, standing in one position. The hole was dug with the hind feet only, by scratching vigorously with legs alternating. As soon as a little pile of loose dirt accumulated, she pushed it out behind her, using both legs together to shove it out of the hole, the dirt coming in contact with the soles of the feet. The hole descended forward at an angle of 60° under her position, the sloping floor of the hole being the inclined plane up which she pushed the loose dirt. As she started to lay she slowly rotated her position to the right, pausing periodically to lay an egg or two, after which she rotated again. With all the eggs laid she was back almost where she started from, having rotated through about 350°. From this position, then, she reached back with one hind leg after the other and, using the anterior (top) of the feet, she raked the loose dirt piled immediately behind her into the hole and filled it completely. For a few moments she patted the dirt down with the soles of her hind feet, then headed back toward the ditch, and was captured. The actual time occupied in laying, as represented by the rotation through 350°, was just seven minutes. The hole was then carefully opened. The nest was 5½ inches deep, with a 2-inch opening at the surface, and terminated in a rounded chamber at the bottom 3 inches in diameter. It contained eleven eggs."

FOOD. The feeding habits are exceedingly interesting because they change with age. The largely carnivorous young eat chiefly thin-shelled snails, other easily crushed mollusks, and an occasional insect larva or worm, whereas the adults feed mostly on tender aquatic plant leaves, stems, and bulbous roots. Cahn, on the basis of his own and Garman's stomach dissections, concludes that the adults are entirely herbivorous, but a troublesome adult captured in northern Louisiana by

Strecker disgorged a small mussel, three univalves, and the remains of a blue-tailed skink nearly five inches long! As a matter of fact, Garman found crayfish in adult stomachs.

CAPTIVITY. Generally considered delicate in confinement, this subspecies, nevertheless, can be kept successfully. Mertens reports good results from the use of "Sanostol," a preparation containing vitamins A through D, and a specimen has lived in the Philadelphia Zoological Garden for nine years and eight months. Lettuce and other greens are eaten at least to some extent.

The vivarium should be either a terrarium with enough water to permit the specimens to eat with submerged heads, which they prefer to do, or an aquarium containing large cork islands.

ECONOMIC VALUE. Along the Illinois River the snapping and soft-shelled turtles are the most valuable market species, but next to them comes the Mississippi Map Turtle, which is used more or less as a substitute for the high-priced Diamond-back.

OCELLATED MAP TURTLE

Graptemys pseudogeographica oculifera (Baur)

IDENTIFICATION. This subspecies of the Mississippi Map Turtle is recognized by the pattern of the carapace, each shield of which has a yellow ring bordered inside and out with olive brown. A yellow stripe covers the entire lower jaw.

DISTRIBUTION. Presumably along the Gulf coast from extreme western Florida into eastern Texas. At present it is impossible to say just where intergradation with the Mississippi and Texas Map Turtles takes place.

The type locality is Mandeville, Louisiana.

REPRODUCTION. The Mississippi Map Turtle has been credited with a very early laying season ever since Agassiz reported eggs deposited by it on June 1 at Natchez in southern Mississippi. In Illinois, at least, that turtle actually lays rather late. The one referred to by Agassiz was probably the present subspecies, which, with its southern distribution, would be expected to lay earlier.

Almost nothing is known about the life-history of this Gulf subspecies.

TEXAS MAP TURTLE
Graptemys pseudogeographica versa Stejneger

IDENTIFICATION. This little-known subspecies is described as differing from the Mississippi Map Turtle by the extension of the postorbital spot backward from the lower outer instead of the upper inner edge of the eye.

DISTRIBUTION. Recorded only from Austin, Texas, which is the type locality.

Nothing is known about its habits.

∵

THE PAINTED TURTLES
Genus *CHRYSEMYS*

The turtles of this genus have several claims to distinction among American chelonians. They are the most widely distributed; they certainly are the commonest in most localities if not always the most conspicuous; although comprising a single genus and species they are readily divided into four subspecies with differences pronounced and obvious enough to strike the eye even of the novice, and therefore each subspecies has a good common name. Since subspecies are strictly geographical units, they may be identified on the basis of the localities from which specimens come. The sections on identification give, for the benefit of those more deeply interested, the actual distinguishing characters.

The most complete account of habits will be found under the Central Painted Turtle because that subspecies has been studied perhaps more than others. No one knows just how much the four forms differ in habits although some differences have been brought out; these are given in their proper places. It is best to read first the pages on the Central Painted Turtle, no matter which kind you are especially interested in. Omission of subheadings under the other subspecies usually means similarity to the Central Painted Turtle. In some cases such omissions may of course indicate a complete lack of information.

EASTERN PAINTED TURTLE

Chrysemys picta picta (Schneider)

[PLATES 52 AND 53]

IDENTIFICATION. The crushing surface of the upper jaw is narrow and there is a tooth-like projection on either side of the notch at the tip of this jaw. The depressed carapace is without a median keel. The front and rear edges of the second and third vertebral shields are in line or almost in line with the corresponding margins of the second and third costals. The large shields of the dark carapace are broadly margined with yellow anteriorly and the plastron is immaculate yellow.

SIZE. Six inches is usually given as the carapace length of a large specimen, but a few seven-inch examples and one that measured 7.12 inches are on record.

YOUNG. In hatchlings the carapace varies from about 23 to 26 millimetres in length, and length and width usually do not differ by more than 2 millimetres. The costal and vertebral shields lack the yellow anterior margins, but there is a fine yellowish line down the middle of the carapace.

THE SEXES. Surface measured Pennsylvania specimens and concluded that "the females are proportionately higher and broader than the males."

EGG. The elliptical eggs range in greater and lesser diameters from 26 to 34 × 16 to 17 millimetres. The shell is white and thin.

GROWTH. Agassiz attempted to determine the rate of growth of *Chrysemys picta* by measuring large numbers of specimens and estimating the ages of the size groups thus detected. His results call for fully twice as much time as the turtles probably need to attain maturity. (See the discussion of growth under the Central Painted Turtle.)

Agassiz does not give the source of his material but it is probable that he worked with intergrades between the Eastern and Central Painted Turtles.

DISTRIBUTION. The Atlantic Coastal Plain from Long Island, New York, to Jacksonville, Florida.

Just how far into the Piedmont Plateau of Georgia, South Carolina, and North Carolina this turtle penetrates has not been determined, but it has been found as far west as Laurens and Greenwood Counties, South Carolina, and Cumberland, Johnston, and Vance Counties, North Carolina. The southern Appalachians apparently stand as a gap between it and the form found on their western side.

An area of intergradation between the Eastern and Central Painted Turtles must extend from the Hudson River valley, New York, southward through central Virginia, but what the limits of this area are has not been accurately determined. Bishop and Schmidt, however, do record an intergrade from the District of Columbia, and this record helps to delimit the area in question.

East of the Hudson Valley the Eastern and Central Painted Turtles intergrade in Massachusetts, Vermont, New Hampshire, and southern Maine; possibly also in Connecticut and Rhode Island. Future studies may show that the north-south valleys of the Hudson, Connecticut, and Merrimack Rivers have produced an extremely irregular area of intergradation in New England.

HABITAT. Along the coast the Eastern Painted Turtle is sometimes common in brackish tidal waters, and Babcock writes of finding Painted Turtles covered with a rusty deposit in New England salt marshes.

HIBERNATION. In the northern part of its range the hibernation of this subspecies is undoubtedly similar in time and place to that of the Central and Western Painted Turtles, whereas farther south the period of retirement must be greatly shortened or even omitted.

MIGRATION. In Connecticut, at the first sharp frost of the year, Seton saw twenty or thirty Painted Turtles (possibly intergrades between the eastern and central forms) crawling under ice toward the inlet of a lake. Apparently they were not associated as a group. This is only a casual observation, but it hints at migration under the influence of temperature.

CENTRAL PAINTED TURTLE

Chrysemys picta marginata Agassiz

[PLATES 54 AND 55]

IDENTIFICATION. In form of jaw and shape of carapace this subspecies is similar to its close ally the Eastern Painted Turtle. The front and rear edges of the second and third vertebral

shields alternate with the corresponding edges of the second
and third costals. The large shields of the dark carapace are
not or only narrowly margined with yellow anteriorly, and
the longitudinal blotch on the yellow plastron is but half or
less than half as wide as the plastron.

SIZE. Some data on size are given under the discussion of the
sexes.

YOUNG. In hatchlings the carapace is about 25 millimetres
long and wide. The longitudinal blotch on the plastron is
darker than it is in the adult.

THE SEXES. When the tail is extended, the anus lies well beyond the edge of the carapace in the male, below it in the female. The longest claws of the male forelimb are two or three
times as long as its hind-limb claws or the forelimb claws of
the female. The longest claws of males with carapaces from
four to five inches long may measure as much as half an inch.

Females attain a much greater size than males. For example,
Cunningham found that males averaged 4.61, females 5.63
inches in length; the largest male and female measured 6.89
and 7.36 inches, respectively. His material came from the region of Madison, Wisconsin, where intergrades between the
Central and Western Painted Turtles occur.

EGG. The elliptical eggs of the Central Painted Turtle range
in greater and lesser diameters from 28 to 32 × 17 to 20 millimetres. The shell is white. (See Plate 55.)

GROWTH. The exact rate of growth of young Painted Turtles has never been determined, but from the researches of
Pearse and of Cunningham a hypothetical rate can be worked
out. The former showed that a young specimen living under
natural conditions will add about 30 millimetres to its length
in a year, and about half that amount annually thereafter until
it is 80 millimetres long. Therefore a male hatched, let us say,
in September 1938 with a 26-millimetre (one inch) carapace
might be expected to measure 30 millimetres at emergence in

the spring of 1939. By the following spring (1940) it would be 60, and two years later (1942) perhaps 90 millimetres (3.5 inches) long. Cunningham found active reproductive cells in males only 88 millimetres long, so our hypothetical male might be ready to breed during 1942, the fourth full season of its life, or when it is three and one half to four years old. Since the smallest breeding female found by Cunningham was 130 millimetres (5.12 inches) long, females either grow more rapidly or become sexually mature at a greater age than males. Guessing that the females do both and granting our male an extra year, we can conclude that the latter would probably mature not later than 1943, its fifth full season, females during their sixth or seventh. Pearse's work does not shed as much light on early growth as it should have because he failed to indicate the sex of his specimens. The astonishingly erratic growth indicated by his results might be explained in part by a marked sexual differential rate.

Once mature, these turtles undoubtedly cease to grow so fast. Pearse's successive size groups show a progressive decrease in annual growth rate. Cunningham's figures indicate that a male when first ready to breed is some 29, a female only 13 millimetres shorter than the average size for full-grown individuals. Few years would be needed to add such small amounts.

Cunningham and Pearse secured their material from southern Wisconsin where, as stated above, the Central and Western Painted Turtles intergrade; therefore their results certainly hold for both forms.

In a novel study Mattox found that the number of growth rings in the long bones of the Central Painted Turtle are correlated with size and probably with age. Just how accurate a determination can be made by this method was not shown.

MOULT. All the Painted Turtles periodically shed their epidermal shields. Because of this, growth rings do not appear on the shell and age-determination is much more difficult than in most other turtles. (See Plate 52, illustrating moult in the Eastern Painted Turtle.)

DISTRIBUTION. Eastern Illinois, northern Kentucky, the southern peninsula of Michigan, Indiana, Ohio, West Virginia, western Virginia, western Maryland, all of Pennsylvania but its southeastern corner, extreme northern New Jersey, all of New York but the valley of the Hudson River, northern Vermont eastward through central and northern Maine, and southeastern Canada, east of the Lake Superior drainage and north to about 47° N. Latitude.

Intergradation with the Western Painted Turtle takes place from southeastern Wisconsin southward through Illinois (Cahn) and, in Canada, presumably at the eastern limit of the Lake Superior drainage. The southern limit of its range is for the most part undetermined. Conditions in the Atlantic states are discussed under the Eastern Painted Turtle.

HABITAT. Ponds, large pools, streams of all sizes, ditches, canals, swamps, marshy meadows, bogs, bayous, river bays and backwaters, and small lakes and bays of large ones are frequented by Painted Turtles. Their chief requirement is quiet warm shallow water supporting an abundance of aquatic vegetation. The sluggish plant-grown stretches of swift streams are often frequented. A marked degree of natural stagnation and pollution is readily withstood, water with a decidedly unpleasant odour being at times inhabited.

HABITS. Whatever habits the Painted Turtles have are obviously good ones from a turtle's point of view since no other American species can be rated as more successful either in extent of distribution or in maintaining a large population in spite of man's civilization.

The four subspecies of *Chrysemys picta* are diurnal. They are timid and shy, as shown by the difficulty of approaching basking individuals without sending them scuttling into the

54. Central Painted Turtles (*Chrysemys picta marginata*) from Lucas County, Ohio. The male, on its back, has a carapace 5.31 inches long, whereas that of the female measures 5.75 inches. (*Courtesy Zoological Society of Philadelphia, photograph by Mark Mooney, Jr.*)

55. Eggs of the Central Painted Turtle laid in the Philadelphia Zoological Garden on July 5, 1938. Dimensions in millimetres: 29.5 x 20 and 31 x 20. (*Courtesy Zoological Society of Philadelphia, photograph by Mark Mooney, Jr.*)

56. Western Painted Turtle (*Chrysemys picta bellii*) with a carapace 5.75 inches long. It is a male. (*Courtesy Zoological Society of Philadelphia, photograph by Mark Mooney, Jr.*)

57 [LEFT]. Western Painted Turtle (*Chrysemys picta bellii*). (*Courtesy Shedd Aquarium, photograph by Douglas Cullen.*)
58 [RIGHT]. Young Southern Painted Turtle (*Chrysemys picta dorsalis*) with a carapace 29 millimetres long. (*Courtesy Zoological Society of Philadelphia, photograph by Mark Mooney, Jr.*)

water, where they exhibit an admirable ability to swim. When picked up they sometimes bite viciously, but are more often content to wave their feet vigorously in the air as if swimming, and in doing so repeatedly scratch a restraining hand. The clawing is more annoying than the rather ineffectual biting. Individuals vary considerably in the persistence with which their defensive tactics are kept up, and exceptionally shy specimens soon draw in their limbs and head with a hiss to await developments quietly. Juveniles are, on the whole, less wary than adults and not so prone to scratch and bite. Grant noticed in the Central Painted Turtle a sexual difference in temperament, the males generally being the more nervous, active, and vicious.

A tendency of both male and female Central Painted Turtles of various ages to wander hundreds of yards from water has been remarked on by more than one observer. Such temporary desertion of their native element is not correlated with sexual activity.

The experiments by Casteel on the discriminative ability of the Central Painted Turtle are now classic among studies of animal behaviour and warrant attention. His object was to determine whether thoroughly tamed individuals could be taught to choose between black and white, lines of different widths and direction, and two designs.

The subjects of the experiment were put in an apparatus giving them the opportunity of entering either one of two boxes, to receive an electric shock in one case, palatable food in the other. The visible sides of the boxes were covered by cardboards of the colours, lines, or designs being tested, the same colour, lines, or design being constantly associated either with the reward or with the punishment. All necessary precautions were taken such as frequently but irregularly shifting the boxes about and always going through the same actions between trials whether the boxes had been moved or not.

The results proved that the turtles learned to discriminate between black and white; between vertical and horizontal lines eight, four, and, for one individual, two millimetres wide; between lines of different widths running in the same direction (both vertical and horizontal): eight opposed to two (horizontal), eight opposed to one, and even two opposed to three millimetre widths (vertical).

Only negative results were obtained in the efforts to teach discrimination in design. The designs used were made up of four similar, three-sided white figures on a black background.

Casteel also gave memory tests: two turtles made a perfect score after two and six weeks, respectively; another showed little loss after a twelve-week interval and did as well still nine weeks later.

The "space reactions" experiments of Yerkes involve Painted Turtles and are summarized under the habit section on the Spotted Turtle.

HIBERNATION. In southern Canada and the northern parts of the United States the Central and Western Painted Turtles spend the winter in mud or débris at the bottom of the water in which they live (unless some populations migrate in the autumn and spring; see the following section). Muskrat houses, holes, and cavities in banks may also be utilized. Judging by the brief descriptions of actual sites, hibernation under water is the rule.

The time of retirement in these same northern regions usually seems to be the last two weeks of October; of emergence the last half of March or the first three weeks of April. Due allowance for difference in latitude and for seasonal variations in temperature must of course be made.

MIGRATION. A scientific study of migration was made by Pearse in Lake Mendota, southern Wisconsin, where the Western and Central Painted Turtles intergrade. Of one hundred and sixty-six individuals marked and recaptured, thirty per cent had travelled and seventy per cent had not. The average distance covered was three hundred and sixty-seven feet per turtle; the average period between marking and recapture, five months and nineteen days. Turtles that had been kept for some time were more apt to travel long distances than those tagged and at once released. One that had spent the winter in the laboratory was found about one and a third miles from the point of release after three years, eleven months, and nineteen days. In contrast to this, a specimen detained only long enough to receive a tag was retaken a few feet from its point of capture two years, one month, and four days later! It was concluded that " painted turtles are rather sedentary animals and, if their environment remains favorable, will remain in one locality for years."

This investigation by no means exhausts the subject, because, as implied, it did not tell us what happens when ponds dry up and other untoward events occur. Moreover, numbers of Central Painted Turtles have been seen to make annual migrations of sorts in northern Indiana not obviously under the influence of unfavourable changes in environment, and other more or less casual observations indicate that mass movements sometimes take place. (See the corresponding section on the Eastern Painted Turtle.)

SUNNING AND GREGARIOUSNESS. The most obvious and certainly one of the really characteristic habits of Painted Turtles is sunning in groups. Various numbers from a few to several dozen crawl out on a log, or any other object floating on or projecting from the water, to enjoy the warmth of the sun. Some of them sprawl, apparently asleep, but the approach of danger proves that, asleep or awake, a careful watch is always kept. Individuals frequently float in open water or lie at its surface in dense masses of aquatic vegetation, presumably doing so as a substitute for out-of-water basking.

Newman noticed that some Indiana specimens so regularly

assumed a characteristic position allowing partial submergence that the algal growth of the shell was limited. Besides being beneficial in the usual way, sunning helps rid the shell of algal growth; both shell and the soft parts, of leeches and other external parasites. Algal growth probably makes concealment relatively easy, but whether it is harmful to the shields I do not know.

In many regions Painted Turtles are the most abundant chelonians, and certainly they can be astonishingly numerous. Evermann and Clark state, without apologies, that two hundred and eighty individuals were taken from Lake Maxinkuckee, Indiana, by one haul of a thirty-five-foot seine! Certainly it is not unusual for an isolated pool only fifteen or twenty feet long and wide to be the home of some twenty-five adult Eastern Painted Turtles.

MATING. The fact that mating occurs during both spring and autumn was established by Cunningham from studies carried on in southern Wisconsin, where the Western and Central Painted Turtles intergrade. This biologist concluded that autumn copulation was ineffectual for fertilization because he could find no spermatozoa in the females taken a few weeks after the close of the autumn season. Subsequent investigations have not been made, but, in view of the fact that autumn copulation in at least one other species results in fertilized eggs, further researches should be instigated.

Few actual dates of courtship or mating in a natural state have been published, but observation of a paired couple in mid-August indicates that such sexual activity may be almost continuous in the northern and central states from soon after spring emergence to shortly before autumn disappearance, with a probable intermission during the laying period.

Courtship was known even to Agassiz in 1857 and has been described more than once since, one writer even calling it a form of flagellation, which it decidedly is not. Taylor, who has given the best account, could detect no essential difference between the courtship in Troost's Turtle and in the Western Painted Turtle. He watched captive individuals whose antics may be considered nearly if not entirely normal:

" On October 16 I observed a male of *Chrysemys* behaving in an unusual manner. He would start following a female of the same species, and by swimming faster would quickly overtake her; then, by whirling himself about in the water, he would start swimming backwards just in front of the female, who continued swimming straight ahead. Then the male would slow down, and as the female approached, he would push himself forward toward her, stretch out his arms full length forward, with the palms turned outward, the claws and fingers straightened, and vibrate them rapidly against the chin and lores of the swimming female. The fingers would touch the female from five to seven times during the continued vibration, which lasted perhaps less than one and a half seconds. He would then withdraw his arms, and continue swimming backward ahead of the female. After an interim of from four to five seconds, this same action would be repeated in practically the same way. In this particular manner the act was repeated twelve times before they were interrupted by another turtle separating them by chance. Then the male turned, sought out another mate, and began the same type of courtship with her."

Oddly enough, actual copulation has almost entirely escaped the eyes of herpetologists. Cunningham mentions couples " taken together, plastron to plastron, the female being above, usually with the head above water," and supposed that they were *in coitu*. To my knowledge no other turtles assume such a position, so I am loath to believe that these pairs were really copulating. Cahn saw a male Central Painted Turtle pursue, overtake, and mount a female, and claw at her head and neck. She quickly evaded him, but when last seen he had again taken up the pursuit. This behaviour is hard to classify, but must have been either courtship or attempted coition.

NESTING. Painted Turtles lay their eggs during June and the first three weeks of July, the height of the season including the last two-thirds of June and the first third of July. There is a British Columbia record for May 31 and some indications that the Central Painted Turtle lays throughout July and even into August, but it would be advisable to await confirmation of this late nesting.

Late afternoon is the laying time of the Western, Central, and Eastern Painted Turtles and almost certainly of the Southern as well, although this part of its life history remains a blank. The females usually start digging between 4.00 and 6.30 p.m., but one from southern Wisconsin, where the Central and Western forms intergrade, was found just finishing a nest as early as 4.00 o'clock, and in Iowa a Western Painted Turtle has been seen to begin as late as 8.17 p.m., or thirteen minutes earlier than the late limit given by Agassiz. These hour and minute records are not, of course, to be taken too literally.

Stromsten tells how another Iowa female, immediately after finishing her nest, was so strongly attracted by the light of an electric torch that she followed it both up and down hill, fast or slow, and only freed herself from its spell when within a few feet of the water into which she promptly disappeared. Whether such attraction is part of the mechanism that carries the gravid female through her nesting reflexes remains to be determined by experimentation. It might well be instrumental in drawing her to a relatively high, open area suitable for laying.

The actual sites chosen are so diverse that they defy classification. Some females laboriously wander hundreds of yards from water, whereas others promptly choose a spot within a few feet of the pond or stream in which they live. The only generalizations that I venture are: a tendency to ascend (which must keep them out of wet situations and usually take them onto hillsides or banks); a desire to lay in an open area (ensuring a spot exposed to the sun). Nevertheless, sites on wooded hillsides have been mentioned. The relation of the nesting slope to the points of the compass has been recorded by some whose observations suggest that southern or eastern exposures are frequently chosen. Weather conditions were noted by Nichols for three layings, all of which took place under a sunny sky. The type of earth seems to make little difference unless there is a slight preference for sandy soil. Lawns or other grassy places are sometimes selected and hard soil is by no means shunned.

As far as known, the nesting process is identical in all the subspecies of the Painted Turtle. This conclusion is based on the one complete and the several partial accounts, although it must be admitted that the nesting procedure of the Southern Painted Turtle is unknown except for a brief reference to it by Cahn and one by Cagle.

The complete account just mentioned is by Stromsten who watched many Western Painted Turtles dig their nests on the side of a small hill in Iowa and admirably describes the behaviour of a June 30 performance as typical:

" A painted turtle measuring about six inches in length appeared at the water's edge at about 8:00 p.m., about sixty feet from where the writer was waiting. She followed an old cowpath up the rather steep slope of the hill for a distance of about thirty feet and then turned at right angles to the path and came directly towards me. After she had traveled for perhaps fifteen feet she stopped and dug into the hard dry clay, first with the right hind foot and then with the left, making the dust fly for a considerable distance. It was only twice, once for the right and then for the left foot, that I could see the dust fly although the animal still continued to dig. She began digging her nest at 8:17 p.m. I gradually approached to within five or six feet of the turtle. This disturbed her slightly, but she soon resumed her operations. At first she inserted one foot into the depression she had started and made four or five digging or scraping motions much as a person would in trying to dig a hole in the ground with his finger nails. She then lifted the dirt out and pushed it as far back from the hole as she could, at the same time shifted her body so that the cloaca was directly over the pit and softened the hard clay with water from her bladders. The water was squirted into the pit with considerable force. Then the body was moved further so that the other foot could be thrust into the hole and she continued to dig as before. This was kept up, first with one foot, then softening the dirt, then with the other foot, for some time. This continuous wetting of the dirt soon made it of about the same consistency as thick cream, at which time she discontinued wetting it. As the dirt began to get dryer she commenced to enlarge the diameter of the hole at the bottom so as to make the nest flask-shaped, the neck being slightly larger than the leg and the spherical body as large as the reach of the leg would permit. In digging the body of the nest the turtle would scrape the sides with her claws three or four times, then press the dirt against the pad of her foot with her claws and carry it out by the handful. It was deposited near the edge of the opening and then pushed out so that the dryer dirt was left near the opening while the soft mud was pushed to the periphery. It took about one hour and thirty minutes for this turtle to complete the digging of her nest from the time she began.

"At 9:47 the turtle began to deposit her eggs. First she inserted her right hind foot into the nest, moved over so that the cloaca was directly over the opening, and then removed her leg from the nest. The egg was deposited so that it rested slightly on the edge of the opening, and gently slipped into the nest. Immediately the turtle inserted her right foot again and apparently placed the egg to one side of the nest. In about another minute a second egg was deposited and placed in the same manner as the first. It took about one-half second for the egg to pass out of the body, and seemed to involve no undue effort on the part of the turtle. The third egg appeared in about thirty seconds, and thirty seconds later, the fourth. The fifth egg did not appear until a minute and a half later, although two unsuccessful efforts were made at the regular intervals of half a minute. The sixth egg appeared on schedule time in thirty seconds. The sixth was the last one laid at this time, but evidently the effort had been made to lay eight or nine. After each egg was laid it was arranged in the nest by the right hind foot. The process of egg-laying was completed at 9:52, so that the entire process took about five minutes and at intervals of about thirty seconds for each egg.

"Immediately the turtle began pulling dirt in from the edges, the dryer dirt going in first. This was pressed down by the hind foot, first dirt from one side and then the other was pulled in, each foot being used alternately. She seemed to press the dirt down with her knuckles much as we might with a loosely closed fist. The wet dirt was the last to be pulled on the nest. The softer mud on top was thoroughly kneaded by the knuckles, and flattened and packed by rubbing the plastron over it. Dry dirt was then scratched in, and grass roots were either accidentally or purposely kneaded in as though transplanted. It almost seemed to the observer that the turtle made a special effort to reach far out for bits of grass and debris to help conceal her nest. When this was completed the turtle appeared startled at our flash light for the first time. It was as though she had awakened from a trance. She stretched out her neck, looked around for an instant and then hurried away towards the lake. It was 10:23 p.m. when she left the nest, so that the entire process of nest-digging and egg-laying took over two hours. She worked quite vigorously most of the time, but towards the end she appeared tired and needed to rest frequently. At no time during the procedure of nest-digging and egg-laying did the turtle seem much disturbed by the presence of three or four observers, even when the flash light was held directly in front of her."

A few points call for remark or amplification: The fore-limbs, once firmly planted for support, are scarcely moved, if at all; the size of the cavity probably varies directly with the leg length of the digger; the arrangement of the eggs in single, double, or even triple layer or layers must depend on their number and size; the female departs without taking so much as one fond glance at her nest, so Stromsten's phrase "looked around" certainly means that she peered at her surroundings.

All observers have been impressed by the frequent ejection of cloacal bladder water during nesting, and the purpose of this water has been the object of much conjecture. Obviously it makes digging in hard soil easier and is responsible for the formation of the plug sealing the upper part of the flask-shaped nest cavity. It has been suggested that the eggs absorb some of it and receive benefit therefrom, but Cunningham showed that Painted Turtle eggs absorb little or no water during the first few days; all moisture in an otherwise dry nest certainly would disappear too rapidly to be absorbed by the eggs.

I can detect no difference between the number of eggs laid by the four subspecies of *Chrysemys picta* unless the Western Painted Turtle has a slightly higher average, perhaps corre-lated with its greater size. For example, ten Iowa nests exam-ined by Blanchard had 13, 12, 12, 11, 9, 7, 7, 6, 6, and 5 eggs, and the record number of 15 is based on a count from this same state. The difference may be only an apparent one due to the greater number of data for the western form.

The common range for the four subspecies is 4 to 11 per clutch, with the upper extreme as 13, exceptionally 15. Lots of 5 to 8 are by far the most numerous. Females are known to lay but once a year.

HATCHING AND BEHAVIOUR OF HATCHLING. On June 26 a clutch of Eastern Painted Turtle eggs was laid on a Long Island lawn and watched by Wilcox until they hatched on September 8. This may be taken as a fairly typical illustration of the incubation period, although, as shown by Nichols, many Long Island nests retain their young until the following spring. The same thing probably happens with nests of the Western and Central Painted Turtles as well, and, indeed, Thacker secured some evidence that in British Columbia eggs of the former actually do not hatch until spring. The frequent discovery of hatchlings in the spring and early summer has led others to conclude that fairly late laying in northern regions constantly forces either the hatchlings or embryos to spend the winter in the nest.

All but one of the Long Island hatchlings of September 8 had shed the egg-tooth by October 5. This structure, found on the tip of the snout of most hatchling reptiles, is supposed to facilitate escape from the egg. The more reptile embryology is studied, the more we learn that often this " tooth " is of little or no help in shell-breaking. For example, Cunningham and Huene have recently found that Painted Turtle eggs split as often at the posterior as at the anterior region of the embryo, rapid absorption of water near the close of incubation appearing to be responsible for the rupture.

The following conclusions of Noble and Breslau, who carried on laboratory experiments to determine how hatchling Eastern Painted Turtles find their way to water, are all the scientific information available on the reactions of the young of *Chrysemys picta*:

" Newly hatched snapping, musk and painted turtles find their way from the nests to the water primarily because they are attracted toward large areas of intense illumination. Their escape from the nest is facilitated by their marked negative geotropism in the dark. These turtles are also attracted toward areas of high humidity but the presence of a source of light in a drier area will counteract any tendency to move into the wet area."

Hatchlings kept in a pail by Wilcox buried themselves in sand at night and emerged in the morning; on one cloudy day, when the pail was covered until noon, they remained in concealment until just after removal of the cover. Although obviously attracted by light, they apparently exhibited no negative geotropism in the dark. Other impulses must have been responsible for their " digging in " at night.

FOOD AND FEEDING. There is abundant information on the feeding habits of Painted Turtles, much of which is scattered, not to say fragmentary. Although no satisfactory picture can be put together from the diverse data, one fact, scarcely determinable by dissection of stomachs, is made clear by them: Painted Turtles have strong scavenger tendencies, which must account in part for the alleged vertebrate-eating habit as well as for the occasional devouring of large invertebrates. In nature individuals have been seen to eat dead birds, mammals, reptiles, fish, and clams.

The two serious attempts to determine just what Painted Turtles eat are summarized separately because, for reasons made clear below, they cannot be combined. In perusing them the last remark in the preceding paragraph must be kept in mind.

Surface studied the contents of eighty-six stomachs containing food; his specimens, coming from the eastern half of Pennsylvania, most likely included Eastern and Central Painted Turtles as well as their intergrades. The fact that his material was secured from many widely separated localities makes his findings of special value.

His results are abbreviated in the following list:

Percentage of stomachs with plant remains	73	(63 stomachs)
" " " " algæ	35	(30 ")
" " " " animal matter	80	(69 ")
" " " " mollusks	27	(23 ")
" " " " insects	71	(61 ")
" " " " vertebrate remains	9	(8 ")

Chiefly the leaves of flowering plants had been consumed, and the number of stomachs with non-flowering plants other than algæ was negligible. The well-represented insects, named in order of importance, were beetles, flies, and dragonflies. Only three turtles had eaten crustaceans.

Pearse, Lepkovsky, and Hintze analysed thirty stomach contents from the vicinity of Madison, Wisconsin, where the Western and Central Painted Turtles intergrade. Their results are summarized in estimates of food percentages by volume:

Percentage of	plant	remains	55.0
" "	animal	"	41.2
" "	insect	"	36.2
" "	vertebrate	"	4.8

The first two items do not add up to a hundred because small percentages of dirt and unknown material have been omitted. Crustaceans and mollusks had scarcely been touched. May- and damsel-fly nymphs constituted by far the most important item among the insects, wild celery and duckweeds among the flowering plants. Roughly a third as much algæ as flowering plants had been consumed.

Painted Turtles, then, seem to devour a slightly greater amount of plant than of animal material.

Food is usually but not invariably swallowed under water, the claws being used to assist the jaws in rending pieces too large to be managed whole. The turtles eat during the day, securing a large part of their fare at or near the surface, but sometimes foraging along the bottom.

ENEMIES. In Indiana adults are not infrequently killed and partly devoured or badly mutilated by an animal, probably the muskrat. Females, while going to or from the nesting site, are often crushed on roads and railroads.

The young of all Painted Turtles are eaten by crows, and at least one baby has been taken from the stomach of a bull-frog. Various egg-loving mammals such as skunks, grey squirrels, and raccoons destroy the nests.

Leeches badly infest Painted Turtles.

CAPTIVITY. Records of Painted Turtles having lived in captivity 135, 112, 93, 82, and 53 months speak for their hardiness in confinement. Individuals will become tame enough to take food out of one's hand.

A sunny vivarium having somewhat more water than land and a temperature range of 72° to 80° F. is advisable. Food is much more readily eaten when it can be swallowed under water. Mealworms, earthworms, raw fish or meat, and lettuce can be used as food in addition to the types named above in the section on food and feeding. Of course any small animal or tender plant can be tried. Wild individuals have even been known to clean out cooking-pots left soaking in a lake by campers!

It is interesting that the Painted Turtles fed on rations of lettuce by Pearse, Lepkovsky, and Hintze lost weight. These workers also found that this species grew better and remained in better condition when supplied with vitamin B in brewer's yeast than when given vitamin A in cod-liver oil.

ECONOMIC VALUE. There are two opposite opinions in regard to the relation of Painted Turtle feeding habits to man. Surface contends that the plants eaten are aquatic, and the few fish destroyed of species with little value, whereas the numerous insects devoured include many obnoxious species. Pearse, Lepkovsky, and Hintze do not specifically mention the insectivorous habit, but state that aquatic plants useful as food for ducks, fish, and other valuable animals are an important part of the diet. Their conclusion is that Painted Turtles, being on the whole injurious, should be destroyed.

I cannot understand how these small turtles could consume enough of the plants in question to make an appreciable difference, and this conviction, to my mind, completely invalidates the reasoning of the joint authors. Even if this species destroyed no harmful insects, I would argue that it at least should go unmolested to remain an interesting part of pond and stream life, so dear to the heart of all nature-lovers.

As an article of diet Painted Turtles are scarcely worth considering. Although sometimes eaten locally, they have never had a market value.

WESTERN PAINTED TURTLE

Chrysemys picta bellii (Gray)

[PLATES 56 AND 57]

IDENTIFICATION. In form of jaw and shape of carapace this subspecies is similar to its near ally the Eastern Painted Turtle. The front and rear edges of the second and third vertebral shields alternate with the corresponding edges of the second and third costals. The large shields of the dark carapace have very narrow yellowish anterior margins, but the entire carapace is more or less conspicuously decorated with a network of markings. The yellow of the plastron is largely replaced by a dark bilateral design which sends branches out along the sutures of the shields.

SIZE. This is the largest of the subspecies of *Chrysemys picta*, specimens with carapaces 9.84, 7.87, and 7.60 inches being on record. Cahn's dimensions of an Illinois female of moderate size follow:

	Inches	Millimetres
Length of carapace	6.30	160
Width of carapace	4.53	115
Length of plastron	5.83	148
Width of plastron	4.02	102
Height of shell	2.32	59
Weight	19 ounces	

YOUNG. In hatchlings the carapace is about as wide as long and the plastral design is darker than it is in the adult.

EGG. Cahn gives the average dimensions of forty-one eggs composing seven lots as 34.7 × 17.8 millimetres. According to Stromsten, however, the greater diameter ranges from 25 to 30, the lesser from 15 to 20 millimetres. The shell is white.

DISTRIBUTION. In the United States, from the northern peninsula of Michigan, central Wisconsin, western Illinois, and central Missouri westward to the Rocky Mountains of central Colorado and western Wyoming. In the southwest it reaches the Rio Grande in southern New Mexico and possibly even the southeastern corner of Arizona. Judging by existing records, however, it avoids Oklahoma and all of Texas but the western border. To the northwest this turtle extends its range through Montana and extreme northern Wyoming to the Cascade Mountains of Washington and Oregon, in the latter state even crossing them via the Columbia River to ascend the Willamette as far as Cottage Grove (Storer, 1937).

In Canada it occurs from the region of Lake Superior westward to Vancouver Island. There are, according to Cowan, definitive Canadian records for Lake Nipigon, Ontario, and the country between Kamloops and Vernon, British Columbia. Seton says that it is found northward to 51° N. Latitude in Manitoba.

HABITAT. Altitudes of at least 6,000 and 3,500 feet are attained in Colorado and British Columbia, respectively, by this western subspecies.

ENEMIES. Dr. Frank A. Stromsten has kindly informed me that he once saw in Iowa a ground squirrel (*Citellus tridecem-lineatus*) dig open a nest, take out an egg, sit up, and drink the contents by tilting the egg after biting a hole in one end. In the same region he counted on one hillside a hundred and ten nests that had been robbed by unidentified night prowlers.

SOUTHERN PAINTED TURTLE

Chrysemys picta dorsalis Agassiz

[PLATE 58]

IDENTIFICATION. In form of jaw and shape of carapace this subspecies is similar to its near ally the Eastern Painted Turtle. The front and rear edges of the second and third vertebral shields alternate with the corresponding edges of the second and third costals. The large shields of the dark carapace are margined with yellow anteriorly, and a conspicuous yellow or red stripe extends down the middle of the back. The plastron is immaculate yellow.

SIZE. The few measurements available suggest that this subspecies is somewhat smaller than either of the other three, the largest individual that I find on record having a carapace only 5.67 inches long. Agassiz describes *dorsalis* as the "broadest and shortest" of the forms of *Chrysemys*.

YOUNG. In hatchlings the carapace is about as wide as long, and the costal and vertebral shields do not have anterior yellow margins. The stripe down the middle of the back is very conspicuous. (See Plate 58.)

EGG. Cahn gives the average dimensions of six eggs from a single nest as 31.3 × 18.8 millimetres. Cagle, on the other hand, records the greater and lesser diameters of five eggs from as many nests as ranging from 30 to 35 and 10 to 18 millimetres, respectively. His material came from extreme northwestern Tennessee. The shell is white.

GROWTH. Because of a longer growing season this southern form would be expected to attain maturity more rapidly than the Central Painted Turtle. (See the discussion of growth under that form.)

DISTRIBUTION. The Mississippi Valley northward to extreme southern Illinois. The range of this form is but poorly indicated by definite records. It appears to occur chiefly on the western side of the Mississippi River (Cahn) and to shun the Gulf coastal strip.

HABITAT. This subspecies, according to Cahn, differs from both the Western and the Central Painted Turtles in strongly preferring ponds to streams and in being a trifle more aquatic than either of the others.

HIBERNATION. The period spent in winter retirement is much shorter than in the two northern subspecies and, in the southern part of its range, individuals probably do not hibernate at all. The sites chosen by all the Painted Turtles are undoubtedly much alike.

MIGRATION. The discovery of hundreds of shells over the bottom of a dried lake near bodies of more permanent water led Cahn to suggest that the relatively strong aquatic tendency of this subspecies had kept the original owners of those shells from striking out on land to find a new home as individuals of the other subspecies probably would have done.

ENEMIES. In western Tennessee the eggs of Painted Turtles are used as bait by fishermen.

FLORIDA TURTLE

Pseudemys floridana floridana (Le Conte)

[PLATES 60 AND 61]

IDENTIFICATION. The ridge extending along the middle of the crushing surface of the upper jaw is high and strongly toothed. This jaw has no notch at nor teeth near its tip, but there is a tooth at the tip of the lower jaw. The lines on the top and sides of the head are usually unbroken and there is, as a rule, no vertical stripe across the ear. In the region above the ears, the lines between the pair extending along the upper temporal regions are noticeably unequal in breadth, two pairs (and sometimes the median line) standing out conspicuously among the remaining narrower to obsolescent ones. The immaculate plastron is yellow or orange yellow and the blotches on the lower parts of the marginal shields enclose light areas.

SIZE. The Florida Turtle attains a plastron length of 11.5 inches. One North Carolina female had a carapace 10.83 inches long, 7.28 inches wide, and a shell height of 4.33 inches. Its plastron length was not recorded.

YOUNG. The colours of young individuals are more strongly contrasted than those of adults. In the very young the carapace is distinctly keeled and about as wide as long; also more highly arched than in the adult.

THE SEXES. The male has greatly elongated claws on the forelimbs (see Plate 60) and a head smaller than that of the female.

EGG. A series of a hundred and three eggs found in the Okefinokee Swamp, Georgia, ranged from 33 to 40.5 and averaged 34.2 millimetres in greater diameter. The corresponding figures for the lesser diameter were 22 to 27 and 24.1 millimetres. The shell is white.

DISTRIBUTION. The southeastern Coastal Plain from eastern North Carolina to Alachua County, northern Florida, and Mississippi.

HABITAT. This turtle is extremely abundant in large swamps such as the Okefinokee, but also frequents ponds, lakes, rivers, and streams. Dense stands of aquatic plants growing in quiet shallow water attract it in great numbers.

HABITS. It is shy and difficult to approach in spite of the fact that its well-developed sunning habits often make its presence rather obvious.

REPRODUCTION. The eggs are laid in May and June, usually numbering from twelve to twenty to a clutch. Sandy open banks are the favourite nesting sites.

FOOD. Strong herbivorous tendencies have been noted.

ENEMIES. In the Okefinokee Swamp many animals from man down make free-lunch counters out of the nesting banks of this subspecies. Francis Harper found the banks of the swamp canal literally torn up in May by bears, raccoons, and other animals and Wright and Funkhouser, reporting on their work in this same wilderness, state:

"A bear, killed May 30, had in its stomach twelve eggs, one of which was whole, and signs were plentiful to prove that the bears dug these eggs from the sand. When an egg complement was found exposed or only partly covered by the sand, or with the complement very small, the natives asserted that the turtle had been disturbed in the midst of egg-laying by the attack of bears or had been frightened from the eggs by these animals. A king snake, captured June 26, 1912, had fourteen eggs in its stomach. Another king snake, taken June 3, had thirteen eggs in its stomach. The stomachs of three other specimens of the same species of snake contained, respectively, one, two, and six eggs. . . ."

The common king snake referred to here apparently subsists largely on turtle eggs in the swamp, probably even waiting on banks for the turtles to lay.

A local decrease in numbers of the Florida Turtle was noticed after pollution of waters by sewage and dye-works refuse of Raleigh, North Carolina.

PENINSULAR TURTLE

Pseudemys floridana peninsularis Carr

[PLATES 62 AND 63]

IDENTIFICATION. This subspecies strongly resembles the Florida Turtle, but may be distinguished by the following differences in coloration: The line extending along the upper temporal region becomes nearly or entirely confluent about as far back as the rear extremity of the eye with a more median line, the two continuing as one to the end of the snout, whereas in the Florida Turtle these lines are separately continuous along the top of the head. In the Peninsular Turtle the immaculate plastron is light greenish white or light greenish yellow (not yellow or orange yellow), and the smudge-like blotches on the lower parts of the marginal shields are solid (do not enclose light areas).

YOUNG. Hatchlings from northern Lake County, Florida, have been described as having a prominently keeled carapace, the width of which is proportionately wider and the edges more flaring than in the adult carapace.

EGG. The hatchlings referred to under the discussion of the young above and reproduction below came from white elliptical eggs measuring 36 to 38 by 25 to 26 millimetres.

DISTRIBUTION. Peninsular Florida from Alachua County to Key Largo, exclusive of that part of the upper west coast inhabited by the Suwannee Turtle.

HABITAT. Lakes, rivers, and streams.

REPRODUCTION. At about one o'clock in the afternoon of February 8 a female was found approximately ninety yards from Lake Griffin, northern Lake County, Florida, in an open space among clumps of grass. She was laying in a hole about five inches deep and as many wide at the bottom. Its mouth was only two inches wide and each hind foot rested in a shallow trench to one side of the mouth. The approach of two observers did not disturb the layer, which produced thirteen more of her total of nineteen eggs at an average rate of one every forty-six seconds. After the appearance of each egg, first one hind foot and then the other was extended into the hole, presumably to arrange the eggs. When deposition had been completed, she filled the hole and tamped the soil down smoothly enough to obliterate almost all evidence of disturbance. These finishing touches took twenty-nine minutes. The nineteen eggs weighed almost one-fourteenth as much as the spent turtle.

Exactly a month later in the same field and one hundred and fifty yards from the lake another turtle, surprised after laying six eggs, lost her nerve and fled.

Fifteen eggs of the first and all six of the second lot were removed and buried in a similar place and at the same depth as when found. On the night of July 8 five of the first and two of the second cluster hatched, the others having been previously opened for examination.

Average soil temperatures from February 8 to July 8, correlated with observations of the stages of development, give pretty conclusive evidence of the dependence of rate of development on temperature, as the following summary shows:

February 8 to March 23: average soil temperature about 61° F.;
  little or no development in the eggs examined on latter date.

March 23 to May 21: average soil temperature 74° F.; marked
  development, embryo from first set 15, one from second set
  10 mm. long.

May 21 to July 8: average soil temperature had risen steadily to
  a maximum average of 88° F. for the first week of July; rapid
  development in all the eggs until the hatching climax on
  July 8, which was the hottest day on record since February 8.

Although the reason for the same hatching date of the two
clutches is not apparent, there is little doubt that temperature
much below 70° F. is not favourable for development.

C. C. and D. S. Goff made this study of development in the
Peninsular Turtle.

RIVER TURTLE

Pseudemys floridana concinna (Le Conte)

[PLATES 64, 65, AND 66]

IDENTIFICATION. The ridge extending along the middle of
the crushing surface of the upper jaw is high and strongly
toothed. This jaw is not or only barely serrate and has no
notch nor teeth near its tip. There is a tooth at the tip of the
lower jaw. The lines on the top and sides of the head are usually unbroken, and, as a rule, there is no vertical stripe across
the ear. In the region above the ears, the lines between the pair
extending along the upper temporal regions are noticeably unequal in breadth, two pairs (and sometimes the median line)
standing out conspicuously among the remaining narrower to
obsolescent ones. A more or less extensive dusky figure is evi-

dent on the plastron. The soft parts are light to dark brown, with yellow or orange or occasionally reddish lines, and the brown carapace usually has extensive light markings.

SIZE. A carapace length of nine inches has been recorded for the male, of twelve for the female. The female with the twelve-inch carapace weighed six and a half pounds.

MOULT. The horny shields are apparently cast off periodically and therefore concentric growth rings do not appear on the growing shell.

DISTRIBUTION. The Piedmont Plateau and Appalachian Valley from northern Georgia and eastern Tennessee through northeastern Virginia.

HABITS. There is virtually no definite information on the habits of this highland turtle other than the fact that it inhabits ponds and rivers and eats algæ (contents of one stomach).

MOBILE TURTLE

Pseudemys floridana mobilensis (Holbrook)

IDENTIFICATION. The strongly serrate edge of the upper jaw in the Mobile Turtle serves most readily to distinguish it from its close relative, the River Turtle. The former also has a higher shell.

There are some lines on the outer surface of the hind limb, four or more on this part of the forelimb, and usually seven or more between the eyes — points in which it differs from the Suwannee Turtle.

SIZE. The carapace of one adult was 8.86 inches long by 5.90 wide.

YOUNG. The carapace in Agassiz's illustration of a very young individual is 39 millimetres long by 40.5 wide.

59. Feeding time for species of pseudemyd turtles (*Pseudemys*) in the Florida Reptile Institute, Silver Springs, Florida. Three and three-fourths bushels of Sagittaria were consumed within twenty-four hours by 105 pseudemyd turtles confined in this pen. (*Photograph by E. Ross Allen.*)

60. Florida Turtle (*Pseudemys floridana floridana*) from the region of Columbia, South Carolina. The long claws of the forelimb prove that this is a male. The carapace is 6.19 inches long. (*Courtesy Zoological Society of Philadelphia, photograph by Mark Mooney, Jr.*)

61. Florida Turtle (*Pseudemys floridana floridana*) from the region of Columbia, South Carolina. The carapace of this male is 6.19 inches long. (*Courtesy Zoological Society of Philadelphia, photograph by Mark Mooney, Jr.*)

62. Peninsular Turtle (*Pseudemys floridana peninsularis*) from Marion County, Florida. This large female has a carapace 12.25 inches long. Some of the pattern can be made out where the plant growth has been scraped off. (*Courtesy Zoological Society of Philadelphia, photograph by Mark Mooney, Jr.*)

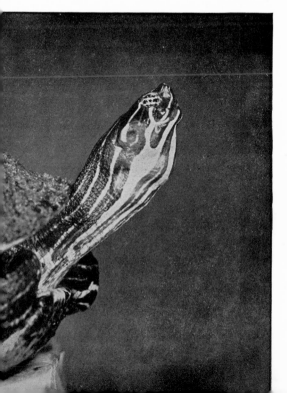

63. Peninsular Turtle (*Pseudemys floridana peninsularis*) from Marion County, Florida. The carapace of this female is 12.25 inches long. (*Courtesy Zoological Society of Philadelphia, photograph by Mark Mooney, Jr.*)

64. River Turtle (*Pseudemys floridana concinna*) with a carapace 4.94 inches long. It is a female. (*Courtesy Zoological Society of Philadelphia, photograph by Mark Mooney, Jr.*)

65–66. River Turtle (*Pseudemys floridana concinna*) with a carapace 4.94 inches long. It is a female. (*Courtesy Zoological Society of Philadelphia, photograph by Mark Mooney, Jr.*)

EGG. Agassiz figures an elliptical egg measuring 43 × 25.5 millimetres. The shell is white.

DISTRIBUTION. The Gulf Coastal Plain from Apalachicola Bay, northwestern Florida, westward into eastern Texas and northward in the Mississippi Valley to northern Louisiana.

HABITAT. Bayous and lagoons and adjacent larger bodies of water.

REPRODUCTION. The turtle dissected by Agassiz on July 12 with twelve eggs in the oviducts is presumably this form. His specimen is listed as being from Natchez, Mississippi, and as having been kept in confinement.

CAPTIVITY. Rust recommends conditions and food similar to those of the Red-bellied Turtle.

ECONOMIC VALUE. An esteemed article of diet, especially in Mobile and New Orleans.

SUWANNEE TURTLE

Pseudemys floridana suwanniensis Carr

[PLATES 67 AND 68]

IDENTIFICATION. The extensive sooty black ground colour of the carapace and soft parts and a corresponding reduction of markings distinguish this subspecies from its close relatives, the River and Mobile Turtles. The Suwannee Turtle has no lines on the outer surface of the hind limb, only two or three on this part of the forelimb, and five between the eyes.

The edge of the upper jaw, like that of the River Turtle, is at most only feebly serrate, whereas the shell is about like that of the Mobile Turtle in degree of elevation.

SIZE. The measurements of the type specimen, a male, follow:

	Inches	Millimetres
Length of carapace	9.92	252
Width of carapace	7.36	187
Height of shell	3.23	82

The carapace of the largest male examined by the describer of this subspecies was 11.10, that of the largest female 16.38 inches long.

THE SEXES. Considerable sexual difference in size is indicated by the measurements given under the discussion of size.

DISTRIBUTION. The Gulf drainage of northern Florida from Crystal River, Citrus County, northwestward to Apalachicola Bay; south in the Withlacoochee drainage to Lake Panasoffkee, Sumter County, and east in the Suwannee drainage to Santa Fe Lake, Alachua and Bradford Counties.

HABITAT. The Suwannee Turtle "attains its maximum abundance in two distinct habitats, the clear calcareous streams of the west coast, and the shallow vegetated flats adjacent to the mouths of these streams."

FOOD AND FEEDING. Literally hundreds may be seen eating water-weed in Levy County, where the waters of Manatee Springs empty into the Suwannee River. At other times they are just as numerous on the eel-grass flats off the mouth of Suwannee Sound.

ECONOMIC VALUE. The people living along the Suwannee River relish this turtle, giving it the complimentary title "Suwannee chicken." The flavour of the meat is said to be equal to that of the Diamond-back of the Atlantic coast. One fisherman put it thus: "The Suwannee chicken eats a hell of a sight better than the Mobilian," or Mobile Turtle. It is indeed interesting that these subspecies may be distinguished gastronomically.

Dr. A. F. Carr, Jr., the describer of this form, has supplied all the foregoing information.

HIEROGLYPHIC TURTLE
Pseudemys floridana hieroglyphica (Holbrook)

IDENTIFICATION. The ridge extending along the middle of the crushing surface of the upper jaw is high and strongly toothed. This jaw usually has a slight to strong notch at its tip, which, however, is never flanked by teeth. A tooth is present at the tip of the lower jaw. The lines on the side of the head usually are not broken to form short bars and spots, and there is, as a rule, no vertical stripe across the ear. On the other hand, many of the numerous lines on the top of the head are discontinuous and connected behind by one to many straight or crescent-shaped transverse bars. Usually eight or more of the lines between the pair extending along the upper temporal regions are about equal in breadth. The very light plastron generally has a more or less complete dusky branching pattern, and the low carapace is flattened.

SIZE. The measurements of an adult female from southern Illinois follow:

	Inches	Millimetres
Length of carapace	12.99	330
Width of carapace	8.50	216
Length of plastron	11.53	293
Width of plastron	6.73	171
Height of shell	4.21	107
Weight	133.8 ounces	

A carapace length of 14.75 inches is often attained.

YOUNG. The carapace of very young individuals is distinctly keeled and about as wide as long. The smallest carapace on record measured 39 millimetres long.

THE SEXES. The longest claws of the male forelimb are two to three times as long as its hind-limb claws or any of the fe-

male's claws. The tail is longer in the male, the anus lying beyond the edge of the carapace when the tail is extended.

EGG. Fully developed eggs taken from a western Tennessee
female were found by Cahn to average 37.6 × 26.1 millimetres
in greater and lesser diameters. The shell was white and hard.

DISTRIBUTION. From central Tennessee, western Kentucky,
the southwestern tip of Indiana, and the adjacent extremity of
Illinois westward to Woodson County, southeastern Kansas,
and southwestward to central Texas. The exact distribution
of this subspecies in Texas has not been worked out; it has,
however, been taken as far to the northwest as Wilbarger
County.

HABITAT. Shallow lakes and bays of big ones, and backwaters and bays of large rivers, are frequented by this decidedly aquatic turtle. A soft bottom supporting an abundance
of aquatic vegetation makes the most congenial haunt for it.

HABITS. It is exceedingly shy and wary, remaining constantly on the look-out for danger while indulging in sun bathing, a favourite pastime. Floating at the surface is another way
in which many hours are spent, but only when the water's
surface is quiet. It is a good swimmer.

On land it moves slowly and awkwardly and, when over-
taken, withdraws into the shell instead of attempting any active form of defence.

REPRODUCTION. The nests are made in sandy places near
water. Early June is the laying season in western Tennessee.
Nine eggs with shells already deposited on them were found
in one female.

FOOD. The above information on habitat, habits, and reproduction is taken from Cahn's account of the Hieroglyphic
Turtle, and the following data on its feeding are quoted directly from this same source:

"This species is largely carnivorous in its diet, feeding upon
almost any animal matter that is available. From the stomachs

67. Suwannee Turtle (*Pseudemys floridana suwanniensis*) from Marion County, Florida. The carapace is 10 inches long, the sex male. (*Courtesy Zoological Society of Philadelphia, photograph by Mark Mooney, Jr.*)

68. Suwannee Turtle (*Pseudemys floridana suwanniensis*) from Marion County, Florida. It is a male with carapace 10 inches long. (*Courtesy Zoological Society of Philadelphia, photograph by Mark Mooney, Jr.*)

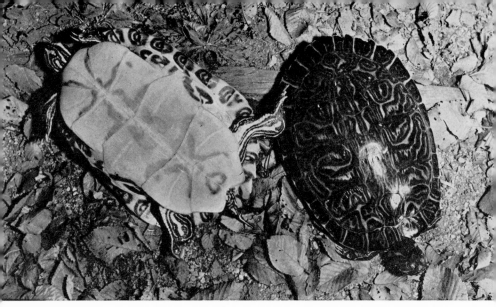

69. Hieroglyphic Turtles (*Pseudemys floridana hieroglyphica*) from Reelfoot Lake, Tennessee. Two females are shown, the carapace of the larger 10.62 inches long, that of the other only one-seventh of an inch shorter. (*Courtesy Zoological Society of Philadelphia, photograph by Mark Mooney, Jr.*)

70. Hieroglyphic Turtle (*Pseudemys floridana hieroglyphica*) from Reelfoot Lake, Tennessee. The carapace of this female is about 10.50 inches long. (*Courtesy Zoological Society of Philadelphia, photograph by Mark Mooney, Jr.*)

71 [TOP]. Red-bellied Turtle (*Pseudemys rubriventris rubriventris*) from Burlington County, New Jersey. The carapace of this dark male is 6.37 inches long.

72 [CENTRE]. Red-bellied Turtle (*Pseudemys rubriventris rubriventris*) from Burlington County, New Jersey, with a carapace 4.72 inches long.

73 [BOTTOM]. Red-bellied Turtles (*Pseudemys rubriventris rubriventris*), from Burlington County, New Jersey, showing reduction of plastral pattern with maturity.

(*Courtesy Zoological Society of Philadelphia, photographs by Mark Mooney, Jr.*)

75. Florida Red-bellied Turtle (*Pseudemys nelsoni*) from Gainesville, Florida, showing its serrate lower jaw and the " teeth " and notches of both jaws. The carapace of this female is 11.87 inches long. (*Courtesy Zoological Society of Philadelphia, photograph by Mark Mooney, Jr.*)

of specimens examined in the field the following items have been noted: crayfish, tadpoles, small fish, gastropods, dragonfly nymphs, corydalis larvæ, water beetles, and an assortment of forms obviously picked from the surface, including grasshoppers, crickets, caterpillars, and various dipterous and hymenopterous insects. The scavenger habit is well developed and I have observed the turtles feeding upon dead fish floating at the surface. They do not, however, practice this scavenger habit along the shore. Some vegetable matter is usually present in the digestive system, this representing aquatic sedges, algæ, and numerous shallow-water plant species."

TEXAS TURTLE

Pseudemys floridana texana Baur

IDENTIFICATION. The ridge extending along the middle of the crushing surface of the upper jaw is high and bears very long teeth. The notch at the tip of this jaw is flanked on either side by a tooth, and the lower jaw has a tooth-like projection on both sides of the prominent tooth at its tip. Some of the very numerous lines on the side of the head are broken to form short bars and spots. A vertical extension of the stripe from the eye to the lower jaw often passes across the ear.

DISTRIBUTION. Southwestern Texas and northern Mexico.

This subspecies ranges westward in Texas to the Pecos River and Guadalupe Mountains. The area of intergradation between it and the Mobile Turtle has not been delimited.

HABITAT. Rivers, creeks, and tanks.

FOOD. Strecker was of the opinion that the Texas Turtle subsists largely on snails.

RED–BELLIED TURTLE

Pseudemys rubriventris rubriventris (Le Conte)

[PLATES 71, 72, AND 73]

IDENTIFICATION. The ridge extending along the middle of the crushing surface of the upper jaw is high and strongly toothed. The notch at the tip of this jaw is flanked on either side by a prominent tooth, and the lower jaw is strongly serrate with a long tooth on either side of the prominent one at its tip. The stripes of the head are not interrupted to form bars and spots. The low carapace is depressed along the median line, and its vertebral shields are concave or flat. As a rule the markings on the lower parts of the marginal shields are either concentric or with light centres. Both common and scientific names refer to the red colour of the plastron.

SIZE. Eleven to twelve inches is the usual adult carapace length of the Red-bellied Turtle, although the form is reported to reach an extreme length of sixteen or even eighteen inches. Brimley gives the carapace length and width and the shell height of a Florida specimen as 9.64, 6.57, and 4.33 inches, respectively.

YOUNG. The young specimen (carapace 32.5 × 32.5 mm.) illustrated by Agassiz has a grey carapace profusely decorated with "hieroglyphic ocelli and curved lines"; a yellow plastron washed centrally with red and having several black blotches widely distributed over its surface (see Plate 73). The young and old are said to be less brilliantly coloured than those of intermediate age.

THE SEXES. The longest claws on the male forelimb are at least twice as long as its hind-limb claws or the forelimb claws of the female. The female attains a greater size. Smith states that the male has a flat plastron, whereas that of the female is convex.

EGG. The elliptical eggs of this turtle vary considerably in size. Smith writes that their average dimensions are 25 × 19 millimetres, but Conant and Bailey found twelve eggs laid by a New Jersey female to range in greater diameter from 34 to 37 millimetres. The shell is white.

DISTRIBUTION. Atlantic Coastal Plain from northern North Carolina to central New Jersey.

Records of the last century indicate that this turtle once inhabited extreme southeastern New York, but those of the last thirty-five years or so carry its range northward only to Toms River (Ocean County) and Milford (Hunterdon County), New Jersey. It was formerly abundant at least as far up the Delaware River as Trenton. Its present scarcity in New Jersey is due entirely to its commercial value. To the west the Red-bellied Turtle has been taken as high up the Potomac as Harpers Ferry, West Virginia. Reports of its occurrence as far south as central South Carolina require confirmation.

HABITAT. Found in streams, rivers, marshes, ponds, and lakes. It sometimes enters brackish water.

HABITS. This species is a good swimmer and fond of rather deep water. It is shy, alert, and active, hisses when annoyed, and has the reputation of being snappy. Captive specimens readily become tame, however. The sunning habit is well developed, banks and various projecting objects being used.

In the Potomac River, below Washington, D.C., many individuals have been known to congregate on shallow bars for hibernation.

REPRODUCTION. The only detailed account of the laying of this turtle is by Smith, who made observations in the region of Washington, D.C., and brings out the following points:

The eggs are laid in June or July. Cultivated land such as a cornfield adjoining the water is usually chosen unless a high steep bank necessitates deposition on shore above high-water line. Nests are made in sand, clay, or loam, most frequently in a sandy clay or loam. Many are often found in a small area and each is shaped like a carafe, with an average total depth as well as an average width at the bottom of four inches.

Three points in Smith's account call for confirmation. He is almost certainly wrong in saying that the digging is done with the forelimbs, and his statement that the female accomplishes the final packing by repeatedly raising her body up and dropping down is certainly interesting. The third point is in regard to the alleged abandoning of the partly completed nest by an alarmed female. Most turtles are not easily driven away once the nesting process is well begun.

He believes that the young hatch during the summer, but spend the winter in the nest, appearing the following April. Probably, however, this occurs only in cases of very late laying.

A New Jersey female caught on June 26 laid six eggs on July 21 and twelve more on August 10. She buried them about four inches deep.

FOOD. The species is said to have omnivorous feeding habits. (See remarks under the treatment of captivity below.)

ENEMIES. A crow has been seen to watch a laying female until her disappearance after completion of her nest and then fly down, dig up the eggs, and start eating them. As shown below, man himself is a major enemy.

CAPTIVITY. This species lives well in captivity, becomes very tame, and ravenously eats fish, earthworms, and various small aquatic animals, such as tadpoles and snails and even water plants. Raw meat should also be relished. Food is preferably swallowed under water.

It ought to be kept in an aquarium and provided with sunning- and hiding-places.

ECONOMIC VALUE. The Red-bellied Turtle (or "Terrapin,"

as it is often called) has long served as an inferior substitute for the Diamond-back Terrapin.

The former once supported a profitable fishing industry between Washington, D.C., and the sea, where in 1883 no fewer than two hundred and forty individuals, apparently assembled for hibernation, were taken in one haul of a seine.

PLYMOUTH TURTLE

Pseudemys rubriventris bangsi Babcock

IDENTIFICATION. This isolated colony of *Pseudemys rubriventris* designated as *bangsi* is described as having a high carapace. In the Red-bellied Turtle its greatest length is usually more than two and one-half times the greatest height of the shell, whereas in the Plymouth Turtle the length is usually less than two and one-half times the height.

For ordinary purposes the two can be considered identical or else specimens may be named on geographical evidence alone.

SIZE. The average adult carapace length is ten to twelve inches. A male with a carapace 11.37 inches long is on record.

DISTRIBUTION. Plymouth County, Massachusetts.

HABITAT AND HABITS. Ponds of various sizes. Boot Pond, for example, with an area of seventy-four acres and a maximum depth of thirty-one feet, is the type locality of this subspecies. Except for breeding a little later and hibernating somewhat longer, this turtle probably has habits identical with those of the Red-bellied Turtle.

FLORIDA RED–BELLIED TURTLE

Pseudemys nelsoni Carr

[PLATES 74, 75, AND 76]

IDENTIFICATION. The ridge extending along the middle of the crushing surface of the upper jaw is high and strongly toothed. The notch at the tip of this jaw is flanked on either side by a prominent tooth, and the lower jaw is strongly serrate, with a long tooth on either side of the prominent one at its tip. The stripes along the head are not interrupted to form bars and spots, and number about four to six, counting from the lower edge of one ear over the head to the corresponding edge of the other ear. The high carapace is elevated along the median line and its vertebral shields are convex. The ground colour of the soft parts and carapace is sooty black. The upper part of each marginal shield has one or two inconspicuous light vertical or longitudinal bars, and the markings on the lower parts of these shields are solid and smudge-like.

SIZE. Measurements of the type specimen, a female, follow:

	Inches	Millimetres
Length of carapace	11.02	280
Width of carapace	7.87	200
Height of shell	5.08	129

DISTRIBUTION. Peninsular Florida.

HABITAT AND HABITS. Common in lakes, ponds, rivers, and streams. Nothing is known of the habits of the species. Its close relationship to the Red-bellied Turtle suggests, but by no means proves, similarity in habits.

ALABAMA TURTLE

Pseudemys alabamensis Baur

IDENTIFICATION. The ridge extending along the middle of the crushing surface of the upper jaw is high and strongly toothed. The notch at the tip of this jaw is flanked on either side by a prominent tooth, and the lower jaw is strongly serrate, with a long tooth on either side of the prominent one at its tip. The stripes of the head are not interrupted to form bars and spots, and number about thirteen to seventeen, counting from the lower edge of one ear over the head to the corresponding edge of the other ear. Usually the carapace is elevated anteriorly and it is not as a rule depressed along the vertebral line. The ground colour of the soft parts and carapace is light to dark brown, and the upper parts of the marginals have concentric figures.

DISTRIBUTION. Gulf coastal strip from Citrus County, Florida, to Louisiana.

HABITAT AND HABITS. Apparently the Alabama Turtle frequents brackish marshes. Almost nothing is recorded about the habits of this species except that, in captivity, it will eat water plants. It has considerable economic value as food for man.

YELLOW–BELLIED TURTLE

Pseudemys scripta scripta (Schoepff)

[PLATES 77 AND 78]

IDENTIFICATION. The ridge extending along the middle of the crushing surface of the upper jaw is smooth or only slightly serrate. The notch at the front of the upper jaw is not flanked on either side by a projection, and the edges of both jaws are smooth. There is a conspicuous oblong or triangular yellow spot behind the eye. The carapace is usually keeled and has brown or black markings and yellow stripes. Each marginal is crossed by a median yellow band. The yellow or brownish plastron has a pair of black smudge-like spots on the gular shields and often another pair on the humerals; occasionally additional shields bear similar spots.

SIZE. In 1907 Brimley wrote that the largest specimen he had ever seen measured 10.71 inches and weighed seven and a half pounds, but two years later he recorded one weighing eight and a half pounds as the largest encountered in Craven County, North Carolina.

YOUNG. Very young individuals have more strongly contrasted colours than the adults, and are about as wide as long (27 × 27 mm. in one case). They possess at least some of the characters seen in both young and old Troost's Turtles but not found in adult Yellow-bellied Turtles. For instance, the plastral spots have a tendency to appear as ocelli or figures composed of concentric rings. This similarity of Yellow-bellied juveniles to Troost's Turtles of all ages shows the close relationship between these two subspecies and indicates that the latter is the more primitive and generalized of the two.

MOULT. According to Agassiz, this turtle periodically sheds its epidermal shields. Consequently concentric rings indicating successive growth stages do not appear on the shell, and age-determination is difficult.

DISTRIBUTION. The southeastern Coastal Plain from eastern North Carolina to southeastern Alabama and through northern Florida. This turtle has also been taken in the Piedmont region of North Carolina at Greensboro.

Intergradation with Troost's Turtle apparently takes place from the Piedmont Plateau of northern central Georgia south-

74. Florida Red-bellied Turtle (*Pseudemys nelsoni*) from Gainesville, Florida. The carapace of this female is 11.87 inches long. (*Courtesy Zoological Society of Philadelphia, photograph by Mark Mooney, Jr.*)

76. Florida Red-bellied Turtle (*Pseudemys nelsoni*) from Gainesville, Florida. The carapace of this female is 11.87 inches long. (*Courtesy Zoological Society of Philadelphia, photograph by Mark Mooney, Jr.*)

77. Yellow-bellied Turtle (*Pseudemys scripta scripta*) from Madison County, Florida, with a carapace 3.56 inches long. (*Courtesy Zoological Society of Philadelphia, photograph by Mark Mooney, Jr.*)

78. Yellow-bellied Turtle (*Pseudemys scripta scripta*) from Madison County, Florida, with a carapace 3.56 inches long. (*Courtesy Zoological Society of Philadelphia, photograph by Mark Mooney, Jr.*)

ward to northern Florida, thence westward to southeastern Louisiana (Carr, 1937). The southern extremity of the Appalachian Mountains seems to separate completely the ranges of Troost's and the Yellow-bellied Turtles northeastward from northern Georgia, the former having been found only as far east as Union County, eastern Tennessee, and Bell and Harlan Counties, southeastern Kentucky.

HABITAT AND HABITS. The few observations on the Yellow-bellied Turtle do not indicate any essential difference in habitat preference and general habits between it and Troost's Turtle.

REPRODUCTION. A female that had just been digging a nest was taken in Craven County, eastern North Carolina, on May 24. It is not surprising to learn that this southeastern Coastal Plain form lays rather early.

FOOD. The catholic appetite of captives indicates rather omnivorous feeding habits. Studies of its food in nature are lacking.

A strong suggestion of scavenger tendencies is found in Brimley's observation that a marked increase in the Yellow-bellied population about Raleigh, North Carolina, followed pollution of local waters by city sewage and dye-works refuse.

ENEMIES. Many broken eggs seen in eastern North Carolina many years ago testified to the destruction of nests by egg-loving animals, probably raccoons.

CAPTIVITY. The record longevity of the Yellow-bellied Turtle for the London Zoological Gardens is six years ten months; for the National Zoological Park, Washington, seven years one month. These figures testify to the hardiness of this subspecies in captivity. It may be kept under conditions similar to those recommended for Troost's Turtle and given the same kinds of food.

ECONOMIC VALUE. Eaten locally and sold in southern markets.

TROOST'S TURTLE
Pseudemys scripta troostii (Holbrook)

[PLATES 79, 80, AND 81]

IDENTIFICATION. The following characters distinguish this subspecies from its close relative, the Yellow-bellied Turtle:

The side of the head has three to seven stripes extending backward from the hind margin of the eye, the uppermost one often including an ovate blood-red expansion.

All or at least most of the shields of the yellow plastron have one or more dark spots.

The carapace, usually without a keel, is smoother, more elongate, and more depressed than that of the other form.

The melanistic males of Troost's Turtle, formerly thought to represent a distinct species, are described under the discussion of the sexes.

SIZE. Viosca found the carapaces of the largest male and female among two hundred and twenty-five Louisiana individuals four or more inches in length to measure 7.5 and 8.5 inches, respectively. The carapace of the biggest male in Cahn's measurements of Illinois specimens is 8.54, that of the biggest female 9.57 inches long; the total weights 42.8 and 71.8 ounces, respectively. Although somewhat larger dimensions (260 mm. plastron length) have been recorded, the above figures give the best idea of the greatest sizes that will be encountered ordinarily.

Measurements of a female of moderate size from Illinois follow:

	Inches	Millimetres
Length of carapace	7.87	200
Width of carapace	6.06	154
Length of plastron	7.28	185
Width of plastron	4.72	120
Height of shell	2.87	73

YOUNG. In very small individuals the conspicuously keeled carapace is about as wide as long (approximately 30 mm.). It is bright green, and all the shields are marked with fine parallel black lines arranged in bands or forming concentric figures. The yellow stripes of the adult are evident on the costals. The head markings, especially the ovate blood-red expansion of the uppermost lateral stripe, are very conspicuous (see Plate 81).

THE SEXES. The larger size attained by the female is shown by the figures given under the discussion of size. When the tail is extended, the anus of the male lies beyond the hind edge of the carapace, whereas in the female it lies below or in front of this edge. The longest claws on the male forelimb are at least twice as long as its hind-limb claws or the forelimb claws of the female. A male with an 8.5-inch carapace may have claws 0.87 inches long.

At least some of the large males of this species exhibit a strong melanistic tendency, or a general darkening of their lighter colours (see Plates 79 and 80). For many years these dark males were recognized as a distinct species, and not until Viosca showed that no females or very young existed among melanistic specimens did their correct status become generally recognized. In extreme cases the carapace and head markings almost if not entirely disappear and even the light colour of the plastron becomes largely obscured by the dark brown which spreads from the plastral sutures, where it first appears.

Viosca seems to be of the opinion that all males become melanistic, the tendency to do so exhibiting itself first when a carapace length of five and a half inches is reached, but Cahn, who records non-melanistic males 7.68 inches long, believes that the matter is not so simple and calls for further investigation.

The relatively rare melanistic males long masqueraded under the scientific name " *troostii*," while the abundant juveniles and females were well known as "*elegans*." The whole lot must now be called *troostii* because that term, although much less familiar, has priority over *elegans*. Such are the exigencies of scientific nomenclature.

EGG. The elliptical eggs of this subspecies vary considerably in size and shape. For instance, Cahn gives the average dimensions of one hundred and twenty-one eggs from seven Illinois sets as 37 × 22 millimetres, whereas, in extreme northwestern Tennessee, Cagle found seven eggs, each from a different nest, to range from 40 to 45 and from 20 to 23 millimetres in greater and lesser diameters, respectively.

GROWTH. In 1927 Grant bought a pair of Troost's Turtles at a pet-shop when they were about the size of a fifty-cent piece (30 mm.). By 1935 or 1936 (Grant does not make his dates clear) the female weighed three and a quarter pounds and had a carapace eight inches long. The preceding year she had been courted by the male and laid fertile eggs. Apparently, then, this pair of turtles, which, since infancy, had lived outdoors at San Diego, California, in semi-captivity, bred during their seventh, eighth, or ninth year. Now, Cahn concluded that females become sexually mature when seven to seven and a half inches long, so Grant's female may not have bred at her first season of maturity. These figures suggest that the female Troost's Turtle requires at least six but not more than eight years to reach maturity, and they also give some idea of its rate of growth.

MOULT. The remark under the Yellow-bellied Turtle applies to this form as well, as both were included in Agassiz's observations on moult.

DISTRIBUTION. From southern Ohio, Indiana, Illinois, southeastern Iowa, Missouri, and a little more than the eastern half of Kansas southward through Texas, northwestern Florida, and the other Gulf states.

In Texas it ranges about as far west as Pecos, near which intergradation with the Rio Grande Turtle is known to occur. Intergrades have also been found in Cameron and Victoria Counties, although those from the latter are nearly typical Troost's Turtle. To the west there is a record for Mora County, northeastern New Mexico, and Agassiz recorded it from the Yellowstone River, a stray record that has not been substantiated. Northern Illinois and Indiana mark the limits of its range to the north; Pickaway and Ross are the only counties of Ohio in which it has been found.

The question of intergradation with the Yellow-bellied Turtle of the southeast is considered under that form.

HABITAT. This is a thoroughly aquatic reptile, inhabiting ponds, lakes, rivers, streams, and large permanent springs. Having a distinct preference for quiet water and muddy, plant-grown bottoms, it is especially common in swamp, slough, and bayou of lake and river. Shallow as well as deep water is frequented, but swift currents are avoided. Very young individuals, however, shun deep water.

HABITS. At most only half-hearted attempts at biting are made by wild individuals caught away from water, because this turtle depends chiefly on its shell for protection when surprised out of its native element. In river or pond it is shy and ever ready to conceal itself in the dense aquatic vegetation which it likes so well. Cahn, however, detected a strain of pugnacity correlated with melanism. (See the discussion of melanism under the account of the sexes above.)

The sunning habit is well developed, great numbers often coming out together on logs or other projecting objects.

There are frequent rather puzzling references to the " piping " notes of various kinds of chelonians, the present form among them. A confined Troost's Turtle was heard by Cahn to whistle repeatedly for three days before suddenly " turning turtle." Dissection showed that a foreign object lodged in the trachea had produced the sound, so here at least is a possible explanation of piping turtles!

MATING. The astonishing subaqueous courtship of Troost's Turtle has been recorded by three herpetologists, but the performers were always captive. Probably the act as witnessed was essentially normal. A composite description follows:

The male places himself in front of the female so that his outstretched forelimbs, their palms turned outward, can just reach her face. He then proceeds to vibrate his long nails against her chin and lores like a hypnotist. The vibrations are kept up for only a second or two at a time, but are repeated at frequent intervals. The male maintains his position by swimming either backward or forward, and the female is described as remaining quite unconcerned. Several males may simultaneously pay court to the same lady in spite of her total lack of interest.

These antics have been observed in March, May, and October, but, since the performers were captive, confirmation of the dates is required.

Some indication of the period that elapses between mating and laying may be had from the case of a captive pair kept by Grant in southern California. The male courted from early in March until the 25th, and laying took place on April 8, the eggs later proving to be fertile.

NESTING. The laying season in western Tennessee extends at least throughout June and July, whereas in Illinois it is reported to be shorter, not beginning until the third or fourth week in June and ending early in July. The nests are made either early in the morning or late in the afternoon, only rarely during the middle of the day.

The site chosen for the nest is usually in an open, sandy area near the water. However, a spot four hundred feet from the nearest pond and one hundred and seventy-five above it was chosen by a colony of Arkansas turtles found by Taylor.

Forty-seven nests examined in western Tennessee contained from 5 to 22 eggs each and averaged 10.5. Cahn, on the other hand, gives the average number for nests of fully mature females as 15 to 18, maintaining that smaller nests with only 6 to 8 are the work of young individuals. Probably persecution by man is an important factor in reducing the number of eggs per nest; the turtle-collector by constantly catching the older females throws the responsibility on the young individuals.

The best description of nest construction and oviposition is by Cagle, who observed numerous turtles in western Tennessee. His account follows:

" The turtle crawls out of the water and seeks an elevated ridge that will insure good drainage. An open area somewhat protected by weeds but exposed to the direct rays of the sun is most often chosen. In the egg-laying season the ground is usually dry and hard; however, the turtle is prepared for this. The bladder and cloaca are distended with water to be used in softening the ground. A portion of the water is released at the chosen spot. In some cases an area of two feet is wet. While the water is soaking into the dry soil, the turtle assumes her digging position. The front feet are braced against weeds, rocks, or any other convenient support, and the back of the carapace is placed over the place to be excavated. Unlike most animals, the turtle uses the rear limbs for digging. Beginning with one of the hind legs, she tests the soil with a sideward, scraping motion of the leg. If it is too hard for comfortable digging, more water is released until the soil is softened. The scraping movements of the hind leg are renewed until a shallow hole has been formed. The turtle then shifts to the other leg and digs. The process is an awkward one and the turtle seems to tire easily. She rests at frequent intervals, lifting her head to watch for possible enemies and changing her position in order to use the other leg. The carapace rubs on the opposite side to the digging leg, making a long depression in the soil. The hind limbs are moved in a half circle, each scraping movement removing a small quantity of dirt.

" After a small hole one inch or slightly more in depth has been formed, the character of the movements change. The turtle has to strain every muscle to dig the nest. Ceasing to enlarge the first opening, she hollows out a jug-shaped cavity below the opening, measuring from three to ten inches in diameter. The left foot is used in digging out the left portion of the nest and the right foot in enlarging the right side. If the turtle is disturbed while she is building her nest, she stops work and remains perfectly quiet until she locates the source of the disturbance. If she senses danger, she leaves the partially constructed nest and flees cumbrously to the water. No turtles were observed returning to a partially completed nest.

" Having completed the excavation of her nest, the turtle removes all excess dirt particles by carefully lifting them out with the hind legs. The author has never observed a turtle using either of her front legs to dig or seal a nest. The eggs are deposited within a few minutes. One turtle was observed moving the eggs about with her foot. Others made no effort to place the eggs in any definite position. Eggs in the nests examined were laid haphazardly in all positions, some horizontally, some vertically.

" The soil that had been removed was packed about the opening to the nest. Although the dirt was already quite wet, the turtle dampened it thoroughly and began to work it over the top of the nest, forming a plug of moist earth. All the loose material was gathered in and padded into place over the entrance and for several inches around it. This layer of mud may be one-half inch to two and one-half inches thick. The back portion of the carapace and the hind feet were used in

79. Troost's Turtles (*Pseudemys scripta troostii*) from Reelfoot Lake, Tennessee. The dark male without pattern strongly contrasts with the gaily striped female. The carapace of the former is 8.25, that of the latter 9 inches long. The long claws of the male are evident. (*Courtesy Zoological Society of Philadelphia, photograph by Mark Mooney, Jr.*)

80. Troost's Turtles (*Pseudemys scripta troostii*) from Reelfoot Lake, Tennessee. The almost entirely black plastron of the male (carapace length 8.25 inches) strongly contrasts with the spotted one of the female, whose carapace is just 9 inches long. (*Courtesy Zoological Society of Philadelphia, photograph by Mark Mooney, Jr.*)

81. Young Troost's Turtle (*Pseudemys scripta troostii*) showing the ovate blood-red expansion of the uppermost lateral stripe extending backward from the eye. The expansion is rather dark in the photograph. (*Courtesy Zoological Society of Philadelphia, photograph by Mark Mooney, Jr.*)

padding the final covering into place. Without a single glance of inspection at her nest, the turtle sidled away through the weeds apparently satisfied with the ability of her posterior working tools."

The finished nest is a jug-shaped hole well sealed above by the closely packed plug of mud, which probably helps to keep the temperature and moisture content of the nest uniform. At least Cagle found that the temperature range in a few nests checked over a period of seven days did not exceed 14.4° F.

According to Cahn, actual physical violence is necessary to cause a female to desert her nest once she has begun to lay. When disturbed slightly, she retires into her shell and suspends action until the annoyance has ceased.

INCREASED ILLUMINATION AND SEXUAL CYCLES. Work in recent years has shown that seasonal changes in the length of daylight or artificially increased periods of illumination affect the sexual cycles in many warm-blooded vertebrate animals living in non-tropical regions. Changes in these cycles may have profound effects on the behaviour of the species. In birds, for example, the initiation of a new cycle starts migration. Recent experiments by Burger on Troost's Turtle indicate that gradually lengthening the periods of illumination affects its sexual cycles, so here we have the first clue to what may prove to be a controlling factor in seasonal breeding activity of this and other turtles. The study of reptile habits is yet in its infancy.

FOOD. This is a largely carnivorous reptile, which eats aquatic forms of big insects, mollusks (especially snails), crayfish, tadpoles, various kinds of small fishes, and a variety of water plants. It is also something of a scavenger, consuming dead animals found in the water.

ENEMIES. Man is the greatest enemy of this turtle, for he not only eats the adults and catches vast numbers of young for the pet-trade but, at least at Reelfoot Lake, Tennessee, uses countless thousands of eggs as fish-bait. In spite of this, Troost's Turtle is a common species in many regions.

But man is only one of the many mammals that digs the eggs; he is certainly, however, the only one that gives them to fish instead of devouring them outright! Raccoons and skunks do their share in keeping down the turtle birth rate.

Moulds, fly larvæ, and possibly ants destroy a small percentage of eggs; still others are spoiled through drying. Presumably the flies reach the eggs before they are covered; the ants eat dried eggs, but whether they actually destroy good ones is not known.

PARASITES. While mammals attack from the outside, numerous parasites work on the "innards," from mouth to rectum inclusive, and without neglecting such delectable organs as the lungs. The average turtle is a veritable collecting-ground for the student of chelonian parasites; in it he can find trematodes, nematodes, cestodes, and various other parasitic invertebrates. The intestine is often crowded by numbers of a little worm with a long family name — Neoechinorhynchidæ. And Troost's Turtle still survives!

CAPTIVITY. This is *the* common turtle of pet-stores, thousands of young being shipped annually out of Louisiana alone. Needless to say, it does well in captivity, often surviving many years; an individual lived five years and eleven months in the London Zoological Gardens.

It should be kept in a sunny vivarium with both land and water, or the young, according to Rust, may be raised in a shoreless aquarium with large cork islands. Suitable temperature range is from 75° to 82° F.

A variety of food can be used: tadpoles, earthworms, insects, chopped raw meat or fish, water plants, and even fruits and tender green vegetables. Swallowing is preferably accomplished with the head submerged.

ECONOMIC VALUE. This turtle not only is eaten locally

wherever it occurs in abundance but also finds its way to the dinner table via large city markets. It is an "important food crop" of Reelfoot Lake, Tennessee.

RIO GRANDE TURTLE

Pseudemys scripta gaigeæ Hartweg

IDENTIFICATION. The ridge extending along the middle of the crushing surface of the upper jaw is smooth or only slightly serrate. The notch at the front of the upper jaw is not flanked on either side by a projection, and the edges of both jaws are smooth. There is a large, subcircular isolated yellow spot in the temporal region. The fundamental pattern of the carapace is composed of irregular figures; light reticulations form distinct light-centred spots on the posterior half of some or all of the shields. A linear or sublinear figure occupies at least half of the median region of the plastron.

With growth the patterns of carapace and plastron become obscured by diffusion of colour and a secondary deposition of dark pigment. A progressive opaquing of the shields of the carapace also modifies its original pattern.

DISTRIBUTION. This recently described subspecies is known only from the Big Bend of the Rio Grande, Brewster County, Texas; southern Coahuila and northeastern Durango, Mexico. Just how extensive is its range in the Rio Grande Valley remains to be determined. Its intergradation with Troost's Turtle is dealt with under that form.

CHICKEN TURTLE

Deirochelys reticularia (Latreille)

[PLATES 82 AND 83]

IDENTIFICATION. The crushing surface of the upper jaw is narrow and without a median ridge. The olive or brown carapace is usually covered with numerous wrinkles or shallow grooves and a large-meshed network of fine yellow lines. When extended, the head and neck are at least two-thirds the length of the carapace. The upper part of each marginal shield is crossed by a yellow bar, and a wide yellow band extends along the front surface of the forelimb. The plastron is yellow, sometimes stained or tinged with red. The upper jaw is notched in front.

SIZE. Ditmars measured a specimen of moderate size as follows:

	Inches	Millimetres
Length of carapace	5.12	130
Width of carapace	3.25	83
Length of plastron	4.37	111
Width of plastron (flat portion)	1.87	47
Length of head and neck	4	102

A very large specimen with a carapace eight and a quarter inches long weighed three and three-quarters pounds.

YOUNG. The carapace of very young individuals is nearly as wide as long (about 32 × 30 mm. at hatching). The colours of the dorsal markings are probably always present and more strongly contrasted than in the adult.

EGG. Elliptical, 36 to 40 by 21 or 22 millimetres. The shell is white.

DISTRIBUTION. The southeastern Coastal Plain from Cumberland County and Beaufort, North Carolina, southward into

82. Chicken Turtle (*Deirochelys reticularia*) from Gainesville, Florida. The carapace is 4.75 inches long. (*Courtesy Zoological Society of Philadelphia, photograph by Mark Mooney, Jr.*)

83. Chicken Turtle (*Deirochelys reticularia*) from Gainesville, Florida. The stripes on the neck are yellow and the carapace is 4.75 inches long. (*Courtesy Zoological Society of Philadelphia, photograph by Mark Mooney, Jr.*)

southern Florida and westward through southern Georgia, Alabama, and Mississippi to Houston, southeastern Texas, and the southeastern tip of Oklahoma. It has been taken in Prairie County, eastern central Arkansas.

HABITS. The Chicken Turtle, a lover of still water, frequents ponds, swamps, and ditches. It is not a river species. Basking individuals, though fond of lying with their long necks stretched out to the fullest extent, are easily alarmed by the approach of man. There is some indication that this species is active at night. When annoyed, it has the unusual habit of partly opening the mouth and hissing without drawing the head in.

CAPTIVITY. A persistent proneness to defend itself by biting makes this species a poor pet. It is said to be an indifferent feeder. However, a specimen in my possession is very docile and eats earthworms and chopped fish ravenously. Rust recommends feeding it on tadpoles, worms, raw meat or fish, mussels or snails; also water plants. It should be kept in an aquarium affording a landing-place or a shoreless one with large cork islands. A place in which to hide should also be provided. Suitable range of temperature is from 70° to 77° F.

A specimen lived in the National Zoological Park, Washington, for more than four and a half years.

ECONOMIC VALUE. It is eaten locally and even sold in southern markets.

CHAPTER VII

THE DESERT, BERLANDIER'S, *and* GOPHER TORTOISES

Family TESTUDINIDÆ
Genus *GOPHERUS*

The gopher tortoises, as these species should be collectively known, are the slow, plodding chelonians of popular fancy and fable, exhibiting the persistence that gave rise to the story of the hare and the tortoise. (A young Berlandier's Tortoise has spent the entire morning in vain efforts to climb onto Romer's *Vertebrate Paleontology* lying on my bookshelf.) They are very closely related to the enormous genus *Testudo*, which, though but poorly represented in the continental New World, has an almost world-wide distribution and boasts fifty species, or fully three times as many as any other genus of the order.

Their habit of excavating extensive burrows distinguishes them from almost all other species of this country. Their strong vegetarian tendencies and preference for dry to desert regions are also unusual, though not unique, characteristics among North American chelonians.

Fossil records carry the genus *Gopherus* back at least a few tens of thousands of years into the Pleistocene, but do not extend its range in North America.

IDENTIFICATION

No one has examined large comparative series of gopher tortoises of the three species in the light of recent conceptions of relationships, so the distinctions between the kinds are but poorly understood. The characters given may not hold, especially when young individuals are involved. Fortunately, the ranges are separate and should be used in preference to the descriptions when dealing with specimens of known origin.

DESERT TORTOISE

Gopherus agassizii (Cooper)

[PLATE 84]

IDENTIFICATION. The carapace is more than twice as long as the shell is high. The head is rounded in front, and the anterior part of the plastron is not bent upward. The distance from the base of the first claw to the base of the fourth claw of the hind foot equals the distance from the base of the first claw to the base of the fourth claw of the forefoot. The carapace is dull brown or horn colour, its shields with or without yellowish centres.

SIZE. Ditmars gives the following measurements of a specimen of moderate size from near Phoenix, Arizona:

	Inches	Millimetres
Length of carapace	9.5	241
Width of carapace	7	178
Length of plastron	9.5	241
Width of plastron	6	152
Height of shell	4.12	105

More information on size will be found below under the account of the sexes.

YOUNG. The carapace of newly hatched specimens varies in length from 41 to 47 millimetres and is nearly as broad as long (41 × 37.5 mm. on the day after hatching in one case). The claws are as sharp as needles and the whole shell is soft because the bones are only partially developed. Specimens two or even three years old are still incompletely ossified. Both the nuchal and caudal shields are incomplete at hatching.

The ground colour of the carapace ranges from dull mustard yellow to warm light brown; variable darker areas of slaty brown appear on each of its shields in symmetrical pattern.

Nearly all of this information about young Desert Tortoises was taken from Miller's excellent account of this reptile.

THE SEXES. Males are a little larger than females. In studying specimens from San Bernardino County, California, Grant found that thirty adult females averaged 9.57 inches in carapace length, whereas the same number of males averaged 11.14 inches. The carapace of the largest male measured 13.27 inches, that of the largest female only 11.26 inches.

The plastron of the male is concave, its gular shields longer and its anals thickened. On the other hand, the plastron of the female extends somewhat farther back toward the hind edge of the carapace. The tail of the male is the longer.

The sexual differences make their appearance as the turtles exceed 4.7 or 5.5 inches in length of carapace.

EGG. The following measurements of two eggs will serve to indicate their range in size and the fact that their transverse as well as their longitudinal sections are elliptical: 41.6 × 36.7 × 34.9 and 48.7 × 39.6 × 38.2 millimetres.

The white shell is extremely thick, hard, and rough. Indeed, Miller found it more difficult to drill than any bird egg of his experience.

The shell contains: first a highly fluid albumen, then a thickly viscid one, and finally a pale cream-coloured yolk.

GROWTH. A juvenile kept in captivity by Miller increased in carapace length 27.6 millimetres (1.04 inches) during three years (from 44.7 to 72.3 mm.), whereas the carapace of another individual, a hatchling taken wild but kept in captivity, increased from 46.9 to 70.4 millimetres, or fifty per cent, in one year.

Bogert has secured the only information on the growth of this tortoise in a natural state. A Mojave Desert adult female with a carapace 250 millimetres (9.84 inches) long was tagged and released on July 7, 1931. When taken 680 days later it had increased 22 millimetres in length. A smaller female when tagged and released in the same place and on the same day had a carapace 150 millimetres (5.9 inches) long. This one grew 70 millimetres before being taken 818 days later, or after approximately one and a half growing seasons. Its increase of about forty-six per cent compares favourably with that of Miller's hatchling.

DISTRIBUTION. Deserts of southeastern California, the southern tip of Nevada, the extreme southwestern corner of Utah, western and southern Arizona, and Sonora, Mexico.

In California it is found in northeastern Los Angeles, eastern Kern, and southeastern Inyo Counties; over most of San Bernardino and much of Riverside and Imperial Counties. Nevada records are confined to Clark County and the southern extremity of Nye. Arizona records fall in Mohave, Yuma, Maricopa, Pinal, Pima, Graham, and Cochise Counties.

HABITAT. This inhabitant of hot, dry deserts prefers gravelly or sandy flats, but also occurs on rocky hillsides and canyon beds. It is found to an altitude of 3,500 feet.

HABITS. This species is shy and inoffensive. Like the Gopher Tortoise, it is strong enough to move with a man on its back. Grant witnessed a race between some children, each carried by two tortoises. The actual speed of its walk has been found to be twenty feet per minute, which is a rate of four or five miles a day.

Being sensitive to both heat and cold, this reptile has to get its active hours in between the cold of the desert night and the cruel heat of the day. Fairly early morning, late afternoon, and cool periods after thunderstorms find it abroad. The hot parts of the day are spent in the shade of bush, rock, or burrow. A specimen placed on its back in strong sun will die in short order. This does not mean that it does not bask in weak rays from time to time.

When turned on its back, a tortoise tries to right itself by bringing one front leg to a sudden halt at the end of a violent flap, an action which causes the whole animal to revolve and may enable it to reach some near-by object or, if the ground is uneven, give it a chance to roll down a slope.

A sleeping individual often sprawls with neck and limbs in such odd positions that it appears to be dead.

The idea of these patient beasts wandering great distances across barren wastes is attractive but without scientific support. Bogert caught and marked several individuals at Lovejoy Springs in the Mojave Desert, California, and immediately turned them loose there. After six hundred and nineteen days the first of the three recovered was found only 150 yards from its point of release; after nearly four years another was taken 300 yards from where it had been set free. A third was captured in the same vicinity, but detailed data for it are not available. The smallest of these three had a carapace 5.9 inches long when first caught. Nevertheless, a strong urge to travel and enormous perseverance in overcoming obstacles in the line of march have been noticed time and again. Ditmars tells how one individual, while walking back and forth across his office, changed its course so that it was forced to clamber repeatedly over a book lying on the floor! Here is a fertile field for experimentation.

HIBERNATION AND ÆSTIVATION. In October or even as late as November the Desert Tortoise goes into hibernation to remain until March. Its winter burrow penetrates a sandy hillside to a depth of two or three feet. Apparently no effort is made to fill the tunnel up after it has been entered.

Æstivation is resorted to during periods of excessive heat, but no detailed study has been made of its æstivating habits.

THE BURROW. As compared with the southeastern Gopher Tortoise, the digging habit is but poorly developed in the desert form, which apparently never goes deeper than eight feet and is usually contented with a straight burrow only two or three feet deep. In fact there are reports of specimens hiding in cavities dug just deep enough to afford protection from the sun. Great difference of opinion exists as to the usual angle of declivity, Camp putting it at forty-five and Grant at twelve degrees.

A site under a bush, in a bank, or at the base of a cliff is generally chosen and moisture is avoided. A burrow harbours a single animal, but no one knows how permanently a hole is occupied. Many other similar questions remain to be answered. The Desert Tortoise does not try to escape into its hole when frightened near by. Indeed, the whole relation of this species to burrows and burrowing is vastly different from that of the Gopher.

Captive tortoises have been seen by Camp to dig into a gravel bank by scraping alternately with the forelimbs and pushing the loose dirt out with their " shoulders."

REPRODUCTION. The following meagre information on the reproduction of the Desert Tortoise has been gleaned partly from accounts of captive specimens, so it must not be taken as final.

Mating occurs in the early spring and possibly continues for some months. Two to six eggs are laid in June or October, or between June and October, and buried in an excavation made three or four inches deep in sand, the female doing all the work with her hind feet, including the arranging of each egg as it is laid. The digging requires about an hour, the actual laying only a quarter as long. A copious amount of water is probably supplied by the cloacal bladder, but no details in regard to this wetting down of the nest are available. Hatchings have been observed from August to November, whereas one in March confirms summer mating and autumn laying. Eggs of other species are known to tide over winter.

MATING. When a male feels sexually attracted toward a female, he approaches her "with his neck extended and the head bobbing rapidly up and down. The female may retract or may go quietly on feeding or dozing in the sun. The male circles about, nipping clumsily at the edges of the female's shell, a most absurd caricature of the traditional ' billing and cooing.' Should the female remain retracted, the male may make a lunge at her with his gular ' horn,' but not with the pugnacity used against a rival." Miller wrote this lively description of a truly remarkable form of love-making.

During copulation the male, mounted on the back of his mate, grunts mechanically with half-open mouth, stamps his feet, and stretches his head and neck down over the forward projection of his plastron, which is the " gular horn " of Miller's description.

FOOD. Oddly enough, as with the Gopher Tortoise, only one scientific attempt to discover what the desert species eats has been made and similar results obtained: the Ortenburgers found only grasses in the stomachs that they examined. On the desert other plants such as blossoms of composite flowers are certainly eaten to some extent. (See the additional remarks under the discussion of captivity below.)

DRINKING. This tortoise is a prodigious drinker. A medium-sized specimen tested by Miller increased its weight slightly more than forty per cent by one long drink, which is the equivalent of a large man getting ten gallons of water down at one time! It is easy enough to appreciate the advantage of this habit in a desert animal that probably encounters water only at long intervals, but the matter does not end there, for the Desert Tortoise is apparently able to derive water from foods and store it in the large anal bladder. Even the thick shell of the egg is remarkably resistent to desiccation, so from the very beginning the individual tortoise is specially adapted for the production, storage, and conservation of water.

DEFENCE. Except in the tender young, which are preyed on by many foes, the shell is sufficient protection from most enemies, man of course excepted. As stated above, this tortoise does not habitually retreat into its burrow at the approach of danger. The voiding of the contents of the anal bladder and the cloaca is another mild means of defence.

The ludicrous fighting of males is described by Camp as follows:

" When one tortoise meets another in the course of its journeying each, whatever the sex, nods its head rapidly up and down as if in salutation, and sometimes noses are touched before passing along. If two males happen to meet, a fight is likely to ensue. After the preliminary nodding the tortoises separate a little distance and then rush toward one another with the heads drawn part way into the shell. The combatants meet head on and the curved horns projecting from the anterior end of the plastron are butted rather violently against the adversary, but do him no damage except sometimes to turn him upon his back; he may then struggle for some time with one fore leg vibrating vigorously in the air and the other pawing for a foothold in the ground before he can right himself."

A capsized combatant is seldom left helpless because his antagonist does not know when to stop or else both tortoises are enjoying the fighting so thoroughly that they want to continue it. At any rate, the issue is usually decided when one fighter becomes discouraged and makes off unharmed, for, like Tweedledee and Tweedledum, these reptile warriors are too well armoured to injure one another.

The significance of these jousts is not clear. One would naturally assume that they are purely the result of sexual rivalry, but Miller has seen an " absurd youngster " with yolk sac still attached to its plastron that without provocation repeatedly lunged at its companions or even at an extended finger!

CAPTIVITY. Away from its native deserts this tortoise is not easily persuaded to live long. One of three kept in the National Zoological Park, Washington, survived more than twenty-seven months, however. A captive soon becomes very tame and seems to enjoy having its head and neck rubbed.

It should be kept in a dry terrarium, given water to drink and sandy soil in which it can burrow. In default of the latter, a dark hiding-place in a shady corner should do. A temperature of at least 75° F. probably must be maintained except perhaps for short periods.

An easy way to feed pet individuals is to allow them to graze on a lawn. Two in my possession do this regularly. Feeding presents no problem, as one can judge from the following incomplete list of plants that have been eaten by Desert Tortoises in confinement: rose blossoms, alfalfa, clover, dandelions, plantain, lettuce, cabbage leaves, tomatoes, watermelons, pears, and cherries. Among the odd things that they will eat are bread, cheese, dry leaves, insects, and dried jackrabbit meat. In fact, I caught one of mine trying to eat a small handkerchief, and this same ravenous tortoise likes to make harmless passes at my three-year-old's bare toes! If the bite ever landed, it might not be so harmless, but the slow movements always allow the boy to escape unscathed and highly amused.

Grant tells of one collector in southern California who let his tortoises hibernate in his cellar under a canvas from December to March.

ECONOMIC VALUE. Indians have no doubt always eaten Desert Tortoises as well as put their empty carapaces to various uses. Under adverse conditions, or when prospecting, white men have also consumed a limited number, and now tortoises are being sold to tourists. This interesting and harmless animal certainly deserves protection by law.

BERLANDIER'S TORTOISE

Gopherus berlandieri (Agassiz)

[PLATE 85]

IDENTIFICATION. The carapace is less than twice as long as the shell is high (disregarding plastral concavity in the male), and the head is wedge-shaped in front. The carapace is dull brown, its shields with or without yellowish centres.

The limited distribution of this tortoise will be a great aid in the identification of specimens of known origin.

SIZE. Ditmars gives the following measurements of a rather small example from Brownsville, Texas:

	Inches	Millimetres
Length of carapace	6	152
Width of carapace	5.37	136
Length of plastron	6.25	159
Width of plastron	4.75	121
Height of shell	3.25	83

There is little information on the maximum size attained by this species, but seven inches seems to be the usual length of the fully grown specimen. Rust, however, gives 8.66 inches as the adult length.

YOUNG. In very young specimens the carapace is as broad as it is long (about 41 × 41 mm.). Each vertebral and costal has a yellow spot in its centre and the marginal shields are edged with the same colour. (See Plate 85.)

EGG. The late John K. Strecker described the eggs as " globular to elongate " in shape and having a hard, white shell. The measurements of three perhaps not entirely normal eggs follow: 49 × 31, 47 × 31, and 45 × 29 millimetres.

DISTRIBUTION. Southern Texas from the vicinity of San Antonio southward through the region of the lower Rio Grande into Tamaulipas, Mexico.

HABITAT. Occurs from sea-level to an altitude of a few hundred feet in Texas, but in Tamaulipas it has been found between 2,600 and 2,900 feet above the sea.

MIGRATION. What appeared to be a migration of these tortoises has been witnessed by Grant in Texas.

REPRODUCTION. The three eggs described above were found on a dry, flinty ridge in Atascosa County, Texas, and under a female which apparently had been forced to lay where the ground was too hard for digging. When discovered, the tortoise clumsily tried to hide her eggs and viciously snapped at a stick thrust toward her. The latter procedure is in strong contrast to the usual docile habits of this species.

CAPTIVITY. A dry terrarium, preferably with a bottom of soft earth about two feet thick in which the occupants can dig, is most suitable. If this is impossible, a dark tunnel-like hiding-place should be provided. A shallow container for drinking-water is preferable and rather high temperatures are of course necessary for this southern animal (about 72° to 80° F.).

Fruit and succulent plant leaves and stems are readily eaten.

Rust recommends species of orpine, and a small tortoise in my possession eats clover, tender grass, lettuce, and bananas. Carnivorous habits are indicated by the fact that captives will also eat raw meat.

Rust calls this a twilight animal, but adds that in course of time it will change its habits. It is not naturally active at night.

A specimen lived fifteen months in the National Zoological Park, Washington.

GOPHER TORTOISE

Gopherus polyphemus (Daudin)

[PLATES 86, 87, 88, AND 89]

IDENTIFICATION. The carapace is more than twice as long as the shell is high. The head is rounded in front, and the anterior part of the plastron is bent upward. The distance from the base of the first claw to the base of the fourth claw of the hind foot equals the distance from the base of the first claw to the base of the third claw of the forefoot. The carapace is dull brown, its shields with or without yellowish centres.

SIZE. A carapace length of twelve inches and a weight of ten pounds is usually stated to be the maximum size attained by this species. Detailed measurements of surprisingly few specimens, however, are on record. Ditmars gives the following dimensions of a large female from Marion County, Florida:

	Inches	Millimetres
Length of carapace	11.5	292
Width of carapace	8	203
Length of plastron	11.5	292
Width of plastron	7.5	190

The height of shell of an individual from Georgia with an eleven-inch carapace was four and three-quarters inches.

YOUNG. The shields of the carapace always have yellow centres.

THE SEXES. The plastron of the male is concave. Other differences apparently have not been accurately determined.

EGG. The eggs are almost spherical (less than 1 mm. difference between greater and lesser diameters in some cases) to somewhat elliptical. The greater diameter is usually about 43, the lesser about 41 millimetres. The shell is white and similar to a bird's in hardness. (See Plate 88.)

GROWTH. Nothing is known of the growth rate of this species under natural conditions. However, in studying the growth of captive young Gopher Tortoise fed on rations of pure foods, Pearse, Lepkovsky, and Hintze secured a maximum gain of sixty-nine per cent in weight over a period of eleven months.

DISTRIBUTION. From Edgefield, Aiken, and Barnwell Counties of southwestern South Carolina, southward through central Florida, and westward along the Gulf coast to the southeastern corner of Texas.

Just how far up the Mississippi Valley this species occurs has not been finally determined, but Stejneger and Barbour (1933) state that it reaches southern Arkansas. There is an old record for Brownsville, Texas, by True, and one for northern Mexico by Lampe, but confirmation of these two records is needed to prove the presence of the Gopher Tortoise so far to the west.

That this species has inhabited Florida for tens of thousands of years has been proved by the discovery of Pleistocene fossil remains of it there.

HABITAT. These tortoises are at home on ridges and the higher ground of dry, sandy pine and oak woods of the Coastal Plain. The elevation must be sufficient to allow them to keep the bottoms of their deep burrows above the water-level of the soil, but not so great that they cannot end their excavations in slightly damp earth. Height above water is of greater significance than distance from it. Closely wooded stretches as well as those with thick underbrush are avoided, open woods being definitely preferred.

HABITS. When surprised away from its burrow, the shy, docile Gopher Tortoise never defends itself by biting at an offender, but retreats into its shell with a hiss, placing its forelimbs so that their hard scaly outside surfaces perfectly protect the head and anterior soft parts (see Plate 86). Thus it patiently awaits further developments. Although the movements are slow and deliberate, it can walk at a moderate rate of speed, holding the body well off the ground and taking steps of good length.

The surprising strength of this chelonian has been repeatedly noted, the general consensus of opinion being that a large adult finds little difficulty in moving with a man on its back. Le Conte even said that one can support a weight of six hundred pounds, a statement that must be taken with a grain of salt. A big individual that I once kept in my house proved, to my dissatisfaction, that it was a first-class furniture-mover.

It is now well established that the daylight hours find it abroad, its nights being spent in the burrow. There is difference of opinion as to the relation of its wanderings to midsummer sun, Hubbard, for example, stating that this sun is no impediment to its activities, whereas Ditmars encountered it prowling during the early morning on sunny days, later only in cloudy weather. The weaker sun of spring and autumn is by no means shunned, however.

A study of " space reactions " by Yerkes proved that this species, like other terrestrial forms, has judgment about walking off of elevated surfaces. At about one foot there was hesitation at the edge, whereas at six times that height great fear was exhibited. Aquatic kinds accustomed to plop into water at the slightest alarm showed much less caution, their drops into pond or river resulting in no harm.

There are only casual observations on its winter habits. In the southern part of its range it apparently remains active, but comes out only on the warmest sunny days; farther north, during severe winters at least, it may really hibernate for a brief spell.

THE BURROW. The Gopher Tortoise is colonial in habits and therefore its burrows occur in groups, the individual holes usually being from twenty or thirty to a few hundred feet apart. Sometimes several hundred are found within a single square mile. This reptile is a good engineer, digging its burrows at slants of fifteen to thirty, occasionally as much as thirty-five degrees to the surface. These are undoubtedly angles at which a minimum of effort is required, caving in being avoided on the one hand and mechanical difficulty in digging and removing loose soil on the other. One burrow seen by Hallinan, to whom we are indebted for the best account of the Gopher's life history, was started at forty-five degrees but abandoned before completion.

A straight course is pursued until a stone, root, or other object forces a turn, and few individuals indeed are fortunate enough to dig without encountering some obstruction. Among twelve burrows excavated by Hallinan, only one was deflected neither to the right nor to the left, and four others turned very little, the rest having one or two sharp bends. Two, in fact, curved so sharply or so often that one ended slightly, the other well back of the starting-point.

The length is largely determined by the distance that must be traversed in order to reach soil of satisfactory dampness. To attain his end, the tortoise spares no pains; one hole was followed for twenty-four feet to a depth of eleven feet with still no end in sight! This individual was outdoing itself, for

84 [LEFT]. Desert Tortoise (*Gopherus agassizii*) from Los Angeles County, California, with a carapace 6.69 inches long. It is a female. (*Courtesy Zoological Society of Philadelphia, photograph by Mark Mooney, Jr.*)

85 [RIGHT]. Young Berlandier's Tortoise (*Gopherus berlandieri*) from Zapata, Texas, with a carapace 66 millimetres long by 60 wide. (*Courtesy Karl P. Schmidt, photograph by Mark Mooney, Jr.*)

86. Gopher Tortoise (*Gopherus polyphemus*) drawn into its shell. The forelimbs can be pressed into the opening of the shell and perfectly protect the head and anterior soft parts. (*Courtesy Zoological Society of Philadelphia, photograph by Mark Mooney, Jr.*)

87 [LEFT]. Gopher Tortoise (*Gopherus polyphemus*) at the mouth of its burrow in Charlton County, Georgia. Reposing thus is a common habit. The carapace of this individual is about 13 inches long. (*Photograph by Francis Harper.*)

88 [RIGHT]. Egg of Gopher Tortoise from Charlton County, Georgia, photographed May 28, 1929. (*Photograph by Francis Harper.*)

89. The Gopher Tortoise (*Gopherus polyphemus*) held by Dr. Sherman C. Bishop has just been dug from its burrow along with its associate, the Gopher frog, which is in Miss Margaret Wright's hand. The site is on an " oak ridge " in Charlton County, Georgia. (*Photograph by Francis Harper.*)

nineteen other burrows averaged only fourteen and one-half feet in length, with a maximum and minimum of twenty and ten and one-half feet, respectively. (See Plate 89.)

The burrows are in either level or sloping surfaces and show no uniformity of direction, entering from all points of the compass. The longer diameter of their cross-section is about twice the shorter one, and each is but slightly greater than the corresponding dimension of the occupant (see Plate 87). Every hole terminates in a small chamber for " elbow room " and turning, although just what traffic rules prevail among Gophers occupying the same domicile has not been determined. Since no more than two individuals live in the same burrow, probably only minor traffic jams occur.

It has not been determined whether pairs occupying one hole are mated male and female. Hubbard has stated, but by no means proved, that an individual may occupy a burrow for twenty-four years. He did, however, determine that the temperature of the chamber varies little from season to season, seldom falling below 74° F. in the winter or rising above 79° in the summer at Crescent City, Florida.

Hallinan's account of the digging cannot well be condensed or improved so it is given in full:

" The material is apparently dug loose with the front feet and pushed out of the burrow with the carapace acting as a shovel-plow. From the small amount of sand at the entrances in comparison to the cubical contents of the burrows it is evident that a large amount is forced aside radially, as the sand is quite compressible. The sand is found to be well packed around the tunnels and this peripheral packing gives greater strength, especially during the heavy rains. In proportion, more sand is found at the entrances of the burrows of smaller tortoises than at the entrances of the larger ones, due no doubt to the lesser strength of the smaller which lessens the amount of sand that they can force aside radially. In burrow No. 12

the sand was flaky, dry, flour-like, and very compressible, with only about one cubic foot placed outside the entrance, but the cubical contents of the burrow was 6 cubic feet showing that about 85% of the sand was forced aside radially and not removed from the burrow."

ASSOCIATES. In addition to being a haven of refuge to almost any small creature in time of trouble, the Gopher's home is regularly inhabited by numerous animals. Abandoned burrows are taken over by skunks, burrowing owls, huge rattlesnakes, and the like. A single hole is on record that harboured at one time a pair of opossums, a raccoon, a rattler more than six feet long, two smaller snakes, and several rats! These holes might well be styled the wild creatures' " flop houses."

That natives of the Gopher's country know its associates well is shown by this part of Fletcher's amusing account of digging one out with the assistance of a local helper:

" After we had made a trench some twelve feet from the entrance large enough to stand and work in, and six feet deep, I asked Henry how far he thought we must go before we got the gopher. ' Well, we must jist go on dis road till we git him, if it takes a hundred yards.' After digging four feet more and still down, Henry handed up a bleached cockroach, remarking, ' We's most' got um; here's one of his " familiars," and when we come to de white frog we's got um shore.' Sure enough it was so, for the spade went four feet more and we could hear it grate on the shell; at the same time a white frog jumped out. It was a bright-eyed little fellow, with transparent legs and toes. A few black specks about his head made a pretty contrast to his sparkling gold-ringed iris. ' Hold on, Henry,' I said, ' let me pull out that gopher; I fear you will scratch him with the spade.' ' You can't pull him out wid an ox team,' was the reply. ' Well, get out of my way and I will show you; he can have no purchase in this wet sand.' So in I went, ' belly flat,' as the boys say when coasting, squeezing myself into the hole until I got my hand on the shell. There were no hind legs to be found, and the wet oval shell was so slippery I had to give it up and be drawn out myself by the legs. ' I'll show you how to get 'im widout scratchin' de shell,' said Henry, and he proceeded to make a cave under the gopher. Into this he dropped, was scooped out and handed over."

Fletcher is more entertaining than accurate, but his mention of a frog " familiar " is important because the Gopher frog is well known to occur chiefly in the burrows of this tortoise, the presence of the latter making little difference to the self-invited amphibian (see Plate 89). Hubbard lists no fewer than fifteen invertebrate " parasites and messmates " of the Gopher, nearly all of which are of course confined to the burrows. Among this sordid assembly are five beetles and a caterpillar moth that live on the dung of their host!

REPRODUCTION. Eggs were found by Hallinan in northern Florida on May 28 and June 4. Nine clutches had from four to seven eggs and averaged five apiece. These lots were deposited in sites well exposed to direct sunlight at an average distance of approximately thirteen inches from the mouth of a burrow and at an average depth of about five. In every nest but one the eggs were laid at the same level.

The breeding male is said by Ditmars to utter a " short, rasping call " at intervals of about two seconds. Hallinan writes that the Gopher at times gives a " low, piteous cry."

FOOD AND FEEDING. The single serious attempt to determine the food of this species was made by Hallinan, who found only grasses in the stomachs opened. Everyone else has been contented to pass on the fact that it is herbivorous, subsisting on succulent plant leaves and stems. Fruits have also been mentioned. An unusually long large intestine confirms its herbivorous habits.

ENEMIES. A large blood-sucking mite lives in the Gopher's

burrow, attacking it as bedbugs do humans; and a species of Adobe tick fixes itself in the sutures between the shields of the shell or to the skin.

Man must be numbered among its enemies. See the remarks below under the heading of Economic Value.

DEFENCE. Retreat into the burrow is the chief means of defence. Withdrawal into the shell is resorted to when the tortoise is surprised away from its home.

CAPTIVITY. Conditions as described under Berlandier's Tortoise are suitable for this Gopher as well. Absolute dryness seems to be bad and yet one must be careful to keep the terrarium from getting wet. There is difference of opinion on this point, so perhaps, in an outside vivarium at least, two sections might be provided, one very dry and the other slightly damp. The tortoises will soon show their preference.

Almost any vegetable, fruit, or grass will suffice as food. Pearse, Lepkovsky, and Hintze fed their turtles on a variety of prepared rations, and Ditmars reports that they will eat raw meat as well as vegetables and fruit.

A specimen lived in the National Zoological Park, Washington, for four years and seven months.

It is said that the Gopher may be caught by digging a deep pit in front of its burrow.

ECONOMIC VALUE. The Creek Indians used to relish this turtle and there are many reports of its being eaten locally in various parts of its range. Even the eggs are sometimes relished. In times past the shells have been used as sun-helmets.

Apparently it sometimes causes trouble by entering vegetable gardens and helping itself to any vegetable striking its fancy.

CHAPTER VIII

THE SEA–TURTLES

Family CHELONIIDÆ

Genera *CHELONIA, ERETMOCHELYS,*
CARETTA, LEPIDOCHELYS,
and *COLPOCHELYS*

Family DERMOCHELIDÆ

Genus *DERMOCHELYS*

Of all the turtles and their kin the giant tortoises of remote tropical islands and the sea-turtles of the warm oceans are the most romantic, the most engaging by far. Man has already sounded the death knell of the former, but the latter, protected by boundless seas, defy his worst machinations and still ascend moonlit tropical beaches in great hordes, turning them temporarily into veritable reptile incubators. Oddly enough, this last link with a terrestrial past is the weakest point of their existence, for it is then that the females, sprawling defenceless and preoccupied on the sand, expose themselves to the greatest risks of their lives. The danger does not end here, since both eggs and young must escape the destruction of lesser enemies which often literally crowd the beaches until dispelled by the arch enemy, man. Although the forsaking of land for water has circumvented many a foe, the perils surrounding the process of procreation, instead of diminishing, have doubtless increased to become, like the waist of an hour-glass, the bottle-neck of survival. Even the one time of their lives when turtle should really enjoy turtle is fraught with danger, since mated pairs are far too oblivious of their surroundings for their own safety.

In spite of all this, sea-turtles have lived long and well over a period stretching back more than sixty million years from the present into the Upper Cretaceous, and the group once boasted giants twelve feet long. Even today few animals surpass them in breadth of distribution or sheer bulk. Fossil species so similar to living forms that they are placed in the genus *Chelonia* were alive in the Oligocene, which began a modest thirty-five million years ago.

In captivity adolescent or mature turtles do best in their native element, but sometimes thrive in the brackish water of estuaries, an aqueous solution of common salt, or even fresh water. The young should be kept only in sea water, which must be frequently changed. According to Rust, it is imperative to give food of marine origin to specimens living in fresh water. The temperature in aquarium or tank must be kept above 65° F., preferably from 68° to 73° F.

No landing-place is required, so perfectly adapted to aquatic life are these reptiles. Parker found that voluntary submergence for forty minutes was not infrequent, and one loggerhead remained under for sixty-four. A Kemp's Turtle survived forced submergence for only a little over an hour and a half, but death was probably greatly hastened by extreme activity.

IDENTIFICATION

The paddle-shaped limbs or flippers of sea-turtles make their recognition as such a simple matter (see Plate 91). The juveniles are even more readily identified because in early youth the flippers are proportionately larger than in later life.

The long tail of the male is seldom mentioned or illustrated and indeed few authors seem to be aware of this striking sexual character. This is evidently because large specimens usually reach museums as shells only, males seldom leave the water, and in many turtle-fishing establishments only females are caught.

At least in the case of adults, carapace measurements are ordinarily taken along the curve of the shell because of mechanical difficulties in getting the straight length and width. The curve is so slight that the method of measurement makes little difference.

The key and classification are based on those of Deraniyagala, who has so admirably worked out the differences between the recent species. Although his results have not yet attained general acceptance, it is high time that they be put to the acid test of wide proof. No other scientist has examined such extensive preserved and living material and Deraniyagala's researches on the group are of unquestionable value.

KEY TO THE AMERICAN SPECIES OF SEA-TURTLES

A1: Shell covered with large horny shields; carapace without longitudinal ridges.

B1: Four pairs of costal shields, the first of each pair not in contact with nuchal.

C1: A single pair of prefrontals on top of head; usually a single claw on each limb; shields of carapace not overlapping (except in the very young). GREEN TURTLE

C2: Two pairs of prefrontals; usually two claws on each limb; shields of carapace strongly overlapping (except in very old individuals). HAWKSBILL TURTLE

B2: Five or more pairs of costal shields, the first of each pair in contact with nuchal (see Pl. 90).

C1: Each bridge with three enlarged poreless infra-marginal shields; limbs two-clawed. (See Pl. 91.)

ATLANTIC LOGGERHEAD TURTLE

C2: Each bridge with four enlarged inframarginals (see Pl. 93) with or without pores.

D1: Each inframarginal with a pore; more than five pairs of costals; limbs two- or one-clawed.

PACIFIC LOGGERHEAD TURTLE

D2: Inframarginal poreless; five pairs of costals; limbs three-clawed.　　　　KEMP'S TURTLE

A2: Shell covered with smooth skin; carapace with seven prominent longitudinal ridges.　　LEATHERBACK TURTLE

GREEN TURTLE

Chelonia mydas (Linnæus)

IDENTIFICATION. The limbs are paddle-shaped and each has one small claw (rarely two). There is a single pair of large shields, the prefrontals, on top of the head between the eyes. Four costal shields are present on each side, and the shields of the carapace are not overlapping (slight overlap evident in the very young).

SIZE. A cast made from a 700-pound Green Turtle caught in the Key West region is exhibited in the New York Aquarium; this turtle is said to be the largest ever taken by the Key West dealers. Babcock, however, gives 850 pounds as the West Indian record. Seventy-five to 150 pounds is the usual weight range of specimens caught at present in American waters. Where this turtle is little molested by man, breeding females have carapaces thirty-eight to forty-six inches long and weigh 300 to 500 pounds.

THE SEXES. In the adult the tail of the female barely reaches beyond the margin of the carapace, whereas that of the male reaches even beyond the tips of the extended flippers.

EGG. The eggs are sometimes spherical, but more often one diameter is from 1 to 3 millimetres greater than the other. For example, the lesser diameters of six typical eggs from Brazil ranged from 40 to 42, the greater from 41 to 44 millimetres. The soft shell is white.

LONGEVITY. A specimen from the Pacific Ocean lived in the New York Aquarium for fifteen years.

GROWTH. Although the growth rate of the Green Turtle has never been fully determined, there is some reliable information on the subject. Moorhouse found that a carapace length of eight inches is reached in one year off the eastern coast of Australia, and Schmidt secured substantiating data in the West Indies. Judging by the findings of these men, this turtle during very early life adds every month about half a pound to its weight and half an inch to its carapace. Moorhouse tentatively states that a female first matures when its carapace is thirty-five inches long and that a length of forty-four inches probably indicates an age of at least ten years.

According to Flower, three specimens in the Aquarium of the Zoological Society of London increased from a weight of less than one to more than fifty pounds in about nine years and four months. Hornell reports a captive individual that reached a carapace length of one and a half feet in twenty-eight months.

DISTRIBUTION. The Green Turtle occurs throughout the Gulf of Mexico and northward along the Atlantic coast to the North Carolina sounds, in which it was abundant before being decimated by turtle-hunters during the nineteenth century. It has been taken as far north as Cohasset, Massachusetts, and is occasionally seen off New Jersey and Long Island coasts. It is now the commonest sea-turtle of Bermuda. In the Pacific it occasionally reaches the bays of San Diego County in extreme southern California and is abundant as far north as southern Lower California.

This valuable turtle has a world-wide distribution in tropical and subtropical seas, usually remaining within 35° of the equator.

Pleistocene fossil remains from Florida prove that it has occurred in the Florida region for perhaps tens of thousands of years.

HABITAT. Shoals and lagoons of oceanic islands and continental shelves. Bays and sounds are often entered, especially in the vicinity of sand beaches. Coral reefs are avoided.

The browsing method of feeding is a strong determining factor in the habitat preference of the Green Turtle, which is prone to frequent fields of sea plants.

HABITS. Just where this turtle sleeps is the most interesting question about its habits. That it does sleep is a well-established fact, for many observers have seen relaxed individuals floating on the surface of the sea. In 1925 Wetmore presented indisputable evidence that great numbers sleep on remote Hawaiian rock ledges and sandy beaches, a fact contradictory to the general belief that sea-turtles die if stranded on their bellies, owing to the lack of sufficient support afforded to internal organs by the lower part of the shell. Breathing is said to be seriously impaired and specimens going to market are always turned on their backs.

Recent observations on the Galapagos Islands confirm Wetmore's evidence, so the beach- and ledge-sleeping habit cannot be considered a peculiarity of the Hawaiian turtles, and remarks on the belief that stranded individuals die unless lying on their backs are in order. Wetmore himself has suggested that the vibration of a ship's deck might have bad effects, but I think that the oxygen requirement of a sleeping turtle may be enough less than that of one struggling from fear and discomfort to account for survival in one case and ultimate death in the other. In this connection it must not be forgotten that laying females of all sea-turtles often remain on a beach for many hours. During much of this time, however, most of the weight rests only on the edge of the carapace.

Deraniyagala states that loggerheads live on land longer than Green Turtles because the plastron and sides of the shell are more completely ossified and better resist the pressure of the upper parts.

Still another point calls for elucidation. Why has no one of the many persons interested in commercial fisheries ever seen Green Turtles asleep on a beach? Again Wetmore's experience is helpful; he noticed that the frequent appearance of human beings on the remote beaches where turtles rested soon caused the reptiles to take their siestas in still more remote places. The habit of sleeping on the strand probably has long since been abandoned wherever turtles have been even slightly molested by man. They must quickly learn that sleep on the bosom of the deep is far safer; certainly it sounds more comfortable and inviting! Fishermen long ago told Bumpus that Green Turtles occasionally sleep off Rhode Island shores with the head resting on lobster-buoys. Are these reptiles astonishingly resourceful or Rhode Island fishermen surprisingly imaginative?

The Hawaiian siestas may also be considered a form of sun bathing, as indeed similar excursions ashore have been called by Deraniyagala in reporting the midday landing of sea-turtles on an uninhabited island in the Maldives.

Although adults drag themselves along on land by laborious strokes of the front limbs moved together and aided (or not?) by alternate pushes of the hind flippers, the gait of the young is relatively nimble for they " walk like most four-footed beasts."

MIGRATION AND INDIVIDUAL RANGE. In spite of a general belief that Green Turtles regularly go back and forth from feeding areas to breeding grounds, sometimes travelling hundreds of miles in doing so, there is no scientific evidence that such mass movements take place. Hornell has brought together the available information supporting the migration hypothesis, but it is not convincing. In fact, the only scientific investigation ever made, the marking experiments of young turtles by Schmidt in the West Indies, gave absolutely no evidence of extensive migrations. Among nine individuals marked and re-taken, only one was found any great distance from its starting-point. That one was discovered fifty miles away after ten months. Others were captured much nearer to or at the common point of release. Although this evidence is limited and largely of a negative character, it is some indication that young Green Turtles are rather stationary.

The problem is a complex one, however, and cannot be so readily dismissed. Working on Heron Island, off the east coast of Australia, Moorhouse found that, although a canning factory had killed all the turtles seen on the island during the 1928–9 laying season, a new crop, including many large individuals, visited the same beaches the following year. Here is strong evidence that females either do not lay every year or else change nesting sites. Such a change would be in the nature of a migration.

A female that landed two consecutive nights on Heron Island was turned each night and actually taken to the factory the second one, before being released. Ten days later she was found laying on an island sixteen miles distant. This change in site was evidently the result of fright, which, however, did not prevent her from making subsequent nests on Heron Island.

Only prolonged investigation on a large scale can solve the many problems of sea-turtle wanderings and individual range.

MATING. The following facts about mating have been well established although actual courtship and copulation really remain to be described: Mating takes place off the nesting beaches during the laying season; many males attempt to copulate at the same time with one female; the mated pairs are oblivious of danger and float on the surface, the male on top with his forelimbs stretched forward and pressing against the carapace of his mate; spent females returning to the sea at least sometimes accept the attention of waiting males and at once copulate.

Judging by Hornell's account, mating takes place not only during but for some time before the laying season, actually beginning with the gathering of the turtles off the nesting beaches. He also states that an ardent male occasionally follows a female a short distance ashore before realizing the futility of his effort and clumsily returns to the water.

Although only diurnal copulation is mentioned, the frequent references to males awaiting females returning from laying is indication of nocturnal mating. Probably the act, usually begun at night, often lasts well into the day.

NESTING. In the Seychelles, east of Africa and some five degrees south of the equator, the Green Turtle lays throughout the year, with a *very* decided peak during March, April, and May; off the west coast of Borneo, about two degrees north of the equator, the peak comes from May to September. In the region of southern Florida and throughout the West Indies the species is reported to nest from April to August; from late October into February on Heron Island, lying about on the Tropic of Capricorn near the eastern coast of Australia.

Nocturnal laying is the universal rule, the majority of females making their nests between the hours of ten and two. The site chosen is usually above the reach of high tide, but many nests were destroyed on Heron Island in 1930 when the high-water mark for January was more than a foot above that of the preceding November. Even if the eggs escape the action of the waves, the salt water quickly coagulates their yolk or drowns the embryos. On this island the layers came on the beach " at any state of the tide," but in the Seychelles Hornell noticed that the females preferred to land on a high tide, the greater number appearing on nights when high tide occurred soon after sunset.

There is considerable disagreement in regard to the actual nesting process, which no one seems to have described in detail from beginning to end. The main facts are fairly clear, however.

In ascending the beach the female pulls herself along with the front flippers (at the same time pushing with the hind ones?), leaving a conspicuous track two to three feet wide made up of parallel depressions separated by a ridge. Her progress is in stages of six or seven steps followed by pauses for rest. When a site has been chosen, she proceeds to sink herself into a large hollow which is made with all four flippers, the front pair throwing the sand out by swimming movements and then resting while the hind pair do their work. After depressions have been made fore and aft, the digger revolves enough to change the centre of action and thus finally works herself into the resulting bowl-shaped excavation.

Next she digs the egg pit, a far more delicate procedure. This secondary excavation is a cylindrical undercut hole some eighteen inches deep and twelve or more across, the exact dimensions depending upon the size of the turtle. We have Beebe to thank for the most detailed account of this supreme accomplishment of the hind flippers without aid of reason or sight. The sand is removed by strokes of the edge of the flippers used alternately, difficulty rapidly increasing with depth. Finally the flipper must be curled inward, gently lowered, uncurled, and forced into the sand by skilful pushes until a load has been dislodged. Then the tip is again curled to completely enfold the sand and bring it out, often with loss of scarcely a grain. A final flick sends the sand flying directly backward and well clear of the hole.

Now the other flipper, which has been held flat against its side of the pit, preventing caving in of the walls, is snapped to throw forward any loose sand that may have fallen on it, curled, and lowered into the hole. (One account describes the waiting flipper as idly outstretched.)

The " exquisite accuracy " of the flipper movements is emphasized by Beebe, who goes on to describe the spraying of the sides and bottom of the hole with a liquid, presumably to reduce the chances of caving in. This undoubtedly is cloacal bladder water, not urine.

When the turtle is ready to lay, the hind flippers are brought together, hiding the tail and covering the mouth of the pit. Accounts of actual deposition are very sketchy, owing no doubt to the difficulty of seeing what goes on after the flippers have been brought together. Usually two eggs are ejected at a time. The end of the laying process on Heron Island is described by Moorhouse:

" As soon as the laying is completed the nest is filled in, the hind flippers patting and kneading the sand into the nest. Then follows a flinging of sand over the body by the fore flippers, the hind ones piling it evenly as it falls. The animal, still throwing sand, moves forward and soon the original spot is obliterated. Then she returns to the water. From the time of the turtle's coming out of the water till her return two to two and a half hours have elapsed, though some animals have taken but one hour, while others have taken as long as seven hours in the process."

Before the investigation on Heron Island it was known that the Green Turtle nests more than once a season, but the maximum number of times was largely a matter of conjecture. Many of the fifty turtles marked there laid seven clutches at intervals of approximately two weeks, and it is possible that some of those that deposited seven times returned to increase the number after the departure of the investigator. Not infrequently females came ashore and dug nests only to return to the water without laying, some vainly wandering distances of six hundred yards besides digging one or two holes.

Moorhouse was also able to show that relatively few females visit one island during a single season. Moreover, he tentatively concludes that turtles do not lay every season and frequently change their laying islands.

A staggering lot of statistics on the number of eggs laid at a time by females on islands off the west coast of Borneo have been made available by Banks. The average for 16,690 clutches taken from one island in 1934 was 108 eggs per clutch, and 107 for 10,726 others from another in 1932. The maximum number of eggs in any one clutch among many tens of thousands was 176. Disregarding round numbers, the highest count that I find for all parts of the world is 195. Banks further detected in the Bornean region a slight tendency for the size of clutches to be larger on nesting beaches visited by relatively few turtles, one such place having an average count of 118 eggs per nest based on only 875 layings. Correlation between the number of turtles depositing in a given area and the annual weather conditions was also discernible, the reptiles being less productive during damp, stormy years.

The average incubation period in the Seychelles is stated by Hornell to be forty-seven days, the greatest but a few more than fifty; but on Heron Island the eggs of eleven marked nests required from sixty-five to seventy-two days to hatch, those that took the longer time being near enough to fringing vegetation to receive some shade. A shorter period for the former locality, which lies only five degrees south of the equator, is what one would predict; Heron Island is about on the Tropic of Capricorn. Nevertheless, the difference is unexpectedly great.

BEHAVIOUR OF HATCHLING. This is a vexed subject because of lack of agreement and somewhat contradictory statements.

Hornell believes that the young of one nest "hatch out the same day and usually within a couple of hours after the first appears," but Moorhouse states that they "do not all emerge on the same day or night," and goes on to explain how various factors such as low temperature and packing of sand by rain cause delay. It might be argued that the difference is one between actual hatching and subsequent appearance at the surface, but Hornell is certainly of the opinion that hatching is rapidly followed by emergence. Moorhouse refers chiefly to delayed emergence.

The next difficulty is the time of emergence, Moorhouse obviously believing that the night is the normal time, hatchlings having even been seen by him to reach the surface during the day only to bury themselves again. In spite of this, he explains that the young are strongly attracted by a bright light and on three occasions saw individuals leave the sea to approach a petrol lamp.

Another point of disagreement is in regard to the diving ability of very young Green Turtles. Hornell writes that "they are a long time in acquiring the art of diving and staying under water for a prolonged period," but Moorhouse makes no mention of any such inability, to the contrary speaking of the young diving after food and rising to the surface of the sea to breathe. In spite of this, he reports dissecting some and finding "a large percentage of the yolk within them." Now, it is just this yolk that Deraniyagala claims makes young sea-turtles unable to dive!

FOOD AND FEEDING. Adults of this species are chiefly herbivorous, subsisting largely on marine grasses and algæ. Mangrove shoots are relished by Galapagos populations. Eel-grass of the genus *Zostera*, often called "turtle grass," is commonly eaten, and masses of floating leaves of this plant are considered a sure indication of turtle feeding grounds. In cutting the plants near the roots to procure the most succulent parts, the turtles set countless numbers of the leaves free to float on the surface.

Small mollusks and crustaceans are also devoured. For example, Beebe found a stomach crammed with hundreds of shell-less flying snails and a small number of munidas or " scarlet lobsterettes." Young oysters are sometimes eaten.

The juveniles are decidedly more omnivorous than the adults.

Deraniyagala determined that stomachs of individuals kept out of water four days still retain masses of undigested algæ, whereas only twelve hours are required to empty the stomachs of those left in their native element. This might be one factor in the alleged quick death of stranded turtles, discussed above in the section on habits.

ENEMIES. As in the case of the Hawksbill, man is without rival as an enemy.

Adult Green Turtles are not infrequently preyed upon by sharks, which either swallow the reptiles whole or nip pieces from the flippers. Beebe estimated the weight of a specimen cut out of a thirteen-foot tiger shark as about fifty pounds, and more than one observer has seen a female hindered in the nesting operation by mutilated flippers. In one case the damage was so great that the turtle could not clamber up the beach, but had to be satisfied with a simple nest at the very edge of the waves. The yolk of eggs laid so near the sea would be quickly coagulated by the salt water. That shark, in addition to injuring one adult, perhaps prevented the hatching of thousands of young.

In the Seychelles the hatchlings suffer from the depredations of raptorial birds and fish just as described in the corresponding section under the Hawksbill, and there is abundant corroboration of the same kind of destruction wrought in other parts of the world. On Heron Island house cats chew off the heads of newly emerged young, while large nocturnal crabs prepare others for eating by holding them with one nipper and removing the shields of the carapace with the other. On this same island Moorhouse relates that, in an effort to determine their destination, twelve hatchlings were released at low water to be followed, but not one survived, as all were soon devoured by fish lurking in the reef.

On beaches of this same island, when crowded at the height of the season by too many arrivals, one female often digs into the finished nest of another, leaving the eggs thus inadvertently uncovered to be eaten by gulls. In North America raccoons sometimes destroy the nests.

CAPTIVITY. This species is hardy in confinement. It is slow and deliberate in its feeding movements, lacking the aggressiveness of the Hawksbill and the loggerheads.

Although chiefly herbivorous in a state of nature, the Green Turtle in captivity is nearly always fed on animal matter, and, oddly enough, seems to relish such food. Raw fish and meat constitute the usual diet, but one individual ate chiefly fiddler crabs. The usual adult fare of marine grasses and algæ can of course be given.

Moorhouse failed to persuade his hatchlings to eat for seven days, after which they refused many kinds of local sea plants but readily ate meat, clams, and fish, even killing fish that were not too lively. After living on a meat diet for some time, they seemed to relish a little seaweed. In feeding, the juveniles push with the fore flippers the part of any piece of food that is not actually between the jaws, thus tearing it loose from the portion already in the mouth.

ECONOMIC VALUE. The Green Turtle is the source of the famous turtle soup, and the species indeed is eaten as well as drunk by man the world over. It is the basis of extensive industries and tens of thousands of dollars' worth of specimens are sold annually in the markets of our large cities. Without doubt this species is the most important of all turtles from an economic point of view.

Oil is made from both the turtle and its eggs, but the shell has only a low commercial value, being too thin for most purposes.

HAWKSBILL TURTLE

Eretmochelys imbricata (Linnæus)

IDENTIFICATION. The limbs are paddle-shaped and each has two small claws (rarely one). There are two pairs of large shields, the prefrontals, on top of the head between the eyes. Four costal shields are present on each side and, except in old individuals, the rear margins of the shields of the carapace are strongly overlapping.

SIZE. Three feet seems to be about the maximum carapace length attained by this small sea-turtle; one and a half to two feet is the average length of adults. An exceedingly large specimen may weigh 160 pounds. It is singularly hard to find dimensions and weight of the same individual, but one with a carapace two feet long has been recorded as weighing 50 pounds; another, a female, with a 30.31-inch carapace, 98.5 pounds.

THE SEXES. Sexual differences in sea-turtles are seldom referred to, but Deraniyagala mentions two found in this species: The extended tail of the adult female barely reaches the margin of the carapace, whereas the tail of the male is much longer. In females of more than 6.3 inches in carapace length, the two shields in the centre of the top of the head (frontal and frontoparietal) are usually fused; in males they remain separate.

EGG. The eggs are spherical or nearly so and measure from 38 to 41 millimetres in diameter. The soft white shell is thinly covered with a mucilaginous secretion which absorbs water and retains it for many hours.

LONGEVITY. A specimen received by the Berlin Zoological Garden in 1921 was still alive in 1936, and another is reported by Hornell to have been reared to an age of fifteen years. The often quoted account of the individual marked by a Dutch official and found thirty years later on the southern coast of Ceylon is interesting, but can hardly be taken as a scientific datum.

GROWTH. Hornell states that six Hawksbill Turtles confined under semi-natural conditions on Assumption Island attained carapace lengths of 12.5 to 13.5 inches in about twenty-three months, and Deraniyagala tabulates detailed measurements of the growth of two individuals kept in Ceylon. One reached a carapace length of 14.29 inches and a weight of 10 pounds 14 ounces in sixteen months; the other during the same period fell short of equal attainments by only 8 millimetres and 1 pound 6 ounces. The two came from a lot of hatchlings with carapaces 39 to 42 millimetres (1.5 to 1.6 inches) long. At such rates the adult size of twenty to twenty-four inches would be reached in a few years. In fact, Townsend wrote about two captive Florida specimens that attained weights of 50 and 60 pounds and carapace lengths of 24 and 26 inches within seven or eight years. They weighed about 3 pounds when made captive.

DISTRIBUTION. The presence of this turtle on the Atlantic coast north of Florida was long questioned, but its not infrequent occurrence in the vicinity of Woods Hole, Massachusetts, is now established. It also enters Long Island Sound. Records for the region from the Carolinas to New Jersey are, however, astonishingly few.

HABITAT. Shoals, coral reefs, and lagoons of oceanic islands

and continental shelves, usually in water not more than fifty
or sixty feet deep. Until able to dive, the young lurk in masses
of floating sea plants.

HABITS. This is an aggressive, pugnacious reptile.

MIGRATION AND INDIVIDUAL RANGE. As yet there is no scientific evidence that the Hawksbill makes extensive migrations.
On the contrary the available information indicates that each
population is local for any given shoal or reef area. For example, on islands off the east coast of Africa, chiefly Seychelles
groups, Hornell found a direct correlation between the number of individuals taken in six months in any one area and the
number of square miles of suitable banks of that area. Moreover, the annual catches over a period of many years proved
to be astonishingly constant. He concluded that the populations of this region are strictly local, each being dependent
upon and proportional to the area of suitable feeding grounds.

Within a local area individuals probably move freely about
in search of food or travel rapidly when frightened in any
way. At least one, wounded by a harpoon, carried the broken
embedded point a distance of twenty-five miles in two and a
half days.

MATING. According to Hornell, copulation begins in shallow water near shore soon after the return of the spent females
to the sea, where the males lie in wait for them. Whether mating takes place at any other time or place is not known, but
males have been seen to follow females ashore, a procedure
which certainly is unusual. Obviously the mating and laying
seasons wholly or in part coincide. It has been fairly well established by Hornell that each female lays three clutches a
year at intervals of thirteen to fifteen days, so copulation must
take place more than once annually.

NESTING. In the Seychelles, east of Africa and about five
degrees south of the equator, the Hawksbill lays throughout
the year with a *very* decided peak during September, Octo-

ber, and November. In the region of southern Florida and throughout the West Indies it is reported to nest from April to July.

Hornell definitely states that the females habitually come out to lay in the daytime on the Seychelles, and Deraniyagala relates how one was found about to do so on a Ceylon beach at 7.00 p.m. of February 16. He carefully noted the nesting process in this individual, which measured 39.37 inches, or 1 metre, from tip of snout to point of tail, and describes it thus:

" After selecting a suitable spot under the fringe of the screw-pine (Pandanus) brush wood, it commenced to dispel the loose sand with a few outward semicircular sweeps from all flippers, after which the animal began to dig methodically and slowly using its feet for the purpose. The sand was grasped by contraction of the under surface of one foot and gently set aside and the process repeated with the other. As the hole deepened a foot would be carefully lowered into the pit where, after a pause of a second or two, it caught up a flipperful of sand. The limb was then slowly withdrawn and the sand gently set aside. This would be followed by a short pause after which the other foot would be lowered. The same foot never dug twice consecutively. Finally, the bottom of the hole was enlarged so that the nest appeared goblet-shaped in section and was about 20 cm. in diameter and about 50 cm. deep. After finishing the nest, the depth of which equalled the length of the leg, the animal placed her feet on either side of the hole and commenced to oviposit. At this stage the sand was scooped by the writer from the side of the hole to obtain a better view, and it was observed that the cloaca was prolongated to a considerably lower level than the caudal appendage, but not everted. The turtle strained prior to the ejection of eggs which were shot out in simultaneous batches of 2, 3 or 4 between pauses of a few seconds' duration. Eggs were not observed to be deposited singly. The number of eggs

ejected at each stricture was verified by receiving each discharge into a coconut shell and it was noticed that the batches
of four appeared early in the process and lasted until oviposition was half finished. After this the eggs issued in threes and
ultimately in twos. Along with each batch of eggs were also
discharged a few drops of mucus.

" All the eggs were taken out of the nest through the side
opening, but the turtle did not take any notice. After the last
egg had been laid the animal strained for another three minutes,
then after a few minutes' rest commenced to fill in the empty
hole with great care. It grasped sand with a foot which was
next lowered far into the hole prior to dropping the sand
gently on the place where she imagined the eggs to be. The
feet were worked alternately in this manner until the animal
considered its eggs well covered. Now it worked faster and
with less care shovelling in sand with alternate sweeps of its
hind limbs. At last the nest was filled in and, placing her feet
together edge to edge, she patted down the loose earth, at first
gently, later rapidly and with increased force. All this time
the animal had remained stationary and had not used its arms,
but now it began to gyrate around the covered hole which it
kept under its belly and scattered sand with strong sweeps
from all four flippers. This gyration produced a small trench
around the filled up nest, but in a short time this was obliterated and the animal began to move off seaward, when it was
captured. The process of digging occupied about three-
quarters of an hour, oviposition about a quarter of an hour and
filling in the nest about another three-quarters of an hour."

Choice of a site above the level of high tide is undoubtedly the general rule, but this selection of one about two hundred and sixty feet from the water and sheltered by fringing
vegetation is especially interesting, the female apparently
showing a desire to nest in a protected spot regardless of the
great distance doing so forced the young to travel to reach the

sea. The presence of four conversing persons with a coconut-leaf torch did not disturb the nesting process.

In the Bermuda region the gravid Hawksbill is said to come ashore on a rising tide.

Only 115 eggs were laid by the Ceylon female, but Hornell gives the number per clutch as 150 to 200. The usual incubation period is sixty days, though periods five days shorter and seven longer have been noted.

BEHAVIOUR OF HATCHLING. Both Hornell and Deraniyagala bring out interesting facts about the behaviour of the hatchling. These are combined and numbered for the sake of brevity and convenience.

1. The eggs of any one clutch hatch almost simultaneously, the turtlets following one another to the surface in quick succession.

2. Once out, they are noticeably influenced by light. Numbers crowd around a lantern placed near a nest from which young are escaping at night, or if many are placed in a basin, they at once tirelessly scramble toward light.

3. If kept in water for a few minutes, they not only become sluggish but are no longer attracted by light.

4. During the first day the forelimbs are used chiefly as balancers, swimming being accomplished largely by alternate strokes of the hind limbs.

5. The presence of internal yolk material renders ineffectual for several days all efforts to dive. This inability to descend materially affects their feeding habits, exposes them to certain enemies, and allows them to be dispersed by wind and current.

6. No effort by confined individuals to avoid being picked up is exhibited for more than a month, but striking the outside of the basin in which they float makes them attempt to dive.

7. Food may be taken as soon as the second day after emergence, floating algæ, sea grass, and even chopped fish being ac-

ceptable. The flippers are used in breaking off parts of pieces too large to be swallowed whole.

8. The sea water in which hatchlings are kept must be changed at least twice daily because of their extreme sensitiveness to impurities.

FOOD AND FEEDING. This aggressive turtle is omnivorous, devouring mollusks, crustaceans, ascidians, fish, marine algæ, and other sea animals and plants. Babcock relates that, while eating the Portuguese man-of-war, the turtle keeps its eyes closed for protection, and during such times hunters readily capture the preoccupied reptile.

Shoals less than sixty feet deep with abundant growth of brown algæ are favourite feeding grounds of large numbers of Seychelles Hawksbills.

ENEMIES. Man is without rival as an enemy of this reptile. Next to him come frigate-birds. These winged enemies are said by Hornell to gather on nesting grounds and feed on countless numbers of hatchlings as they emerge and toddle down the beach in vain efforts to reach the sea. Even after a few lucky survivors have attained their goal, the inability to dive leaves them still exposed to the same tormentors, while fish attack them from below. Other raptorial birds, rats, and crabs do their bit in raising the turtle infant mortality rate.

Barnacles often encrust shell and flippers, and cirripedes frequently cause great damage by boring into these same parts. The female whose nesting behaviour is described above was in bad condition, apparently the effect of the countless barnacles and cirripedes which had adopted her as their host.

CAPTIVITY. The information given above in the sections on longevity and growth is sufficient proof of the hardiness of this species in captivity. In spite of this, numerous attempts at Hawksbill culture have failed, owing perhaps rather to lack of a scientific approach than to any inherent or insurmountable difficulty. The delicacy of the young and their pugnacity probably are the chief obstacles, crowded individuals being prone to bite one another's eyes. Ripe eggs if carefully handled can be removed from the female or nest and successfully hatched.

Captive adults or adolescents have been known to eat seaweed, garden plants, ascidians, young oysters, clams, acorn barnacles, conchs, crabs, and chopped fish.

ECONOMIC VALUE. The shell of the Hawksbill is the source of the renowned " tortoise shell," and numerous industries are based on this product in various parts of the world. Methods of capture and removal of the shields differ from place to place.

All the shields have value, but those of the carapace are the thicker. The average weight of shields per shell from sixty Seychelles turtles was found to be:

Carapace	2.4 pounds
Plastron	0.43 "
Marginals	0.74 "
Total	3.57 "

A question of great interest is whether a turtle from which the shields have been carefully removed will survive and regenerate a new lot if set free. Fishermen often release peeled specimens with this hope in mind, but no one seems to have a final answer. The power to renew at least parts of the shell, however, was exhibited by a young captive that lost the seventh left costal shield together with the upper halves of the sixth and seventh marginals on October 29, 1928, and so completely healed the wound by June 20, 1929 that only a slight dent in the margin of the carapace remained as evidence of the injury. Again we are indebted to Deraniyagala.

ATLANTIC LOGGERHEAD TURTLE

Caretta caretta (Linnæus)

[PLATES 90 AND 91]

IDENTIFICATION. The limbs are paddle-shaped and each has two claws. There are two pairs of large shields, the prefrontals, on top of the head between the eyes. Five or more costal shields are present on each side, the first one of each row making contact with the nuchal. The shields of the carapace do not overlap (a slight overlap is evident in the very young). Three enlarged poreless shields (the inframarginals) extend across the bridge along the edges of the lower parts of the marginals.

SIZE. A weight of 450 pounds is occasionally recorded for Atlantic Loggerheads taken in American waters, but an individual weighing 300 pounds and having a three-foot carapace is considered very large.

True describes one taken in 1871 that weighed about 850 pounds and measured nine feet across the back from tip to tip of front flippers and had a head eleven inches long by eight broad. These astonishing dimensions are confirmed by a skull of the same length found recently on one of the Florida Keys.

THE SEXES. In *Caretta gigas*, a species closely related to the Atlantic Loggerhead, the tail of the male reaches beyond the extended hind flippers, whereas that of the female barely reaches the edge of the carapace. Similar relations almost certainly exist in the Atlantic Loggerhead.

EGG. An egg figured by Agassiz measures 41.5 × 42.5 millimetres. The soft shell is white.

LONGEVITY. A female (presumably of the Atlantic Loggerhead) brought to the Berlin Aquarium in 1913, when approximately two years old, was still thriving there in 1936. Some loggerheads, probably also of this species, lived in the Vasco da Gama Aquarium, Lisbon, Portugal, from about 1898 to 1931, when they died during a spell of extremely hot weather.

GROWTH. Nothing is known about the growth of the Atlantic Loggerhead in a natural state, but Parker has summarized by far the best data on its growth in captivity. Among the six individuals discussed in his paper, one stands out by reason of the rapid rate at which it grew. Parker is inclined to consider its rate unusual, whereas I, to the contrary, think its rate probably approximates that of the normal unconfined individual. The specimens that grew so much more slowly were, I believe, like so many other captive turtles, retarded in development by some unknown cause. There is a remote possibility that a differential sexual growth rate was in part responsible for the puzzling difference.

The fast growing individual attained a weight of 42 pounds and a carapace length of 20.87 inches in the first three years of its life; when four and a half years old, it measured 24.8 inches and weighed 81 pounds 8 ounces. Thus it grew 3.94 inches and about doubled its weight during that last year and a half. No one knows at what size this species matures, but it most likely does so when weighing somewhere between 200 and 250 pounds, if not before. Obviously the individual in question was within a very few years of maturity.

DISTRIBUTION. This hardy sea-turtle occurs abundantly along the shores of our Gulf states and commonly ranges northward along the Atlantic coast to North Carolina and Virginia. It is found as far north as Cape Cod every summer. The fact that it lays on North Carolina and even Virginia beaches is further proof of its hardiness.

It is widely distributed in the tropical and subtropical Atlantic, also occurring in the Mediterranean Sea.

Pleistocene fossil remains from Florida prove that it has lived in the Florida region perhaps tens of thousands of years.

HABITAT. Marine, probably preferring the waters of archipelagos, continental shelves, estuaries, and animal- and vegetation-laden ocean currents.

HABITS. Two Atlantic Loggerheads kept in the Fisheries Biological Station at Beaufort, North Carolina, were gentle during the first two years of life, after which they became decidedly aggressive and frequently fought each other or bit at any hand held within reach. The adults are elsewhere described as active and vicious.

Although the information on the general habits of this species is meagre, several odd observations are of some interest.

Sleep is apparently indulged in while floating on the surface. Musk glands, secreting a substance presumably of a defensive nature, are located in the hatchling at the edge of the carapace: an anterior double one with two ducts opening at the fourth marginal shield, and a posterior one, its single duct beneath the eighth marginal.

The species is occasionally found as far north as Long Island, New York, during the warmer six months of the year beginning with June. No impulse to hibernate or secure protection from cold by burying themselves in bottom mud or vegetation was exhibited by three individuals weighing from forty to sixty pounds and kept in shallow water outdoors at Beaufort, North Carolina. Two succumbed on December 14, when the air temperature reached 26° F., the third on February 3, when a drop to 13° F. was recorded. All remained active until killed by the cold.

NESTING. The only first-hand account of nest construction in this species is quoted in full from Mast:

"On July 11, 1910, I was fortunate enough to be present when a turtle came out to lay on Loggerhead Key, Florida, while it was still daylight (7^h5^m p.m.). This individual was about 3 feet long and 2 feet wide. She came out at right angles to the water line and proceeded directly up the beach 50 to 60 feet, where she immediately began to make her nest. There was no indication whatever of a process of selection of the place for the nest, as some have asserted in describing the breeding habits of this turtle. When the turtle reached the nesting-place she stopped and began at once to move the posterior end from side to side, throwing the sand out sidewise and forward alternately, with the two hind flippers, to a distance of 5 to 6 feet. Thus a crescent-shaped trench was made, wide and deep in the middle and narrow and shallow at either end. This trench was over 4 feet long and nearly 10 inches deep in the middle. The lateral movement of the turtle during this process of digging was largely due to the action of the muscles connected with the front flippers, which remained stationary as the body turned on them.

" After the trench was finished the turtle took a position so that the right hind leg was very nearly over the middle of the bottom of it. This flipper was then thrust vertically down into the sand (the flat surface being nearly parallel with the long axis of the body) and the end turned in under the sand so as to form a cup much like one formed by a human hand partly closed. The posterior end of the animal was then raised by the action of the left leg and pushed to the right. During this process the right flipper, containing a fair-sized handful of sand, was of course raised and as the posterior end of the body moved to the right the flipper gradually rotated so as to face backward; it was then thrust out to the side and inverted so as to empty the sand in a heap, just in front of which the foot was placed on the ground in the customary position. The left flipper was now directly over the hole made by the right one and used in removing sand just as described, except that it took the sand from the right side of the hole while the right flipper took it from the left side. Before the body was pushed back to the left by the right leg it made a sudden movement forward and threw out a considerable bit of sand, making a hole just in front of the place where the sand taken from the nest had been deposited. This sand was pushed into the hole in front of it when the turtle moved back to the right again and thrown out just before it moved to the left the following time. Thus the two hind flippers alternated in scooping the sand from the nest until a cylindrical hole was dug nearly as deep as their length. The alternation from right to left was perfectly regular. Neither flipper ever took sand from the hole twice in succession.

" After the hole was completed the turtle assumed a position so that the cloaca was very nearly over the center of it and began to lay at once. The cloaca projected fully 2 inches during the process of laying. The head was well extended and flat on the ground. The anterior end of the body was raised so that the ventral surface made an angle of about 20° with the horizontal. There was no arrangement of the eggs in the nest as fishermen sometimes assert. The eggs were dropped from the cloaca into the hole in a series of one or two at a time at intervals of from 4 to 8 seconds. Two were deposited together about every fourth time. During the discharge of the eggs the hind flippers were slightly raised, and in one case (witnessed at night earlier in the summer) there was heavy breathing which was very distinctly heard. In the turtle under present consideration, however, not the slightest sound was detected.

" Fishermen often say that after a turtle begins to lay it will continue even if it is turned on its back. I did not try this, but I did strike the turtle a sound blow on the head with a heavy stick, using both hands, at two different times while she was laying. She withdrew her head, moved slightly to one side and stopped laying, but only for a few moments. Noise and gentle contact did not appear to affect her in the least.

" It is commonly thought that the loggerhead turtle ordinarily lays three times during each summer, about 150 eggs the

90. Atlantic Loggerhead Turtle (*Caretta caretta*) with a carapace 17.87 inches long. It is a female. (*Courtesy Philadelphia Aquarium and Zoological Society of Philadelphia, photograph by Mark Mooney, Jr.*)

91. Atlantic Loggerhead Turtle (*Caretta caretta*) with a carapace 17.87 inches long. The tips of the man's fingers just touch, on either side, the first of the three enlarged inframarginal shields. The smaller claw nearer the end of the flipper cannot be clearly seen. (*Courtesy Philadelphia Aquarium and Zoological Society of Philadelphia, photograph by Mark Mooney, Jr.*)

92. Kemp's Turtle (*Colpochelys kempii*) with a carapace 20.87 inches long. It is a female. (*Courtesy Philadelphia Aquarium and Zoological Society of Philadelphia, photograph by Mark Mooney, Jr.*)

93. Kemp's Turtle (*Colpochelys kempii*) with a carapace 20.87 inches long. Four enlarged inframarginal shields can be seen on either bridge. It is a female. (*Courtesy Philadelphia Aquarium and Zoological Society of Philadelphia, photograph by Mark Mooney, Jr.*)

first time, fewer the second time, and about 80 the third. I did
not ascertain precisely how many eggs were laid by the turtle
under observation. It is almost impossible to remove the eggs
from the nest without killing the embryos, and, since there
have been many trustworthy observations on the number of
eggs laid, it seemed unnecessary to destroy the young for the
sake of learning the exact number in this particular nest.

" Immediately after the eggs were discharged the turtle began to cover them. In doing this she moved the posterior end
back and forth much as she did in digging the hole. As this
end proceeded to the right the left flipper was thrust backward
into the sand and then suddenly moved inward so as to throw
and scrape the sand on to the eggs immediately back of it. As
it proceeded to the left the right flipper acted in the same way,
but of course it threw the sand in the opposite direction. Thus
the turtle filled the trench as well as the hole, stopping frequently to pack the sand, especially that over the eggs. This
she did by placing the posterior pointed end of the body on
the sand and elevating the anterior end so as to bring her full
weight to bear upon it. After the trench was nearly filled she
turned about over the region several times and threw and scattered the sand in every direction with all four flippers so as to
conceal the place, especially that where the eggs were laid.
This completed she returned to the sea and entered only a few
feet from the spot where she came out. On the way down the
beach I stood on her back and she carried me (165 lbs.) apparently with but little effort. From what has been said re-
garding the concealment of the nest of the loggerhead turtle
it must not be assumed that the nesting-place is difficult to
find – quite the contrary, for the turtle-tracks leading to and
from it are very conspicuous and can not be mistaken. The
place where the eggs are buried is, however, not easy to find.
In the case of the nest described I had considerable difficulty
in finding the eggs, even after carefully watching the whole

process of laying and noting the position of the turtle in detail; and this is quite in harmony with the experience related to me by several fishermen who collect the eggs for food.

" The eggs in this nest were 11 inches below the surface, and they occupied a space 6.5 inches in depth and 9 inches in diameter, making the bottom of the nest 17.5 inches from the surface. The turtle under observation was out of water 42 minutes, approximately 3 of which were required to come from the water to the nest, 4 to make the trench, 8 to dig the hole, 12 to lay the eggs, and 15 to fill the hole and trench, smooth off the place and get back to the sea. The rate of locomotion on land is about half a mile an hour."

The most detailed information on the time of nesting has been secured for North Carolina by Coker, who found that the height of the season there is during June and July; some laying, however, takes place in late May and early August. As far south as Florida laying is said to begin much earlier. There is general agreement that nests are made at night, the female watched by Mast having made hers unusually early.

The site chosen is generally just above the high-tide mark and near the vegetation or dune line, the distance from water of course depending on the slope of the beach. The eggs must be above the usual level of high tide or else they will be spoiled by the salt water or the embryos drowned. Nevertheless, the eggs of one nest washed by a very high tide before Coker's eyes, and marked, later hatched successfully. The eggs of most of several nests examined by him, however, were about three or four feet above the level of high tide.

Coker found that the topmost eggs are about thirteen inches below the surface. The egg pocket of one nest carefully opened was eight inches deep by ten in diameter; the top, of course, was flat. These figures agree well with those given by Mast. The number of eggs per nest in seven reported cases ranged from 118 to 152 and averaged 135. Nests with 87 and

60 eggs have been recorded. Whether, in accordance with Mast's suggestion, these small clutches are second or third layings of the same season cannot even be presumed until more studies have been made.

BEHAVIOUR OF HATCHLING. The young emerge from the nest after an incubation period which, though varying with conditions of temperature and moisture, usually lasts about two months.

Young loggerheads have been used in experiments to determine just how hatchling sea-turtles manage to find their way from nest to sea. The results obtained by Hooker and Parker prove that the young move downhill away from a broken and toward an open horizon. It is obvious that, once out of the nest, such behaviour, in nearly every case, would cause the turtles to go down the beach and finally into the ocean. Hooker further detected a tendency to move away from transparent and opaque red, orange, and green toward transparent or opaque blue, concluding therefrom that vegetation above the beach helps to speed the hatchling in the right direction; also that " the darker blue of the deeper water attracts it out of the dangerous fish-infested shoals of the reefs."

Surprisingly enough, the position of the sun, the sound or odour of the ocean, and proximity to water were shown to be without effect.

The impulse to go downhill would only hinder the upward escape from the depth of the nest to the surface through the sand covering the eggs. It is probable that, like some freshwater turtles, the newly hatched loggerhead ascends in the dark. Once the light is reached, this negative geotropism must soon be lost or else overcome by the stronger positive one already written of.

FOOD AND FEEDING. Although always described as only " chiefly " carnivorous, I find no definite record of any plant food having been taken. Hermit crabs, shell-fish, and conchs

(*Strombus*) are favourite articles of diet, but "loggerhead sponge," the Portuguese man-of-war, borers (*Natica*), and fish are also eaten.

Great strength of jaw enables this rapacious reptile easily to crush shell-fish and eat conchs by biting off the small end of the shell and extracting the animal through the hole thus made.

ENEMIES. Man is certainly the chief enemy of the Atlantic Loggerhead. Hogs and raccoons have been known to destroy the nests.

The shell is usually well covered with barnacles, which even fix themselves in the mouth.

CAPTIVITY. The two individuals kept for six years in the Fisheries Biological Station, Beaufort, North Carolina, and reported on by Hildebrand and Hatsel, were fed chiefly on fish, but blue crabs were occasionaly given. When a considerable size had been obtained, this diet was supplemented now and then by hard clams in the shell. Sand dollars (*Mellita*) have also been fed to captives. Before these two were able to dive, their food (fish) was suspended at the surface.

Aside from the two records related under the section on longevity above, loggerheads have been known to survive twelve and fourteen years of confinement. Unfortunately, in all four cases there is some doubt as to the species concerned. In view of the lack of general agreement in regard to the status of these turtles, no harm can result from putting down the records for what they may be worth.

ECONOMIC VALUE. Although decidedly inferior to that of the Green Turtle, the flesh of young individuals is eaten locally and sometimes even sold in city markets. The eggs have long been an esteemed local table delicacy. In 1893 True reported that oil is extracted from the animal itself as well as from its eggs; the former kind of oil, too rank for cooking, is smeared on ships and used to soften leather.

PACIFIC LOGGERHEAD TURTLE
Lepidochelys olivacea (Eschscholtz)

IDENTIFICATION. This species differs from the Atlantic Loggerhead in many characters. The most obvious of these are: one or two claws on each flipper, six or more costals on each side, and four enlarged inframarginals, each perforated by a pore.

SIZE. This turtle has been so consistently confused with the recently described *Caretta gigas* that one cannot tell which descriptions of loggerheads from the Pacific apply to the one or to the other. Deraniyagala, however, gives the carapace lengths of seven adults taken in the region of Ceylon as ranging from 25.59 to 35.43 inches. It is impossible to tell whether these figures apply to *gigas*, *olivacea*, or a mixture of the two; in all probability they indicate the average dimensions of both, since Deraniyagala nowhere gives size as a distinguishing character.

THE SEXES. Although I have no proof to offer, there can be little doubt that the male is distinguished by a much longer tail. (See the remark under the same heading in the account of the Atlantic Loggerhead.)

EGG. Spherical or nearly so, and 38 to 44 millimetres in diameter. One diameter may be as much as two millimetres longer than the other, but the greater one is nearly always at least 40 millimetres.

DISTRIBUTION. There seems to be no really concrete evidence that this inhabitant of the tropical and subtropical Pacific actually reaches the shores of California, but its accidental occurrence there is likely. Strauch recorded a specimen from "California," but this may refer to Lower California, for which there is at least one (other) good record.

REPRODUCTION. On Ceylon coasts, according to Deraniyagala, this turtle deposits from 90 to 135 eggs during the period from August through January, the young emerging after about two months' incubation.

KEMP'S TURTLE

Colpochelys kempii (Garman)

[PLATES 92 AND 93]

IDENTIFICATION. The limbs are paddle-shaped and each has three claws. There are two pairs of large shields, the prefrontals, on top of the head between the eyes. Five costal shields are present on each side, the first one of each row making contact with the nuchal. The shields of the carapace do not overlap (a slight overlap is evident in the very young). Four enlarged shields (the inframarginals) extend across the bridge along the edges of the lower parts of the marginals. These inframarginals are poreless.

Oddly enough, this American turtle has never been adequately described and examination of more specimens may show that some of the points given above are not really diagnostic of the species.

SIZE. Individuals with carapaces two feet long are already sexually mature, and the largest carapace on record measures just under twenty-eight inches. This species seems to be even smaller than the Hawksbill Turtle.

DISTRIBUTION. The northern Gulf of Mexico and the Atlantic from Velasco, eastern Texas, to North Carolina.

It also ranges along the coast to New Jersey every summer and not infrequently reaches Massachusetts, where it has been taken as far north as Swampscott. To the south it has been

recorded from Jamaica. Babcock recently failed to find concrete evidence of the existence of this species in Bermuda, but
fishermen report catches of a " mulatto turtle " there which
may be it. There is indisputable evidence, however, of its occurrence off Ireland.

The almost negligible information on the habits of this turtle is hard to explain. It is said to breed during the winter in
the region of Florida. Stomach dissections convinced De Sola
that the spotted lady crab (*Platyonichus ocellatus*) is the main-
stay of its diet in Georgia waters.

The flesh, superior to that of the Atlantic Loggerhead, is
eaten locally.

LEATHERBACK TURTLE

Dermochelys coriacea (Linnæus)

IDENTIFICATION. The paddle-shaped limbs are devoid of
claws, and the shell is covered with smooth skin instead of
large horny shields. Seven prominent ridges extend down the
back, which is dark brown or slaty black, uniform or with
spots or blotches variously described as white, bluish white, or
pale yellow.

SIZE. This is the largest of living turtles. In 1923 a 1,286-
pound specimen eight feet long and having a front flipper
spread of as many feet was taken off the California coast, and
much more recently one weighing 1,450 pounds was secured
near Vancouver Island. There are a few additional records of
individuals from North American waters weighing over 1,000
pounds. The average adult weight, however, is certainly less
than half, the maximum probably somewhat more, than three
quarters of a ton.

YOUNG. Very young specimens differ from the adult chiefly in being covered by small irregular scales, which begin to disappear at the age of a few weeks, and in having white shell ridges and flipper margins.

THE SEXES. In the male the hips are narrow, the profile depressed, the plastron concave, and the tail reaches well beyond the hind limbs when these are placed edge to edge; whereas in the other sex the hips are wide, the profile convex or straight, the plastron convex, and the tail shorter than the hind limbs (Deraniyagala, 1932).

EGG. The spherical eggs range from 50 to 54 millimetres in diameter and have a soft white shell. Ten to twenty abnormal eggs, small or variable in shape and lacking yolk, are the last of each clutch to be laid.

GROWTH. Deraniyagala describes the growth of a specimen that was kept alive in Ceylon for six hundred and sixty-two days, during which time it attained a carapace length of approximately seventeen inches and a weight of about sixteen pounds. At hatching, its carapace was not less than 58 nor more than 60 millimetres (about 3.32 in.) long. Another captive reached a carapace length of 6.30 inches in a hundred and sixty-nine days. This reptile has the astonishing ability of increasing its hatching weight some fifteen thousand fold. If human beings did the same, a man would weigh fifty tons, and beside him King Kong would be merely a Lilliputian ape instead of a terrible monster.

DISTRIBUTION. The Leatherback Turtle strays farther to the north than any other marine chelonian. It has been recorded from Nova Scotia, and two individuals were taken near Nootka Sound, Vancouver Island, British Columbia, in 1931. There are no fewer than six Maine locality records for it, the northernmost being Naskeag Point. Marin County, California, is the farthest north record for the west coast of the United States, but four other California counties have yielded specimens. It occurs, however, only occasionally along our coasts, being nowhere common.

This species is widely distributed in tropical and subtropical seas.

HABITAT. More highly adapted to marine life than any other turtle, this reptile apparently prefers water more than a hundred and fifty feet deep, which it voluntarily leaves only to lay its eggs. The very young were rare and early adolescents unknown until Deraniyagala's enlightening reports appeared during the last decade. Even now but a single juvenile seems to have been found in its native marine habitat. This one was taken at 10.00 p.m. on September 30, 1934, twelve and a half miles from a Ceylon shore and a little over one mile from the edge of the continental shelf in water a hundred and sixty-four feet deep. The carapace measured 3.34 inches and its age was probably about three weeks.

HABITS. The great strength of this giant among turtles is shown by the actions of the laying female described below in the section on nesting. The power that sends such a huge bulk ploughing through sand must be prodigious. The weight of a man on its back is not even noticed. Once the quick movements of an individual confined in a room upset stove, tables, and barrels and were likened to those of a Texas wild steer. When injured or tormented, a stranded Leatherback utters a sound audible at a quarter of a mile, " an indescribable kind of noise such as is heard at a menagerie." Naturally, the removal of an adult from its native element is a task of no small magnitude.

Sleep is at least sometimes indulged in while floating on the surface.

NESTING. On the coasts of Ceylon the Leatherback's laying season extends throughout the year, but reaches its height in May and June after the beginning of the southwest monsoon. The females lay at night, usually between 9.00 and 11.00 p.m.,

on broad beaches of fine sand, preferably those without fringing reefs. Ordinarily the nests, the deepest dug by any sea-
turtle, are fifty to sixty-five feet from the sea. The same small
stretch of beach often bears the trails of several females at one
time, and each one lays several clutches a year. A clutch contains 90 to 150 eggs, requiring 58 to 65 days to incubate.

We have Deraniyagala to thank for all these facts about
nesting, and unfortunately can present little New World information for comparison. Females have been known to lay
on West Indian shores, one on March 30, another probably on
April 19. (The former returned to the same spot on April 10,
presumably to lay again, but was captured.) The number of
eggs laid in one case was five or six dozen, in the other seventy-
eight. Long ago Prince of Wied reported that on Brazilian
shores the Leatherback lays four times a year at intervals of
fourteen days.

Nest construction has been well described by Deraniyagala;
the date was May 29, 1934, the time 9.30 p.m., the place
Ceylon:

"Glistening silvery in the moonlight, the turtle ascended
the beach in a straight line to the sandy embankment created
by the scouring action of the waves. Through this obstacle
she cut her path with simultaneous jerks of her powerful fore
flippers and gained the dry sand. Here, she commenced what
Sinhalese fishermen term a 'sand-bath' flinging up a shower of
sand over her back to a distance of about three metres by
strong simultaneous jerks of her fore limbs. The upward
direction of these movements differed from her usual shuffle.
The turtle probably tested the density of the sand while 'sand
bathing' for each jerk of her fore flippers excavated hollows
which were 16 to 26 cm. deep. Her course was zig-zag and
she even doubled back upon her track searching for a suitable
place in which to nest. Meanwhile she was completely coated
with sand, except for her eyes, which were washed by a copi-

ous flow of tears. After a satisfactory place was found, she dispelled the loose sand with a few preliminary sweeps of the flippers; a shallow cavity was next hollowed out posteriorly with a side to side movement of her carapace, facilitated by the out-stretched hind limbs and cruro-caudal fold of skin. During this operation, her fore flippers sank into the sand and apparently acted as anchors, while a cushion-like mound of sand lay heaped behind each. After these preliminaries she excavated a smaller nest hole within the crater by working the hind limbs alternately, flinging the sand to a distance of 30 cm. or more as it was brought up. When the combined depth of the crater and the nest hole was about 100 cm. and she could no longer reach the bottom of the pit, she began to lay.

" Anchored by the fore limbs, the turtle sloped her body into the pit at an angle of about 35 degrees, protruded her cloaca, and then deposited the eggs in batches of two or three at a time, moving her head up and down as she strained. Her breathing was somewhat stertorous and a peculiar fishy odour was noticeable. Her eggs laid, she began to fill in the nest hole working the hind limbs alternately, each taking up a flipperful of sand which was gently placed upon the eggs. This was continued until the eggs were well covered, after which the sand was pushed in rapidly. Eventually, with her fore limbs still buried, the animal demolished the brink of the nest pit by swinging her outstretched hind quarters and tail rapidly from side to side, although the carapace was stationary. During this procedure, every time a hind flipper touched the ground, it flung the sand crosswise towards its fellow with a rapid scooping movement.

" Although the turtle is said to be cautious in her approach to land, once oviposition commenced the animal was completely indifferent to the presence of man, noise or lights, and this indifference persisted even after she had covered up the eggs and had begun to churn up the beach all round the nest, in spite of blows.

"When the nest was nearly covered, she moved her front limbs for the first time since oviposition commenced. Both were jerked back simultaneously, showering sand over her back and into the pit, but without visibly altering her position. She worked the front and hind limbs in turn over five minute intervals, the former always with a simultaneous jerk, the latter generally alternately. Eventually she gyrated on her plastron upon the nest area and flung up great scoopfuls of sand with her fore flippers, occasionally employing her head to push down any ridges of sand created during this process. Throughout this phase the turtle did not appear to move from the nest and it was only by comparing the animal's position with a haversack I had laid down when first she commenced to dig, that it became apparent that she had moved quite two metres during ten minutes. At this stage I struck her a sharp blow on the head with a stick and sat upon her, but undeterred she continued to churn up the sand and worked shoreward instead of towards the sea.

"After a time she doubled back on her tracks and slowly and laboriously repeated the process. Finally she decided that her duty was done, and it was certainly very thorough, for after she had gone, three of us dug for an hour with our hands but were unable to locate the eggs. The departing turtle no longer showered sand with her fore limbs, but wearily made for the sea stopping after every two·or three shuffles, blowing most of the time. Gradually she recovered her energy and rested only after every ten or fifteen shuffles. She approached the wave line and there paused. The breakers were rough on the night of May 29, 1934, at Tangalla (Southern Province). When the surf reached her, she allowed herself to be washed away into the waves without exerting herself. At her first attempt she failed to get past the breakers, but as·the next wave rose she hugged the ground, escaped under the wave, and was gone.

" The track of *Dermochelys* is of interest. In marine The-cophora the nest is generally at the bend of a V formed by the ingress and egress trails of the animal. In *Dermochelys* the track roughly resembles the three sides of a rectangle of which the middle one is a long churned up area of sand in which the nest may be located anywhere. The marks left in the sand were as follows: — each time the long fore flippers shifted forward their tips cut thin arcs in the sand, and as the animal jerked herself forward, each limb impressed a wide furrow with a ridge of earth heaped along its posterior margin. The push off with the hind limbs formed an inner row of shallower furrows. As in most marine Thecophora, the tip of the tail ploughed a thin median furrow in the sand. The majority of tracks showed the ingress and egress trails about six to twenty metres apart, while the churned up area was generally five to ten metres long and two or three wide. In this instance, however, the turtle returned to the sea by the ingress trail, though this seldom happens."

In this account the term " marine Thecophora " refers to all the other sea-turtles.

The throwing of sand on the back is presumably a protective measure, rendering the female's slaty black back less conspicuous against the sand in moonlight. The turtle itself probably has few enemies, but the eggs have many. The even more valuable habit of making the vicinity of the actual nest resemble " the arena of a buffalo fight " renders discovery of the eggs next to impossible. Deraniyagala relates that a giant lizard or monitor was disturbed after it had dug three holes in a futile attempt to find the newly laid eggs of a Leatherback. Presumably the monitor depends on its sense of smell, but the strong fishy odour emitted freely by the nesting turtle permeates the churned-up sand so thoroughly that any odour of the eggs is completely lost amid that of the disturbed area.

Wind and rain soon obliterate all outward sign of the huge turtle's efforts, leaving the eggs in almost perfect concealment.

BEHAVIOUR OF HATCHLING. According to Deraniyagala, "Newly hatched Dermochelys dive easily and swim rapidly with long downward sweeps of their relatively enormous fore flippers, while the hind limbs act mainly as balancers. . . . Observation of 40 and 62-day old Dermochelys showed that when moving fast it employs only its fore flippers and spreads out the hind limbs in a horizontal plane to act in the dual role of rudder and balancers." The membranes connecting the hind flippers with the tail help these limbs and the caudal appendage in their combined dual role.

Unlike other juvenile sea-turtles the young do not learn that the walls of their aquarium are solid, but persist in swimming against them, thus injuring snout and flippers. As if to make up for this stupidity, the hatchling Leatherback enjoys the distinction of being apparently the only sea-turtle that dives readily during the first days of existence. The internal yolk of other species keeps the body afloat in spite of efforts to descend.

FOOD. The stomach of a Ceylon male contained jellyfish (Scyphomedusæ). Dissections of females from the same place revealed only small quantities of fine blue-green algæ. Sears found Amphipod crustaceans in a Massachusetts individual, but thought that they might have been eaten when attached to jellyfish.

CAPTIVITY. No large Leatherback has survived more than a few weeks of confinement. The two young individuals kept alive under the direction of Dr. Deraniyagala in Ceylon have already been written about in the section on growth. These specimens ate chopped fish, which apparently was not especially suitable food. They required frequent changes of sea water daily and careful attention to diet.

(See also the remarks on the behaviour of the hatchling above.)

ECONOMIC VALUE. The Leatherback has no commercial value in the United States. In many parts of the world a useful oil is extracted from its skin and corselet. Deraniyagala tasted excellent curry made from its flesh in Ceylon, where the oil has considerable value as a canoe varnish.

CHAPTER IX

THE SOFT–SHELLED TURTLES

Family TRIONYCHIDÆ
Genus *Trionyx*

Although not especially old as turtles go, this family can, nevertheless, trace its tree back a cool eighty million years in the United States and fully twenty million more in Mongolia, where it lived during the Lower Cretaceous. Compared to them, man is a recent settler on this globe. The living species, some twenty-five in number, though but a poor representation of the kinds that have existed, are still widely distributed in Asia, the East Indies, North America, and Africa. All of the New World species are found in the United States.

Because the life histories of the American *Trionyx* have been so incompletely worked out, I cannot resist giving some information about the reproductive habits of the Japanese species of the genus. For about sixty years this turtle has been successfully bred in Japan, and from observations of specimens in confinement the following facts have been reported by Mitsukuri: At hatching, the carapace is 1.06 inches long; by the fifth year the length has increased to 6.9 inches, and the females begin to lay during their sixth year. Copulation takes place at the surface of the water, and each female deposits from two to four clutches a season (last of May to middle of August), each clutch having from seventeen to twenty-eight or more eggs. A nesting female abandons her task at the slightest disturbance.

298

94 [TOP]. Southern Soft-shelled Turtle (*Trionyx ferox*) from Florida with a carapace 13.75 inches long. It is a female. (*Courtesy Zoological Society of Philadelphia, photograph by Mark Mooney, Jr.*)

95–96 [CENTRE]. Young Southern Soft-shelled Turtle (*Trionyx ferox*) from Gainesville, Florida, with a carapace 41 millimetres long. (*Courtesy Zoological Society of Philadelphia, photograph by Mark Mooney, Jr.*)

97 [LOWER]. Egg of the Southern Soft-shelled Turtle from the Okefi-nokee Swamp, Georgia, photographed on May 29, 1930. (*Photograph by Francis Harper.*)

98. Spiny Soft-shelled Turtle (*Trionyx spiniferus*) from the region of
Columbia, South Carolina, with a carapace 14.25 inches long. It is a female.
(*Courtesy Zoological Society of Philadelphia, photograph by Mark
Mooney, Jr.*)

99. Young Spiny Soft-shelled Turtle (*Trionyx spiniferus*) from the region of Columbia, South Carolina, with a carapace 5.69 inches long. It is
a female. (*Courtesy Zoological Society of Philadelphia, photograph by
Mark Mooney, Jr.*)

Physiological and anatomical studies have explained how the highly aquatic soft-shelled turtles are able to remain under water for hours on end. While submerged, these reptiles pump water in and out of the mouth and pharynx by alternately raising and lowering the hyoid apparatus at the average rate of sixteen times a minute. The highly vascular lining of the pharynx removes oxygen from the water and unloads carbon dioxide into it. The classical work on this pharyngeal respiration was done by S. H. and S. P. Gage some fifty years ago. *Trionyx muticus* and *T. spiniferus* were used, but doubtless any species of *Trionyx* would have given much the same results.

IDENTIFICATION

No turtle is more easily placed in its group than a soft-shell, the name alone being a give-away. In addition to the flexible leathery shell entirely lacking the usual hard shields, the long, soft snout or proboscis (see Plate 99) and fleshy lips are points not readily overlooked.

All of the fourteen or fifteen species of the genus *Trionyx* look much alike to the casual glance because of their similar pancake form and lack of distinctive or " contrasty " adult patterns. The young, unlike most juvenile turtles, have the adult shape and are much more readily identified than a mature individual because of their distinctive coloration; it is to these small specimens that the turtle hobbyist would best turn his attention. Baby soft-shells are among the most singular and lively of turtles and might even be described as " cute," an adjective that can scarcely be applied to the rather forbidding adults.

The key given below is not very satisfactory, as only slight acquaintance with it will show. The situation is saved, however, by the mitigating fact that *T. muticus* is a really distinct animal not closely related to the others and readily distinguished from them by its round nostrils and smooth carapace. It is worthy of note that the callosities of its plastron are more strongly developed, according to Siebenrock, than in any other member of the family. With this species removed from the puzzle, specimens of known origin can nearly always be identified on the basis of distribution alone, as a perusal of the ranges will show.

When geographical data are lacking, the key will have to be relied upon or else recourse may be had to the time-honoured but weak character of the point of union of the stripes that start from the eyes and extend toward the snout. In Emory's Soft-shelled Turtle these two stripes unite between the eyes (that is, they come together immediately); in the Southern Soft-shell they join just in front of the eyes; in the Spiny Soft-shell they do not unite until the base of the snout is reached. These stripes fade with maturity and rightly belong with the other juvenile colour characters, of which there is no lack.

KEY TO THE AMERICAN SPECIES OF *Trionyx*

A1: Anterior border of carapace with tubercles (see Pl.
     99); a longitudinal ridge projecting in each crescent-
     shaped nostril from dividing septum.
  B1: Anterior border of carapace with small tubercles;
       carapace much wider behind.
                         Emory's Soft-shelled Turtle
  B2: Anterior border of carapace with small tubercles;
       carapace somewhat elongate.
                       Southern Soft-shelled Turtle
  B3: Anterior border of carapace with prominent spine-
       like tubercles; carapace neither much wider behind
       nor somewhat elongate.   Spiny Soft-shelled Turtle

A2: Anterior border of carapace smooth; nostrils round, without longitudinal ridges.

SPINELESS SOFT-SHELLED TURTLE

EMORY'S SOFT-SHELLED TURTLE

Trionyx emoryi (Agassiz)

IDENTIFICATION. Each crescent-shaped nostril has a longitudinal ridge in it projecting from the septum dividing the nostrils. The carapace is relatively wider behind than in the other species of the genus, and there are small tubercles along its anterior border as well as whitish ones distributed over its surface posteriorly. Remnants of the juvenile pattern are more or less in evidence on the olive carapace.

The southwestern distribution of this species will serve to identify many specimens of known origin.

SIZE. A Lower California specimen with a carapace 14.57 and a plastron 10.55 inches long is on record, but the adult carapace usually measures from ten to twelve inches.

The greater posterior width of the carapace is illustrated below by Siebenrock's measurements of a female:

	Inches	Millimetres
Anterior width of carapace	7.36	187
Width at middle	9.33	237
Width behind the middle	9.64	245
Posterior width	8.86	225
Length	11.50	292

YOUNG. Agassiz figures a specimen with a carapace measuring only 36.5 millimetres long by 31.5 millimetres across its widest point. According to him, in the young the white dorsal tubercles are relatively small, the pale rim of the rear margin of the carapace is set off by a distinct black line which later fades, and the faint black lines encircling the white tubercles of the back rapidly disappear.

EGG. An egg of this species figured by Agassiz is spherical and measures 29 millimetres in diameter. The shell is white.

DISTRIBUTION. This turtle is common in the highlands of central and western Texas. It also descends the rivers flowing through the southeastern lowlands of that state, reaching the coast as far east as Liberty County. To the northeast it has been recorded for Le Flore Country, southeastern Oklahoma; to the south it ranges to central Tamaulipas, northeastern Mexico; to the west it ascends the Rio Grande into Doña Ana County, southern New Mexico.

Recent discoveries prove that Emory's Soft-shelled Turtle has attained the Gila-Colorado system of the southwest. It is established from near the mouth of the Colorado River, Lower California, to Pierce Ferry, Arizona, just below the lower end of the Grand Canyon. A record for the Phoenix, Arizona, vicinity shows that it ascends the Gila River at least as far as that city.

HABITAT AND HABITS. Rivers, streams, and, at least in Arizona, canals and irrigation ditches are frequented. Agassiz was informed by a first-hand observer of this species that " it delights in clear, bold, and rocky streams, and possesses nothing of the sluggishness of other Testudinata, but is brisk and vivacious in all its movements, running rapidly on land when dropped from the hook of the angler, and swimming with great velocity."

Captive specimens prefer fish, but will take raw beef.

ECONOMIC VALUE. Recently seen for sale in the market at Ciudad Juárez, northern Mexico. Presumably its meat is as delicious as that of other soft-shelled turtles.

SOUTHERN SOFT-SHELLED TURTLE

Trionyx ferox (Schneider)

[PLATES 94, 95, 96, AND 97]

IDENTIFICATION. There is a row of tubercles along the anterior border of the somewhat elongate carapace, and each crescent-shaped nostril has a longitudinal ridge in it projecting from the septum dividing the nostrils. Remnants of the striking juvenile coloration are more or less in evidence on the plastron and the olive carapace.

The southeastern distribution of this species will serve to identify many specimens of known origin.

SIZE. Agassiz states that the largest Southern Soft-shelled Turtle that he ever saw or heard of had a carapace eighteen and a half inches long and sixteen wide. A Florida female weighing thirty-four and a quarter pounds is also on record. Wright and Funkhouser, however, give the following dimensions of a Georgia specimen of average size:

	Inches	*Millimetres*
Length of carapace	15.5	394
Width of carapace	11	279
Length of plastron	11.5	292
Width of plastron	10	254
Height of shell	5	127
Width of head	2.5	63

They also describe a head three and a half inches wide! No other soft-shelled turtle of North America rivals this species in size.

YOUNG. The very young have a yellow-margined carapace covered with large dark spots narrowly separated by light ground colour, a dark grey or black plastron, and yellow markings or longitudinal stripes on the greyish black limbs, neck, and posterior part of the head. As growth proceeds, these bright colours rapidly fade or change, only the dorsal spots sometimes persisting as dim remnants after a carapace length of six inches has been reached. The tubercles of the carapace, however, instead of disappearing become relatively more prominent with age.

The carapace of a very young specimen is about 41 millimetres long and nearly circular in shape. (See Plates 95 and 96.)

THE SEXES. The extended tail of the male projects beyond the edge of the carapace; that of the female does not, and the latter sex apparently attains the greater size; at least all the very large specimens whose sex is recorded are females. Siebenrock says that the female has the larger head, a less distinct snout pattern, and better-developed tubercles on the anterior border of the carapace, whereas Agassiz states that the tubercles on the male are more numerous and larger than those on the female carapace. Agassiz adds that the male has a more oblong carapace. Obviously the sexual differences in this species call for further study.

EGG. The spherical eggs range from 24 to 31 millimetres in diameter and have a hard brittle white shell, which is usually described as thin (see Plate 97). Agassiz's table, however, indicates a rather thick shell.

LONGEVITY. One of these turtles has lived twenty-five years in the Frankfurt am Main Zoological Garden, Germany.

DISTRIBUTION. The southeastern Atlantic and Gulf Coastal Plain from the Peedee River, eastern South Carolina, southwestward throughout Florida, and to Houston, southeastern Texas.

The exact inland limits of its range have not been determined, but the following records give some indication of them: Abbeville County and Columbia, South Carolina; Tuscaloosa

County, Alabama; Waco region, eastern central Texas; Rogers and Le Flore Counties, extreme eastern Oklahoma. The last two and probably the first of these records prove that this species sometimes penetrates a short distance into uplands bordering the Coastal Plain.

Fossil remains from the Pleistocene of Florida show that this turtle has lived in the extreme southeast for at least tens of thousands of years.

HABITAT. The Southern Soft-shelled Turtle lives in rivers, streams, lakes, ponds, and large swamps. It likes a soft bottom, and large specimens often inhabit deep water. According to Ditmars, it even enters brackish water.

HABITS. Surprisingly active on land as well as in the water, this turtle can jump forward a distance equal to its length and dig remarkably well in sand. It is vicious and, when cornered, ever ready to defend itself by snake-like jabs with its head, which enable the keen-edged jaws to inflict painful bites on an incautious offender. A baited hook is readily taken.

Three other habits in which it likes to indulge for hours on end are floating lazily at the surface, lying buried in mud or sand under shallow water, and basking along the edges of its haunts.

REPRODUCTION. A female weighing thirty-one and a quarter pounds was taken twenty-five yards from the shore of a lake in Lake County, Florida, at 11.00 a.m. on May 19. Two days later she was found to contain twenty fully developed eggs, so without doubt she had left the water just before her capture to look for a nesting site. These facts, reported by Goff and Goff, are all we know about the laying time of the Southern Soft-shelled Turtle in Florida.

In the Okefinokee Swamp of southeastern Georgia, Francis Harper saw a female deposit her eggs in June. After digging a hole in soft ground with her hind feet and carefully burying the eggs in it, she went a few yards and " scuffled " —

that is, vigorously scratched up the ground and scattered the earth about. By thus leaving a conspicuous sign of her presence some distance from her well-concealed nest she presumably misled egg-eating marauders. This laying and "scufflin'" was described to Harper in picturesque language by Allen Chesser of the Swamp:

"The ol' Soft-shell Turtle is given sense. It's a sharp trick. One wouldn' ketch on ter it.

"In the fust outset, when they come out, they locate a place where they want ter dig their hole. An' they ain't like ev'rything else. Ef I wuz goin' ter dig a hole, I'd use muh fore feet, but he digs with 'is hind feet. He takes one handful er dirt at a throw, an' throws it out *thataway*. Then 'e'll change, an' throw it out the other way. He gits 'is hole dug, an' lays 'is aigs, then kivers 'em with 'is hind feet. Then 'e starts off.

"Come ter the scufflin' part now. He won't start ter scuffle till 'e gits off ten er twelve feet. Then starts scufflin'. Keeps movin' erlong, an' scufflin', then 'e'll stop that, an' go on ter 'is home again in the water. I suppose he does that ter save 'is aigs, ter fool them that wants ter eat 'em. I know it fooled me, till I got ketched on ter it."

The nest is usually in a sandy spot exposed to the sun and contains from twenty to twenty-two eggs. The clutch removed from the Lake County female already referred to hatched sixty-four days after burial under three to five inches of sandy soil, or sixty-six days after removal from the female.

FOOD. Scanty is the information on the feeding habits of this turtle. Snail and mussel remains were found by Agassiz in the stomach of one specimen and in the fæces of others. There are general statements to the effect that it eats crayfish, frogs, fish, and even waterfowl.

ENEMIES. Alligators have definitely been known to eat the Southern Soft-shelled Turtle, and a young one was once found in the stomach of a water moccasin (*Agkistrodon*).

The eggs and hatchlings doubtless make dainty morsels for many mammals and birds, so in lieu of scientific data we can fall back on Allen Chesser's graphic account, which is certainly based on wide experience:

" The Jackdaw, the Raccoon, an' the Bear will eat the aigs. They shore love a aig. They're drilled ter it. They go right ter the place. They know where it is.

" The Jackdaw will sit aroun' while the turtle's at work; wait on 'im; fight up in the tree with each other. I reckon they are all hongry, an' all want ter git there fust.

" Coon, he small feller, digs a small hole [to get the eggs]. But the Bear, with 'is paws he'll *dig a hole.*

" The ol' gip, when she finds pups, 'll be hongry, an' range these woods, diggin' turtle aigs."

Chesser's " Jackdaw " is the fish crow, and his " gip " a female dog; " finds " means to him " bring forth."

CAPTIVITY. An aquarium with a thick layer of sand on the bottom and a perfectly smooth slope onto which the turtles may crawl without bruising their tender plastrons is advisable. Temperatures from 75° to 82° F. and frequent feeding are recommended by Rust. For food, earthworms, chopped large, or whole small fish, tadpoles, small frogs, and pieces of beef are suitable.

ECONOMIC VALUE. The flesh is delicious, and Ditmars states that quantities of specimens are sold in southern markets.

SPINY SOFT-SHELLED TURTLE

Trionyx spiniferus Le Sueur

[PLATES 98 AND 99]

IDENTIFICATION. There is a row of prominent conical tubercles along the anterior border of the carapace, which is neither somewhat elongate nor widened behind, and in each crescent-shaped nostril a longitudinal ridge projects from the septum dividing the nostrils. Remnants of the juvenile pattern are more or less in evidence on the olive or brown carapace.

SIZE. Although several specimens of this species with fourteen-inch carapaces are listed or described, I find this length to be the maximum recorded. Siebenrock's measurements (of a female) for comparison with Emory's Soft-shelled Turtle follow:

	Inches	Millimetres
Anterior width of carapace	6.70	170
Width at middle	8.82	224
Width behind the middle	8.66	220
Posterior width	6.89	175
Length	11.81	300

Evermann and Clark give these dimensions of a large Indiana female:

	Inches	Millimetres
Length of carapace	13	330
Width of carapace	10.5	267
Length of head and neck	9	229
Length of tail	3.5	89
Weight	7 pounds	

YOUNG. In very young specimens the light, somewhat greenish carapace is dotted with numerous conspicuous dark black-encircled spots which become entirely black toward its margin. The carapace in turn has a yellow border set off by a black line. This border and its black line are widest posteriorly. As growth proceeds, the dorsal spots increase in size and fade into irregular, more or less persistent blotches. The yellow and black of the margin also fade. The tubercular spines along the anterior border of the carapace are relatively larger in the adult than in the young.

Agassiz figures a juvenile with a carapace 43 millimetres long by 38 wide.

THE SEXES. The female attains a much greater size, sometimes being two to three times as bulky as the adult male. In the latter sex the tail is thicker and, when extended, projects well beyond the hind edge of the carapace, whereas in the female it scarcely projects beyond this edge. The tubercles of the carapace are larger and more numerous in the female. De Sola states that the carapace of this sex is wider across its forward edge, and Siebenrock describes the female's head as larger and thicker.

EGG. The eggs are spherical or nearly so and have a thick white shell which is hard and brittle. Cahn gives the average diameter of two hundred and seventeen eggs as 28.3 millimetres, the greatest 29.3 millimetres, whereas Force found that thirty-two mature eggs taken from a female averaged 32 millimetres in diameter, and Agassiz figures one with a diameter of only 25.5 millimetres. Evermann and Clark, on the other hand, describe non-spherical eggs measuring 34 × 25.5 millimetres.

GROWTH. After an examination of ovaries, Cahn is inclined to believe that females are sexually mature at a carapace length of about nine and a half inches. The facts about the growth of the Japanese Soft-shelled Turtle recorded near the beginning of this chapter give a clue to what rate may be expected for the American species.

DISTRIBUTION. From West Virginia, western Pennsylvania, and the Lake Erie region westward through the southern half of the lower peninsula of Michigan, all of Ohio, Kentucky, Tennessee, Indiana, Illinois, Wisconsin, Iowa, Missouri, and Kansas to Cache la Poudre River, northern Colorado. To the northwest it has been taken in the Missouri River at the eastern border of Montana; to the south, near the southern border of Arkansas and in four counties of eastern Oklahoma.

In the northeast this species occurs rarely as follows: the

western and southern bays and shores of Lake Ontario and the Lake Champlain borders and river mouths of Chittenden and Franklin Counties, Vermont. It presumably reached Lake Champlain via the St. Lawrence. Old records indicate that the Spiny Soft-shelled Turtle once attained the Finger Lakes of New York, the Mohawk River, and even the upper Hudson, but its present existence in central and eastern New York lacks the substantiation of recent records.

Its recent discovery in the Broad River, near Columbia, South Carolina, is puzzling, to say the least, because it is generally conceded to belong to the Ohio and Mississippi drainages. See Plates 98 and 99.

HABITAT. The habitat of this, the commonest of the Soft-shelled Turtles, has been described by many field workers. Without doubt rivers and large streams are its favourite haunts, but lakes and smaller streams are also frequented, the latter chiefly by the young. There are occasional records for large ponds, and one each for sloughs and a drainage ditch. Relatively shallow water with a sandy or soft muddy bottom free of rocks and gravel is preferred. Dense aquatic vegetation does not seem to be an attraction.

An altitude of at least 5,000 feet is reached in the western part of its range.

HABITS. This thoroughly aquatic reptile is a powerful and agile swimmer. In spite of the fact that it seldom leaves the water, its movements on land are astonishingly quick and it can readily climb steep banks.

Much time is spent lying shallowly buried in mud under water which is often just deep enough to allow the snout to reach the surface. Such a position is attained by rocking the body from side to side and flipping the sand or mud up so that it settles on the back. The inconspicuous head alone is allowed to remain visible. This concealment is of inestimable value to the tender young, which undoubtedly are relished by a variety of furred, feathered, and scaled enemies. The ability of this reptile to remain completely submerged for hours on end is explained near the beginning of this chapter.

Floating at the surface of calm water is another favourite pastime.

HIBERNATION. The winter is spent under a few inches of mud or sand at the bottom of the water inhabited. The time of appearance and disappearance is either very variable or difficult to ascertain, as shown by the following reported dates of emergence and retirement or early and late activity:

April 20 and September 20	Monroe and Wayne Counties, New York
March 19 and December 11	Vigo County, Indiana
Early April	Northern Indiana
Late April or early May and late October	Illinois

There are even a few reports of finding these turtles in the depth of winter presumably out of hibernation and more or less active.

SUNNING. During the hot parts of the year, basking on sand or grassy beaches or banks is often indulged in; objects protruding from the water are less frequently used. Where the species is abundant, great numbers are seen out together, but such a constant vigil is kept that the slightest disturbance produces a general scuttling toward the water, which is never more than a few feet away. A habit of turning to face the water before settling down greatly facilitates this quick escape. A completely relaxed posture may be assumed, the legs and neck stretched out and the toes widely spread.

Lying in very shallow open water is another method of warming up.

REPRODUCTION. In Indiana and Illinois the eggs are laid from the second week in June to or even through the third week of

July, making, of course, due allowance for unusual seasons. The young appear in September or late August. Somewhat earlier nesting in northeastern Oklahoma is indicated by the discovery there of thirty-two mature eggs in a female on May 20. On the other hand, very late laying or greatly retarded development may force the embryos to pass the winter in the egg. A nest with advanced embryos found in northern Indiana on November 16 was reported by Evermann and Clark. From the information now available, this record is extremely unusual, at least for its latitude.

The number of eggs deposited by a female at one time is rather variable and also not always easily determined either by dissection or by counts of eggs in nests. Mature and immature eggs found in one animal are confused by some investigators, and nests are sometimes double or not easily separated one from another. Few persons are fortunate enough to be on hand to count the eggs as they come out. In spite of all difficulty, independent examination of series by three men agree well in putting the average number at 18 or 19, the range as 12 to 25, with as many as 32 rarely produced. Small and young females probably are responsible for the nests containing fewer than 12 eggs.

NESTING. The laying antics of this astonishing turtle have been described twice. The fuller of these accounts, quoted from Cahn, follows:

" When the female comes out to lay, so cautious and alert is she that it is almost impossible to observe her activities from a point sufficiently close to see what is actually going on. This difficulty Mr. Combs overcame by sitting up in a tree for hours at a time, observing the turtles through powerful binoculars. The nesting performance is as follows: A female about twelve inches long left the water at 11:15 on the morning of July 11, 1931. She progressed only about four feet from the water when she turned and went back into the river, entering, however, only the shallows. A few minutes later she repeated the performance and returned again to the water. A third time she came out some five feet up stream, at a point where the willow brush was less dense and the sand more abundant. She held her neck erect and very stiff, and advanced with extreme caution. After traveling 18 feet from the water, a distance which it required about 15 minutes to cover, she came to rest and remained entirely motionless, neck fully extended, for two minutes. Then, very deliberately, she planted her fore feet firmly in the sand, and began scratching slowly with her hind feet. From the time she planted her front feet until the eggs were laid and the nest covered, she never moved the fore feet from this spot. In digging the hole she made two or three slow, heavy scratches with one hind foot; this was followed by a sudden, violent kick which sent the dirt flying four or five feet behind her. Scratching then began with the opposite foot in exactly the same manner. Thus for 16 minutes she dug, alternating in the use of her hind feet, every third or fourth stroke shooting out the loose dirt which the preceding scratchings had loosened, building up a pile of dirt immediately behind her. During all the digging she held her head high, carefully watching.

" As soon as the digging ceased, she drew in her neck and remained very quiet for 8 minutes, during which time the subsequent examination of the nest showed she laid 12 eggs. Then, her front feet still in their original position, she began filling in the nest. This she accomplished by extending her hind feet backward and raking into the hole the loose sand her excavating had piled up. With the front feet acting as a fixed pivot, she rotated her body and hind legs through an arc of about 90°, dragging in all the loose sand within reach. As soon as this was completed to her satisfaction, she wheeled quickly about and without a glance behind her at the nest which she never saw, hurried back into the water.

"Then the nest was examined. It was found to consist of a hole descending at an angle of about 60°, the opening at the surface lying under what was approximately the middle of the plastron while the animal was digging. Thus the eggs when laid were deposited upon an inclined plane down which, being spherical, they rolled. It could not be determined from the point of observation whether or not the hind legs were used in lowering the eggs into the hole. A second interesting fact was that the sand which surrounded the eggs was very much wetter than the surrounding material. From this the obvious conclusion must be drawn that the female, as she packed in the sand around the eggs while filling up the hole, wetted it down, undoubtedly with water stored in the cloacal region. The utilization of water in this manner has been observed in the case of other turtles. The sand at the surface was so neatly packed down that the nest site was almost invisible."

The female watched by Newman behaved in much the same way, yet different enough to make his account worth reading too:

"June 22, 1903, 11.10 A.M. — A warm sun-shiny day. Place: the ' old road ' about ten feet from the water's edge and concealed from view on one side by tall grass. A large female Aspidonectes [*Trionyx*] has just emerged from the grass and is commencing to make a nest. No time is lost in selecting a spot. She scratches out footholds for the fore-feet and begins to excavate with the hind-feet, using right and left feet alternately with a circular gouging movement. At intervals she pushes aside the accumulated earth with the hind-feet. As the hole becomes deeper it is necessary for her to raise the anterior part of the body to its full height in order to give a more nearly perpendicular thrust with the hind-feet.

" In less than forty minutes the nest is completed and she has commenced to lay her eggs, letting the tail down into the narrow hole as far as possible. After depositing several eggs she arranges them with the hind-feet and then rakes in some earth previously wet up with water from the accessory bladders. The earth is gently packed in before any more eggs are laid. The remainder of the eggs are deposited and the hole is filled up with earth and tramped down quite firmly with the knuckles of the hind-feet, right and left feet being used alternately. This treading movement continues for some minutes and seems to be quite thorough. Although not in any way disturbed, the tortoise left without attempting to cover up the traces of scratching feet, and anyone who is familiar with the appearance of a tortoise nest would have no difficulty in detecting this one. At 12.25 she turned and started for the water but was captured with a landing net. The nest was examined and found to be flask-shaped with a narrow neck only an inch and a half in diameter. The depth of the nest was a trifle over six inches and the diameter at the bottom about three inches."

Although Cahn does not mention treading with the knuckles during the filling process, he does say that the sand was neatly enough packed to make the nest site almost invisible. Presumably, then, his turtle packed the sand in the same way that Newman's did. The extreme nervousness described so carefully by Cahn is not brought out in the other description, but Newman remarks on it elsewhere. Most turtles are anything but shy while making their nests. Newman tells of an ideal bank near a hayfield in which men worked except from noon to 1.00 p.m., a fact that the turtles seemed to realize, none appearing before noon, but numerous ones hurrying out during the absence of the men to complete nest construction before their return. This incident also brings out the rather unusual time of day chosen by this species.

Even though soft sandy beaches are generally selected, nests are made in almost any soil in which the turtle is able to dig.

Near the beginning of this chapter a few data on the repro-
duction·of the Japanese Soft-shelled Turtle are given for comparison.

FOOD AND FEEDING. Examinations of stomach contents prove
that the Spiny Soft-shelled Turtle subsists largely on crayfish. Many other small animals, chiefly aquatic forms, have
also been found in its stomach: minnows or young of larger
kinds of fishes, big insect larvæ, mollusks, earthworms, frogs,
and tadpoles. Herbivorous and scavenger tendencies are very
weakly indicated. Surface even writes of one stomach that
was stuffed with grains of corn!

From the vantage-point of a high bank Newman watched
individuals catch their prey. He relates: " They crawl or swim
along the bottom, thrusting their snouts under stones and into
masses of aquatic vegetation, occasionally snapping up a crayfish or larva that they have succeeded in dislodging. They do
not tear up their food, but swallow it whole, using the fore·
feet to assist in forcing it down." Fishermen sometimes claim
that large-mouth black bass often accompany these turtles.
The explanation seems to be that the bass are either after minnows feeding on food stirred up by the turtles or intent on
devouring crayfish missed by the reptiles.

ENEMIES. Man is no doubt the chief destroyer of adults.
The eggs are certainly eaten by various mammals, and the
young probably by mammals, birds, fishes, and reptiles. Almost no scientific information is available on this subject, however.

DEFENCE AND DISPOSITION. The vicious habits of these turtles have given rise to many humorous stories of persons taken
unawares or bitten on particularly sensitive parts of their anat-
omy. Again we have Newman to thank for a serious summing
up of the defensive actions:

" Although their ability to elude pursuit furnishes them with
a most efficient method of defense, they are not limited to this

alone. Their bite is vicious in the extreme. When captured they hiss violently and thrust out the head, snapping vigorously with a sudden precise darting movement. Their aim is accurate and if the objective point is within reach they seldom miss. One learns to grasp them by the tail, as this is about the only part of their body that is beyond the reach of their fierce jaws.

" Unlike other species they keep the eyes uppermost when snapping at objects back of them. They refuse also to retire into the carapace when captured, but continue to struggle violently for some time. After an exhausting struggle, however, they seem to become discouraged and lie quietly as long as they are watched. If confined in a room they never wander around, but remain in some dark corner, watching one's actions with an alertness quite characteristic.

" When first captured there exudes from the inguinal glands a thick yellow semi-fluid excretion resembling in appearance the yolk of an egg. This substance has no perceptible odor, but is undoubtedly homologous with the emission of the inguinal glands of the musk and snapping tortoises, that has such a nauseating odor. Of course it is problematical that even this malodorous excretion serves a protective function, but it at least tends to disgust a captor."

Young individuals do not often display such fierce and sullen behaviour as the adults.

CAPTIVITY. This species lives well in confinement if provided with the same environment that suits the other species of *Trionyx*. It has been successfully fed on crayfish, worms, snails, fish, meat, and similar foods. Newman found that the tender young are attacked by the Common Musk Turtle as well as the Central Painted Turtle and therefore should not be confined with such aggressive species.

A specimen survived ten and a half years of confinement in Paris, and another lived five years in the New York Aquarium.

ECONOMIC VALUE. Clark and Southall's report stating that soft-shelled turtles do not reach the large city markets is discussed in the corresponding section of the treatment of the Spineless Soft-shelled Turtle and of course applies to the present species as well. In spite of this, there is good evidence that the Spiny Soft-shell is widely sold in local markets within its area of abundance.

SPINELESS SOFT-SHELLED TURTLE

Trionyx muticus Le Sueur

IDENTIFICATION. The carapace is entirely devoid of tubercles and the round nostril does not have a longitudinal ridge in it projecting from the septum dividing the nostrils. Remnants of the juvenile pattern are more or less in evidence on the olive or brown carapace.

SIZE. The greatest carapace length reported for the Spineless Soft-shelled Turtle is fourteen inches. This species is, nevertheless, generally described as the smallest North American soft-shelled turtle, seldom seen with a carapace more than ten inches long. A large Ohio female is recorded as having a carapace 9.21 inches long by 7.91 wide.

YOUNG. The carapace of the hatchling is about 35 millimetres long by 32 wide. It is uniform olive with a sprinkling of small dark dots and dashes and a yellow lateral and rear margin set off by a black line. As growth proceeds, the dots and dashes spread to form obscure, more or less persistent blotches, and the yellow and black of the margin grow dim or vanish entirely.

THE SEXES. The female attains a much greater length and bulk than the male, and in the latter sex the extended tail projects well beyond the hind edge of the carapace, whereas in the female it fails to reach or scarcely projects beyond this edge. The male plastron has much more pronounced callosities.

In addition to these well-known sexual characters, Cahn describes the claws of the hind feet as usually longer in the female, those of the forefeet as usually longer in the male; and De Sola says that the carapace of the former sex is wider across its forward edge.

EGG. The spherical eggs have a thick brittle white shell. Cahn gives the average diameter of one hundred and sixteen eggs as 22.6 millimetres.

DISTRIBUTION. There has been some confusion over the identity of this turtle, so its distribution is not easily determined. It is, however, known to range from northern Louisiana over all of Oklahoma, Arkansas, and Missouri, across eastern Kansas, and into western Tennessee. To the southwest it has even been taken as far as Tom Green County, western Texas, but Texas records are extremely few. It ascends the Missouri into South Dakota and the Mississippi at least to Pepin County, Wisconsin. In the east it follows the Ohio River system to occur throughout the southern third of Ohio, and it is found along the Wabash to Delphi, Indiana. Numerous records prove its presence over all of Illinois but the northeastern section.

HABITAT. Rivers and streams of all sizes and rates of flow are typically inhabited by this thoroughly aquatic species, which is sometimes found in lakes as well. A sand or silt bottom devoid of rocky areas and dense aquatic vegetation is preferred and stagnant water avoided.

The vicinity of a windfall, submerged roots, logs, or driftwood in otherwise clear, smoothly flowing water is the favourite haunt.

HABITS. Like the other members of its genus, the Spineless Soft-shelled Turtle is an agile, powerful swimmer and a fast runner on land, where it is said to be able to outrun a man. Although extremely shy, if cornered it will defend itself vigorously by shooting the head forward like an angry snake and biting with its sharp-edged jaws. It is less vicious, however, than the Spiny Soft-shelled Turtle.

Hours are spent lying barely covered by sand of river or stream, often at a depth that just allows the snout to reach the air. Such a position is attained by flipping the sand up and allowing it to settle on the back. Only the inconspicuous head is kept out, so the turtle is virtually invisible. The ability of this reptile to remain completely submerged for hours is explained near the beginning of this chapter.

Sunning is indulged in to a limited extent. Muller studied the behaviour of great numbers about an island in the Mississippi River near Fairport, Iowa. During June and July they came out to lie chiefly on beaches with northern exposure, keeping within ten feet of the water and turning about now and then. The usual time chosen was before 2.00 p.m.

Though relaxed with outstretched neck and drooping carapace margins, basking individuals remain ever on the alert.

MIGRATION. The congregation of large numbers below river dams indicates that upstream migration takes place, but nothing has been determined about the nature of such mass movement.

REPRODUCTION. The laying season in Illinois extends from the middle of June, or possibly a little earlier in the southern part, to the middle of July. A large female lays about twenty, rarely as many as thirty-one eggs at a time; smaller and younger ones produce fewer. The incubation period is approximately seventy days, but varies considerably with different conditions of moisture and temperature.

On the island near Fairport, Muller carefully studied nest construction and describes it as follows:

" In building her nest, the female selects a spot with an unobstructed view of the open water, and from ten to sixty feet inland. Here she scoops out a hole in the sand, about five inches in diameter, and ten inches deep, using her fore paws in the operation, and piling up the loose sand around the hole. The necessary conditions for incubation are sufficient dampness so that the sand will just cling together, and absence of clayey or earthy matter which might cause the sand to pack and thus prevent the escape of the young. Often in her search of proper conditions the female will dig three or four holes before laying her eggs. A suitable nest being dug the turtle assumes a position with her hind feet down the hole, and dropping her eggs into her hind paws, arranges them neatly upon the floor of the nest. The hole is then filled in with the sand removed from it, the hind feet being used. . . . The finished nest appears as a small crater on the sand, about a foot in diameter, or, where the surface is covered with pebbles, as a circular area of clear sand. The temperature of the nests is quite constant — about 90° F."

Muller's reference to digging with the forepaws is apparently an error. As far as I can determine, all turtles dig their nests with the hind limbs.

Hatching always occurs at night or early in the morning. Instead of using its egg-tooth, Muller continues, the hatchling escapes from the egg by means of its forelimbs. It then tunnels upward, leaving the shell behind. Having a desire to go downhill and in the direction of an open horizon, it walks toward the water inhabited by its parents. In technical language, it is both geotropic and phototropic. It is interesting to speculate as to what becomes of these tropisms once the water is reached; the former would make it go downstream and into deep water, whereas the latter would pull it to the surface or even out of the water again! Presumably both impulses are rapidly lost or at once overwhelmed by stronger ones. Muller found that very young individuals when frightened bury themselves in the sand of an aquarium bottom or bite if held. They also eat readily.

Near the beginning of this chapter a few data on the reproduction of the Japanese Soft-shelled Turtle are given for comparison.

FOOD AND FEEDING. The food consists chiefly of worms, large insect larvæ, thin-shelled bivalves and snails, crayfish, frogs, tadpoles, and various kinds of fishes. This species has been accused of devouring "young fowl," presumably waterfowl.

Even fruit and nuts have been found in its stomach, and potato stems are said to be one of its favourite foods. Confirmation of this odd love of potato stems would be most gratifying.

It is assumed that these turtles bury themselves in sand, as already described under the account of habits, partly at least to lie in wait for prey, but Cahn has seen one in a large tank pursue and catch a brook trout by sheer superior agility. Bearing in mind the speed of the brook trout, one can well understand that these turtles have no great difficulty keeping their stomachs full!

ENEMIES. No fewer than forty nests that had been dug into by hungry animals were found by Muller on his island in the Mississippi. He saw raccoon tracks near some and believed that "ground moles" and crows were perhaps responsible for the destruction of others. Skunks are well known to be fond of turtle eggs. Leeches, in Cahn's opinion, do not often attack this species, because its habitat is not especially congenial to them. Man is, of course, the chief enemy of the adult. Unfortunate indeed is the turtle whose meat happens to be pleasing to the human palate.

CAPTIVITY. Conditions similar to those described for the Southern Soft-shelled Turtle are suitable for this species too.

Captives have actually been observed to eat insects, earthworms, crayfish, fish, and meat.

Muller hatched eggs in artificial nests, "prepared in small sandpiles placed in the angle of the floor and wall of an empty cement pond bed." The northern wall was used and the eggs hatched July 29, 30, and 31. Excessive moisture made the eggs rot, whereas too little only retarded development.

ECONOMIC VALUE. Although there is general agreement in regard to the great popularity of this turtle because of its delicious flavour, I find no evidence that it reaches the large city markets. Clark and Southall, who reported on the economic resources of our fresh-water turtles in 1920, explain its absence from markets thus: The soft-shelled turtles are too well liked locally and too little known in the markets. The fishermen keep and eat them or sell them near by. Moreover, their habits make the capture of many specimens at a time very difficult.

BIBLIOGRAPHY

There is no other book on the turtles of the United States in print. The information found in the foregoing pages has been gleaned chiefly from some eight hundred technical articles and books, the most important of which are cited in the text by the names of the authors and listed below.

AGASSIZ, LOUIS: *Contributions to the Natural History of the United States of America.* Boston: Little, Brown and Company; 1857.

ALLARD, H. A.: "Notes on Two Common Turtles of Eastern United States." *Science,* New series, Vol. 30 (1909), pp. 453–4.

——: "The Natural History of the Box Turtle." *The Scientific Monthly,* Vol. 41 (October 1935), pp. 325–38.

ALLEN, MORROW J.: "A Survey of the Amphibians and Reptiles of Harrison County, Mississippi." *American Museum Novitates,* No. 542 (1932), pp. 1–20.

BABBITT, LEWIS H.: "Some Remarks on Connecticut Herpetology." *Bulletin, Boston Society Natural History,* No. 63 (1932), pp. 23–8.

BABCOCK, HAROLD L.: "The Turtles of New England." *Memoirs, Boston Society Natural History,* Vol. 8 (1919), pp. 325–431.

——: "New England Turtles." *Bulletin, Boston Society Natural History,* No. 39 (1926), pp. 5–9.

——: "The Turtles of the Northeastern States." *Copeia,* No. 1 (1932), pp. 42–3.

——: "The American Snapping Turtles of the Genus *Chelydra* in the Collection of the Museum of Comparative Zoology, Cambridge, Mass., U. S. A." *Proceedings, Zoological Society London,* 1932, pp. 873–4.

———: "The Sea-turtles of the Bermuda Islands, with a Survey of the Present State of the Turtle Fishing Industry." *Proceedings, Zoological Society London*, Series A, Vol. 107 (1938), pp. 595–601.

BANKS, E.: "The Breeding of the Edible Turtle (*Chelone mydas*)." *Sarawak Museum Journal*, Vol. 4, Part 4 (1937), pp. 523–32.

BEEBE, WILLIAM: "Turtle Sanctuary." *Harper's Magazine*, November 1937, pp. 653–60.

BISHOP, SHERMAN C., and W. J. SCHOONMACHER: "Turtle Hunting in Midwinter." *Copeia*, No. 96 (1921), pp. 37–8.

——— and F. J. W. SCHMIDT: "The Painted Turtles of the Genus Chrysemys." *Field Museum Zoological Series*, Vol. 18 (1931), pp. 123–39.

BLAKE, S. F.: "Sexual Differences in Coloration in the Spotted Turtle, Clemmys guttata." *Proceedings, United States National Museum*, Vol. 59 (1921), pp. 463–9.

BOGERT, CHARLES M.: "Note on the Growth Rate of the Desert Tortoise, *Gopherus agassizi*." *Copeia*, No. 3 (1937), pp. 191–2.

BREDER, RUTH BERNICE: "Notes on the Drinking Habits of Terrapene carolina (Linnæus)." *Copeia*, No. 131 (1924), pp. 63–4.

———: "Turtle Trailing: A New Technique for Studying the Life Habits of Certain Testudinata." *Zoologica*, Vol. 9 (1927), pp. 231–43.

BRENNAN, L. A.: "A Check List of the Amphibians and Reptiles of Ellis County, Kansas." *Transactions, Kansas Academy Science*, Vol. 37 (1934), pp. 189–91.

BRIMLEY, C. S.: "Notes on Some Turtles of the Genus Pseudemys." *Journal, Elisha Mitchell Science Society*, Vol. 23 (1907), pp. 76–84.

———: "Notes on *Pseudemys scripta* Schoepff, the Yellow-bellied Terrapin." *Copeia*, No. 87 (1920), pp. 93–4.

BROWN, J. ROLAND: "A Blanding's Turtle Lays Its Eggs." *Canadian Field-Naturalist*, Vol. 41 (1927), p. 185.

BUMPUS, H. C.: "Reptiles and Batrachians of Rhode Island." *Random Notes on Natural History, Providence, R. I.* Vol. 1,

Bibliography 327

Nos. 10–12 (1884); Vol. 2, Nos. 1–12 (1885); Vol. 3, Nos. 1–2 (1886).

BURGER, J. WENDELL: "Experimental Sexual Photoperiodicity in the Male Turtle, *Pseudemys elegans* (Wied)." *American Naturalist*, Vol. 71 (1937), pp. 481–7.

CAGLE, FRED R.: "Egg Laying Habits of the Slider Turtle (Pseudemys troostii), the Painted Turtle (Chrysemys picta), and the Musk Turtle (Sternotherus odoratus)." *Journal, Tennessee Academy Science*, Vol. 12 (1937), pp. 87–95.

CAHN, ALVIN R.: "The Turtles of Illinois." *University Illinois Bulletin*, Vol. 35 (1937), pp. 1–218.

—— and EVERT CONDER: "Mating of the Box Turtles." *Copeia*, No. 2 (1932), pp. 86–8.

CAMP, CHARLES LEWIS: "Notes on the Local Distribution and Habits of the Amphibians and Reptiles of Southeastern California in the Vicinity of the Turtle Mountains." *University California Publications Zoology*, Vol. 12 (1916), pp. 503–44.

CARR, ARCHIE F., JR.: "A New Turtle from Florida, with Notes on *Pseudemys floridana mobiliensis* (Holbrook)." *Occasional Papers, Museum Zoology University Michigan*, No. 348 (1937), pp. 1–7.

——: "The Status of Pseudemys scripta and Pseudemys troostii." *Herpetologica*, Vol. 1 (1937), pp. 74–7.

——: "A New Subspecies of *Pseudemys floridana*, with Notes on the *floridana* Complex." *Copeia*, No. 3 (1938), pp. 105–9.

CASTEEL, D. B.: "The Discriminative Ability of the Painted Turtle." *Journal Animal Behavior*, Vol. 1 (1911), pp. 1–28.

CLARK, H. WALTON, and JOHN B. SOUTHALL: "Fresh-water Turtles: a Source of Meat Supply." *Report U. S. Commissioner Fisheries for 1919, Appendix VII* (1920), pp. 1–20.

COKER, R. E.: "The Cultivation of the Diamond-back Terrapin." *North Carolina Geological Survey*, Bulletin No. 14 (1906), pp. 1–69.

CONANT, ROGER: "The Reptiles of Ohio." *American Midland Naturalist*, Vol. 20 (1938), pp. 1–200.

—— and REEVE M. BAILEY: "Some Herpetological Records from Monmouth and Ocean Counties, New Jersey." *Occasional*

Papers, *Museum Zoology University Michigan*, No. 328 (1936), pp. 1–10.

COWAN, IAN M.: "A Review of the Reptiles and Amphibians of British Columbia." *Report, Provincial Museum, British Columbia, 1936* (1937), pp. K16–K25.

CRAGIN, F. W.: "Second Contribution to the Herpetology of Kansas." *Transactions, Kansas Academy Science*, Vol. 9 (1885), pp. 136–40.

CUNNINGHAM, BERT: "Some Phases in the Development of Chrysemys cinerea." *Journal, Elisha Mitchell Scientific Society*, Vol. 38 (1923), pp. 51–73.

—— and ELIZABETH HUENE: "Further Studies in Water Absorption by Reptile Eggs." *American Naturalist*, Vol. 72 (1938), pp. 380–5.

DAVIS, WILLIAM T.: "The Common Land Turtle." *Proceedings, Natural Science Association Staten Island*, Vol. 6 (1897), pp. 20–2.

DERANIYAGALA, P. E. P.: "The Testudinata of Ceylon." *Ceylon Journal Science*, Section B, Vol. 16 (1930), pp. 43–88.

——: "Notes on the Development of the Leathery Turtle, Dermochelys coriacea." *Ceylon Journal Science, Section B*, Vol. 17 (1932), pp. 73–102.

——: "Some Postnatal Changes in the Leathery Turtle Dermochelys coriacea." *Ceylon Journal Science, Section B*, Vol. 19 (1936), 225–39.

——: "The Nesting Habit of Leathery Turtle Dermochelys coriacea." *Ceylon Journal Science, Section B*, Vol. 19 (1936), pp. 331–6.

DE SOLA, RALPH: "Sex Determination in a Species of the Kinosternidæ, with Notes on Sound Production in Reptiles." *Copeia*, No. 3 (1931), pp. 124–5.

——: "The Turtles of the Northeastern States." *Bulletin, New York Zoological Society*, Vol. 34, No. 5 (1931), pp. 131–60.

——: "Herpetological Notes from Southeastern Florida." *Copeia*, No. 1 (1935), pp. 44–5.

—— and FREDRICA ABRAMS: "Testudinata from South-eastern

Georgia, Including the Okefinokee Swamp." *Copeia*, No. 1 (1933), pp. 10–12.

DITMARS, RAYMOND L.: "A Review of the Box Turtles." *Zoologica*, Vol. 17 (1934), pp. 1–44.

——: *The Reptiles of North America*. New York: Doubleday, Doran & Company; 1936.

EVERMANN, B. W., and H. W. CLARK: "The Turtles and Batrachians of the Lake Maxinkuckee Region." *Proceedings, Indiana Academy Science, 1916* (1917), pp. 472–518.

EWING, H. E.: "Reproduction in the Eastern Box-turtle *Terrapene carolina carolina* (Linné)." *Copeia*, No. 2 (1933), pp. 95–6.

——: "Further Notes on the Reproduction of the Eastern Box-turtle, *Terrapene carolina* (Linné)." *Copeia*, No. 2 (1935), p. 102.

——: "Notes on a Florida Box-turtle, *Terrapene bauri* Taylor, Kept under Maryland Conditions." *Copeia*, No. 2 (1937), p. 141.

FLETCHER, WILLIAM B.: "The Florida Gopher." *Proceedings, Indiana Academy Science, 1899* (1900), pp. 46–52.

FLOWER, STANLEY SMYTH: "Contributions to Our Knowledge of the Duration of Life in Vertebrate Animals. — 3. Reptiles." *Proceedings, Zoological Society London* (1925), pp. 911–81.

——: "Further Notes on the Duration of Life in Animals. — 3. Reptiles." *Proceedings, Zoological Society London*, Vol. 107 (1937), pp. 1–39.

FORCE, EDITH R.: "The Amphibians and Reptiles of Tulsa County, Oklahoma, and Vicinity." *Copeia*, No. 2 (1930), pp. 25–39.

FROTHINGHAM, LANGDON: "Observations on Young Box Turtles." *Bulletin, Boston Society Natural History*, No. 78 (1936), pp. 3–8.

GAGE, SIMON H. and SUSANNA P.: "Aquatic Respiration in Softshelled Turtles (Amyda mutica and Aspidonectes spinifer); a Contribution to the Physiology of Respiration in Vertebrates." *Proceedings, American Association Advancement Science*, Vol. 34 (1886), pp. 316–18.

GARMAN, H.: "The Differences between the Geographic Turtles." *Bulletin, Essex Institute,* Vol. 22 (1890), pp. 70–83.

GOFF, C. C. and DOROTHY S.: "Egg Laying and Incubation of *Pseudemys floridana.*" *Copeia,* No. 2 (1932), pp. 92–4.

GOFF, DOROTHY S. and C. C.: "On the Incubation of a Clutch of Eggs of *Amyda ferox* (Schneider)." *Copeia,* No. 3 (1935), p. 156.

GRANT, CHAFFEE: "Breeding of *Pseudemys elegans* in California and Notes on Other Captive Reptiles." *Copeia,* No. 2 (1936), pp. 112–13.

GRANT, CHAPMAN: "Secondary Sexual Differences and Notes on the Mud Turtle, Kinosternon subrubrum in Northern Indiana." *American Midland Naturalist,* Vol. 16 (1935), pp. 798–800.

——: "Notes on the Spotted Turtle in Northern Indiana." *Proceedings, Indiana Academy Science,* Vol. 44 (1935), pp. 244–7.

——: "Herpetological Notes from Northern Indiana." *Proceedings, Indiana Academy Science,* Vol. 45 (1936), pp. 323–33.

——: "The Southwestern Desert Tortoise, *Gopherus agassizii.*" *Zoologica,* Vol. 21 (1936), pp. 225–9.

GREEN, HAROLD T.: "Notes on Middle States Amphibians and Reptiles." *Copeia,* No. 122 (1923), pp. 99–100.

HALLINAN, THOMAS: "Observations Made in Duval County, Northern Florida, on the Gopher Tortoise (*Gopherus polyphemus*)." *Copeia,* No. 115 (1923), pp. 11–20.

HALTOM, WILLIAM L.: "Alabama Reptiles." *Alabama Museum Natural History, Paper* No. 11 (1931), pp. 1–145.

HARPER, FRANCIS: "Tales of the Okefinokee." *American Speech,* Vol. 1 (1926), pp. 407–20.

HARWOOD, PAUL D.: "The Helminths parasitic in the Amphibia and Reptilia of Houston, Texas, and Vicinity." *Proceedings, United States National Museum,* Vol. 81, Article 17 (1932), pp. 1–71.

HAY, W. P.: "A Revision of Malaclemmys, a Genus of Turtles." *Bulletin, U. S. Bureau Fisheries,* Vol. 24 (1905), pp. 1–19.

HILDEBRAND, SAMUEL F., and CHARLES HATSEL: "Diamond-back

Terrapin Culture at Beaufort, N. C." *U. S. Bureau Fisheries*, *Economic Circular*, No. 60 (1926), pp. 1–20.

—— and CHARLES HATSEL: "On the Growth, Care and Behavior of Loggerhead Turtles in Captivity." *Proceedings, National Academy Sciences*, Vol. 13 (1927), pp. 374–7.

——: "Review of Experiments on Artificial Culture of Diamond-back Terrapin." *Bulletin, U. S. Bureau Fisheries*, Vol. 45 (1929), pp. 25–70.

——: "Growth of Diamond-back Terrapins, Size Attained, Sex Ratio and Longevity." *Zoologica*, Vol. 9 (1932), pp. 551–63.

HONIGMANN, H.: "Zur Biologie der Schildkröten." *Biologisches Zentralblatt*, Vol. 41 (1921), pp. 241–50.

HOOKER, DAVENPORT: "Certain Reactions to Color in the Young Loggerhead Turtle." *Papers, Tortugas Laboratory, Carnegie Institute Washington*, Vol. 3 (1911), pp. 69–76.

HORNELL, JAMES: *The Turtle Fisheries of the Seychelles Islands.* London: H. M. Stationery Office; 1927.

HUBBARD, HENRY G.: "The Florida Land Tortoise-Gopher, Gopherus polyphemus." *Science*, Vol. 22 (1893), pp. 57–8.

HURTER, JULIUS: "Herpetology of Missouri." *Transactions, Academy Science St. Louis*, Vol. 20 (1911), pp. 59–274.

LAMPE, ED.: "Catalog der Reptilien-Sammlung (Schildkröten) des naturhistorischen Museums Wiesbaden." *Jahrbüchern Nassauischen Vereins Naturkunde*, Jahrg. 54 (1901), pp. 177–222.

LATHAM, ROY: "Notes on Cistudo carolina from Orient, Long Island." *Copeia*, No. 34 (1934), pp. 65–7.

MAST, S. O.: "Behavior of the Loggerhead Turtle in Depositing Its Eggs." *Papers, Tortugas Laboratory, Carnegie Institute Washington*, Vol. 3 (1911), pp. 63–7.

MATTOX, NORMAN T.: "Annular Rings in the Long Bones of Turtles and Their Correlation with Size." *Transactions, Illinois State Academy Science*, Vol. 28 (1936), pp. 225–6.

MERTENS, ROBERT: "Schildkröten-Beobachtungen im Freiland-Terrarium." *Blätter Aquarien Terrarienkunde*, Jahrg. 47 (1936), pp. 253–7, 268–72.

MILLER, LOYE: "Notes on the Desert Tortoise (Testudo agas-

sizii)." *Transactions, San Diego Society Natural History*,
Vol. 7 (1932), pp. 189–208.
MITSUKURI, K.: "Cultivation of the Snapping-turtle, or Soft-shell
Tortoise 'Suppon,' in Japan." *Bulletin, U. S. Bureau Fish-
eries*, Vol. 24 (1905), pp. 260–6.
MOORHOUSE, F. W.: "Notes on the Green Turtle (*Chelonia
mydas*)." *Reports, Great Barrier Reef Committee*, Vol. 4,
Part 1 (1933), pp. 1–22.
MULLER, J. F.: "Notes on the Habits of the Soft-Shell Turtle —
Amyda mutica." *American Midland Naturalist*, Vol. 7
(1921), pp. 180–4.
NETTING, M. GRAHAM: "Muhlenberg's Turtle in Western Penn-
sylvania." *Annals, Carnegie Museum*, Vol. 17 (1927), pp.
403–8.
——: "Blanding's Turtle, *Emys blandingii* (Holbrook), in Penn-
sylvania." *Copeia*, No. 4 (1932), pp. 173–4.
——: "Hibernation and Migration of the Spotted Turtle, *Clem-
mys guttata* (Schneider)." *Copeia*, No. 2 (1936), p. 112.
NEWMAN, H. H.: "The Habits of Certain Tortoises." *Journal
Comparative Neurology Psychology*, Vol. 16 (1906), pp.
126–52.
NICHOLS, JOHN T.: "Further Notes on Painted Turtles." *Copeia*,
No. 1 (1933), pp. 41–2.
NOBLE, G. K., and A. M. BRESLAU: "The Senses Involved in the
Migration of Young Fresh-water Turtles after Hatching."
Journal Comparative Psychology, Vol. 25 (1938), pp. 175–93.
ORTENBURGER, A. I. and R. D.: "Field Observations on Some Am-
phibians and Reptiles of Pima County, Arizona." *Proceed-
ings, Oklahoma Academy Science*, Vol. 6 (1927), pp. 101–21.
ORTENBURGER, A. I., and BERYL FREEMAN: "Notes on Some Rep-
tiles and Amphibians from Western Oklahoma." *Publica-
tions, University Oklahoma Biological Survey*, Vol. 2 (1930),
pp. 175–88.
OVER, WILLIAM H.: "Amphibians and Reptiles of South Dakota."
Bulletin, South Dakota Geological Natural History Survey,
Series 23, No. 10 (1923), pp. 5–34.

OVERTON, FRANK: "Aquatic Habits of the Box Turtle." *Copeia*, No. 26 (1916), pp. 4–5.

PARKER, G. H.: "The Crawling of Young Loggerhead Turtles toward the Sea." *Journal Experimental Zoology*, Vol. 36 (1922), pp. 323–31.

——: "The Time of Submergence Necessary to Drown Alligators and Turtles." *Occasional Papers, Boston Society Natural History*, Vol. 5 (1925), pp. 157–9.

——: "The Growth of the Loggerhead Turtle." *American Naturalist*, Vol. 63 (1929), pp. 367–73.

PATTERSON, THOMAS L.: "Comparative Physiology of the Gastric Hunger Mechanism." *Annals, New York Academy Sciences*, Vol. 34 (1933), pp. 55–272.

PEARSE, A. S.: "The Growth of the Painted Turtle." *Biological Bulletin*, Vol. 45 (1923), pp. 145–8.

——: "The Abundance and Migration of Turtles." *Ecology*, Vol. 4 (1923), pp. 24–8.

——, S. LEPKOVSKY, and LAURA HINTZE: "The Growth and Chemical Composition of Three Species of Turtles Fed on Rations of Pure Foods." *Journal Morphology Physiology*, Vol. 41 (1925), pp. 191–216.

RISLEY, PAUL L.: "Anatomical Differences in the Sexes of the Musk Turtle, *Sternotherus odoratus* (Latreille)." *Papers, Michigan Academy Science Arts Letters*, Vol. 11 (1930), pp. 445–64.

——: "Observations on the Natural History of the Common Musk Turtle, *Sternotherus odoratus* (Latreille)." *Papers, Michigan Academy Science Arts Letters*, Vol. 17 (1933), pp. 685–711.

ROSENBERGER, RANDLE C.: "Notes on Some Habits of *Terrapene carolina* (Linné)." *Copeia*, No. 3 (1936), p. 177.

RUCKES, HERBERT: "Studies in Chelonian Osteology." *Annals, New York Academy Sciences*, Vol. 31 (1929), pp. 31–120.

RUST, HANS-THEODOR: "Ergänzung zum 'Verzeichnis der bisher gepflegten Schildkröten.'" *Wochenschrift Aquarien Terrarienkunde*, Jahrg. 47 (1936), pp. 163–5.

——: "Verzeichnis der bisher gepflegten Schildkröten." *Taschen-*

334   *Bibliography*

kalender Aquarien Terrarienfreunde, Jahrg. 28 (1936), pp. 159–208.

——: " Interessante Schildkröten. III Sternotherus minor (Agassiz), 1857, die kleine Moschusschildkröte." *Wochenschrift Aquarien Terrarienkunde*, Jahrg. 34 (1937), pp. 637–9.

SCHMIDT, JOHS.: " Marking Experiments with Turtles in the Danish West Indies." *Meddelelser Kommissionen Havundersogelser*, Serie: Fiskeri, Vol. 5, No. 1 (1916), pp. 1–26.

SCHMIDT, K. P., and WALTER NECKER: " Amphibians and Reptiles of the Chicago Region." *Bulletin, Chicago Academy Sciences*, Vol. 5 (1935), pp. 57–77.

SEARS, J. H.: " *Dermatochelys coriacea*, Trunk Back or Leathery Turtle." *Bulletin, Essex Institute*, Vol. 18 (1886), pp. 87–94.

SETON, ERNEST THOMPSON: " A List of the Turtles, Snakes and Batrachians of Manitoba." *Ottawa Naturalist*, Vol. 32 (1918), pp. 79–83.

SIEBENROCK, F.: " Die Schildkrötenfamilie Cinosternidæ." *Sitzungsberichten, Akademie Wissenschaften Wien*. Mathem.-naturw. Klasse, Vol. 116 (1907), pp. 527–99.

——: " Die nearktischen *Trionychidae*." *Verhandlungen, Zoologisch-Botanischen Gesellschaft Wien*, Vol. 73 (1924), pp. 180–94.

SMITH, HUGH M.: " Notes on the Breeding Habits of the Yellow-bellied Terrapin." *Smithsonian Miscellaneous Collections* (Quarterly Issue), Vol. 45 (1904), pp. 252–3.

SNYDER, L. L.: " Some Observations on Blanding's Turtle." *Canadian Field-Naturalist*, Vol. 35 (1921), pp. 17–18.

STEJNEGER, LEONHARD: " Rehabilitation of a Hitherto Overlooked Species of Musk Turtle of the Southern States." *Proceedings, United States National Museum*, Vol. 62, Art. 6 (1923), pp. 1–3.

—— and THOMAS BARBOUR: *A Check List of North American Amphibians and Reptiles*. Third Edition. Cambridge: Harvard University Press; 1933.

STORER, TRACY I.: " Notes on the Range and Life-history of the Pacific Fresh-water Turtle, Clemmys marmorata." *Univer-*

sity *California Publications Zoology,* Vol. 32 (1930), pp. 429–41.

——: " Further notes on the Turtles of the North Pacific Coast of North America." *Copeia,* No. 1 (1937), pp. 66–7.

STRAUCH, ALEXANDER: " Bemerkungen über die Schildkröten-sammlung im zoologischen Museum der kaiserlichen Akademie der Wissenschaften zu St. Petersburg." *Mémoires, Académie Sciences St.-Pétersbourg,* VIIᵉ Série, Vol. 38, No. 2 (1890), pp. 1–127.

STRECKER, JOHN K.: " The Reptiles and Batrachians of McLennan County, Texas." *Proceedings, Biological Society Washington,* Vol. 21 (1908), pp. 69–84.

——: " Observations on the Food Habits of Texas Amphibians and Reptiles." *Copeia,* No. 162 (1927), pp. 6–9.

——: " Chapters from the Life-histories of Texas Reptiles and Amphibians." *Contributions, Baylor University Museum,* No. 10 (1927), pp. 1–14.

——: " Random Notes on the Zoology of Texas." *Contributions, Baylor University Museum,* No. 18 (1929), pp. 1–12.

——: " Field Notes on the Herpetology of Wilbarger County, Texas." *Contributions, Baylor University Museum,* No. 19 (1929), pp. 1–9.

——: " Notes on the Zoology of Texas." *Baylor Bulletin,* Vol. 38, No. 3 (1935), pp. 1–69.

STROMSTEN, FRANK A.: " Nest Digging and Egg Laying Habits of Bell's Turtle, Crysemys marginata bellii (Gray)." *University Iowa. Studies Natural History,* Vol. 10 (1923), pp. 67–70.

SURFACE, H. A.: " First Report on the Economy of Pennsylvania Turtles." *Zoological Bulletin, Pennsylvania Department Agriculture,* Vol. 6 (1908), pp. 106–96.

TAYLOR, EDWARD H.: " Observations on the Courtship of Turtles." *University Kansas Science Bulletin,* Vol. 21 (1933), pp. 269–71.

——: " Arkansas Amphibians and Reptiles in the Kansas University Museum." *University Kansas Science Bulletin,* Vol. 22 (1935), pp. 207–18.

THACKER, T. L.: "Notes on Bell's Painted Turtles (Chrysemys marginata bellii) in British Columbia." *Canadian Field-Naturalist*, Vol. 38 (1924), pp. 164–7.

THOMAS, EDWARD S., and MILTON B. TRAUTMAN: "Segregated Hibernation of *Sternotherus odoratus* (Latreille)." *Copeia*, No. 4 (1937), p. 231.

TINKLEPAUGH, O. L.: "Maze Learning of a Turtle." *Journal Comparative Psychology*, Vol. 13 (1932), pp. 201–6.

TOWNSEND, CHARLES H.: "Growth of Confined Hawksbill Turtles." *Bulletin, New York Zoological Society*, No. 22 (1906), p. 291.

TRUE, FREDERICK W.: "On the North American Land Tortoises of the Genus Zerobates." *Proceedings, United States National Museum*, Vol. 4 (1882), pp. 434–48.

——: "Useful Aquatic Reptiles and Batrachians of the United States." *Fisheries Fishery Industries United States*, Section 1 (1893), pp. 141–62.

VAN DENBURGH, JOHN: "The Reptiles of Western North America." *Occasional Papers, California Academy Sciences*, No. 10 (1922), pp. 1–1028.

VAN HYNING, O. C.: "Batrachia and Reptilia of Alachua County, Florida." *Copeia*, No. 1 (1933), pp. 3–7.

VIOSCA, PERCY: "The *Pseudemys troostii-elegans* Complex, a Case of Sexual Dimorphism." *Copeia*, No. 4 (1933), pp. 208–10.

WALLS, G. L.: "The Reptilian Retina. I. A New Concept of Visual-cell Evolution." *American Journal Ophthalmology*, Vol. 17 (1934), pp. 892–915.

WETMORE, ALEXANDER: "Bird Life among Lava Rock and Coral Sand." *National Geographic Magazine*, Vol. 48 (1925), pp. 77–108.

—— and FRANCIS HARPER: "A Note on the Hibernation of *Kinosternon pennsylvanicum*." *Copeia*, No. 45 (1917), pp. 56–9.

WICKHAM, M. M.: "Notes on the Migration of *Macrochelys lacertina*." *Proceedings, Oklahoma Academy Science*, Vol. 2 (1922), pp. 20–2.

WILCOX, LE ROY: " Incubation of Painted Turtle's Eggs." *Copeia*, No. 1 (1933), p. 41.

WRIGHT, ALBERT H.: " Notes on Clemmys." *Proceedings, Biological Society Washington*, Vol. 31 (1918), pp. 51–8.

——: " Notes on the Muhlenberg's Turtle." *Copeia*, No. 52 (1918), pp. 5–7.

—— and W. D. FUNKHOUSER: " A biological reconnaissance of the Okefinokee Swamp in Georgia. The Reptiles. I. Turtles, Lizards, and Alligators." *Proceedings, Academy Natural Sciences Philadelphia*, Vol. 67 (1915), pp. 107–39.

YERKES, R. M.: " The Formation of Habits in the Turtle." *Popular Science Monthly*, Vol. 58 (1901), pp. 519–29.

——: " Space Perception of Tortoises." *Journal Comparative Neurology Psychology*, Vol. 14 (1904), pp. 16–26.

LIST OF THE TURTLES
of the United States and Canada

<table>
<tr><td></td><td>Common Names</td><td>Chapter and Page</td></tr>
</table>

Family KINOSTERNIDÆ

Genus *STERNOTHERUS*

<table>
<tr><td>S. odoratus</td><td>COMMON MUSK TURTLE</td><td>II · 37</td></tr>
<tr><td>S. minor</td><td>SOUTHERN MUSK TURTLE</td><td>II · 47</td></tr>
<tr><td>S. carinatus</td><td>KEELED MUSK TURTLE</td><td>II · 49</td></tr>
</table>

Genus *KINOSTERNON*

<table>
<tr><td>K. baurii</td><td>STRIPED MUD TURTLE</td><td>II · 51</td></tr>
<tr><td>K. flavescens flavescens</td><td>YELLOW MUD TURTLE</td><td>II · 52</td></tr>
<tr><td>K. sonoriense</td><td>SONORAN MUD TURTLE</td><td>II · 55</td></tr>
<tr><td>K. subrubrum subrubrum</td><td>COMMON MUD TURTLE</td><td>II · 57</td></tr>
<tr><td>K. subrubrum hippocrepis</td><td>MISSISSIPPI MUD TURTLE</td><td>II · 62</td></tr>
<tr><td>K. subrubrum steindachneri</td><td>STEINDACHNER'S MUD TURTLE</td><td>II · 63</td></tr>
</table>

Family CHELYDRIDÆ

Genus *MACROCHELYS*

<table>
<tr><td>M. temminckii</td><td>ALLIGATOR SNAPPING TURTLE</td><td>III · 66</td></tr>
</table>

339

INDEX

✳

i

A NOTE ON THE TYPE
IN WHICH THIS BOOK IS SET

This book was set on the Linotype in Janson, a recutting made direct from the type cast from matrices (now in possession of the Stempel foundry, Frankfurt am Main) made by Anton Janson some time between 1660 and 1687.

Of Janson's origin nothing is known. He may have been a relative of Justus Janson, a printer of Danish birth who practised in Leipzig from 1614 to 1635. Some time between 1657 and 1668 Anton Janson, a punch-cutter and type-founder, bought from the Leipzig printer Johann Erich Hahn the type-foundry which had formerly been a part of the printing house of M. Friedrich Lankisch. Janson's types were first shown in a specimen sheet issued at Leipzig about 1675. Janson's successor, and perhaps his son-in-law, Johann Karl Edling, issued a specimen sheet of Janson types in 1689. His heirs sold the Janson matrices in Holland to Wolffgang Dietrich Erhardt.

HALFTONE ENGRAVINGS OF THE ILLUSTRATIONS
WERE MADE BY
Eagle Photoengraving Co., NEW YORK